CHOCTAW BY BLOOD

ENROLLMENT CARDS

1898-1914

VOLUME III

TRANSCRIBED BY

JEFF BOWEN

NATIVE STUDY
Gallipolis, Ohio
USA

Originally published:
Baltimore, Maryland
2015

Reprinted by:

Native Study LLC
Gallipolis, OH
www.nativestudy.com

Library of Congress Control Number: 2020911767

ISBN: 978-1-64968-003-7

Made in the United States of America.

This series is dedicated to
Mike Marchi,
who keeps my spirits up.

CREEK CENSUS.

SECOND NOTICE.

Members of the Dawes Commission will be present at the following times and places for the purpose of enrolling Creek citizens, as required by Act of Congress of June 10, 1896:

At Muskogee, Nov. 8 to 30, 1897, inclusive.
At Wagoner, Nov. 8 to 13, " inclusive.
At Eufaula, Nov. 8 to 13, " inclusive.
At Sapulpa, Nov. 15 to 20, " inclusive.
At Wetumpka, Nov. 15 to 20, " inclusive.
At Okmulgee, Nov. 22 to 30, " inclusive.

All persons who have not heretofore enrolled before the Dawes Commission should appear and enroll. Parents and guardians can enroll their families and wards.

TAMS BIXBY,
FRANK C. ARMSTRONG,
A. S. McKENNON,
THOS. B. NEEDLES,
Commissioners.

The above illustration is similar in nature to what was found throughout Indian Territory for different tribes as far as postings on bulletin boards, public centers, or wherever they could be read so people would be notified of where and when they needed to be for enrollment with the Dawes Commission.

This is a picture of the Dawes Commission at Camp Jones in Stonewall, Indian Territory on September 8, 1898.

The images below are of two of the original cards given on the microfilm. The cards given in this book have been formatted to fit on one page and still give all the information found on the original cards.

Introduction

This series of Choctaw Enrollment Cards for the Five Civilized Tribes 1898-1914 has been transcribed from National Archive Film M-1186 Rolls 39-46.

The series contains more than 6100 Choctaw enrollment cards. All of the cards list age, sex and degree of blood, the parties' Dawes Roll Numbers, and date of enrollment by the Secretary of Interior for each person. The contents also give the enrollee's parents' names as well as miscellaneous notes pertaining to the enrollee's circumstances, when needed. Most entries indicate whether or not a spouse is an Intermarried White, with the initials I.W.

Enrollment wasn't as simple a process as most would think just by going through these pages. The relationships between the Five Tribes and the Dawes Commission were weak at best. There were political battles going on between the tribes and the U.S. Government as it was, but the struggles didn't stop there. Each tribe had its own political factions pulling it from every direction. On top of everything else, people from every corner of the United States were trying to figure how to get in on the spoils (Money and Land Allotment) by means of political favor. Kent Carter, author of *The Dawes Commission*, describes the continuous effort required to enroll the different tribes and the pressure the Commission incurred from people all over the country who tried to insinuate themselves into the equation:

"In May 1896 the Dawes Commission Returned To Indian Territory for its third visit, establishing its headquarters at Vinita in the Cherokee Nation. It now had to process applications for citizenship in addition to negotiating allotment agreements; these circumstances make the narrative of events more confusing because the commission attempted the two tasks concurrently. The commissioners resumed making their usual speeches to tribal officials and public gatherings to promote negotiations, but now they inevitably had to respond to questions about how the application process for citizenship would work. They also began receiving letters from people all over the United States asking how they could 'get on the rolls' so they could 'get Indian land'."[1]

For the actual process of Choctaw enrollment, "A commission was appointed in each county of the Choctaw Nation under an act of September 18 to make separate rolls of citizens by blood, by intermarriage, and freedmen; it was to deliver them to recently elected Chief Green McCurtain by October 20, but he rejected them even before they were completed because of charges that people were being left off for political reasons. On October 30, the National Council authorized establishment of a five-member

---

[1] *The Dawes Commission* by Kent Carter, page 15, para. 1

ix

commission to revise the rolls within ten days and then directed McCurtain to turn them over to the Dawes Commission on November 11, 1896. The Choctaws hired the law firm of Stuart, Gordon, and Hailey, of South McAlester to represent the tribe at all proceedings held by the Dawes Commission,"[2] another indication that throughout the Commission's efforts there was always controversy between the tribes and the negotiators.

When completed, this multi-volume series will contain thousands of names, all of them accounted for in the indexes carefully prepared by the author. Hopefully this work will help many researchers find their ancestors and satisfy the questions that so many have had about their Native American heritage.

Jeff Bowen
Gallipolis, Ohio
NativeStudy.com

---

[2] *The Dawes Commission* by Kent Carter, page 16, para. 5

Choctaw By Blood Enrollment Cards 1898-1914

RESIDENCE: Red River   COUNTY. **Choctaw Nation**   **Choctaw Roll**   CARD NO.
POST OFFICE: Kullituklo, I.T.   *(Not Including Freedmen)*   FIELD NO. **601**

Dawes' Roll No.	NAME		Relationship to Person First Named	AGE	SEX	BLOOD	TRIBAL ENROLLMENT		
							Year	County	No.
1376	1 Maytobe, Rayburn	51	First Named	48	M	Full	1896	Red River	8660
1377	2 ", Nancy	39	Wife	36	F	"	1896	" "	8661
1378	3 ", Benson	21	Son	18	M	"	1896	" "	8662
1379	4 ", Samaie	19	Dau	16	F	"	1896	" "	8664
1380	5 ", Selin	16	"	13	"	"	1896	" "	8665
1381	6 ", Harrison	14	Son	11	M	"	1896	" "	8663
~~1382~~	7 DIED PRIOR TO SEPTEMBER 25, 1902 ~~, Peter~~		"	9	"	"	1896	" "	8666
~~1383~~	8 DIED PRIOR TO SEPTEMBER 25, 1902 ~~, Wellington~~		"	7	"	"	1896	" "	8667
1384	9 ", Mattie	7	Dau	4	F	"	1896	" "	8668
14572	10 ", Zuintus	5	Son	2	M	"			

11 ~~No7 died June,1900; Proof of~~
12 ~~death filed Dec 3,1902~~
13 No8 died June 25,1900; Proof of
    death filed Dec 3, 1902.
14
15 ENROLLMENT
16 OF NOS. 12345678and9 HEREON APPROVED BY THE SECRETARY
17 OF INTERIOR Dec 12, 1902

TRIBAL ENROLLMENT OF PARENTS

	Name of Father	Year	County	Name of Mother	Year	County
1	May-tobe	Dead	Red River	Amy	Dead	Red River
2	Jim Sukkey	"	" "	Sallie Sukkey	"	" "
3	No 1			No 2		
4	No 1			No 2		
5	No 1			No 2		
6	No 1			No 2		
7	No 1			No 2		
8	No 1			No 2		
9	No 1			No 2		ENROLLMENT
10	No 1			No 2		OF NOS. 10 HEREON APPROVED BY THE SECRETARY OF INTERIOR May 20, 1903

11 No5 on 1896 roll as Felin Maytobe
12 For child of No5 see NB(Apr 26-06) Card #514
13 No10 affidavit of birth to be supplied; Recd May 24/99
14 No2 is the husband of Annie Thomas on Choc Card 1023, Feby 17, 1902
15 Surname of Nos 1to9 inclusive is Maytube on 1896 roll
   No10 Proof of birth received and filed Sept 25, 1902.
16 No7 died June-1900: No8 died June 25,1900: Enrollment cancelled by Department Sept 16, 1904
   For child of No4 see N.B (Mar 3,1905) #900.

Date of Application for Enrollment.   April 20/99

1

Choctaw By Blood Enrollment Cards 1898-1914

| RESIDENCE: Red River | COUNTY. | | | | | |
| POST OFFICE: Kullituklo, I.T. | **Choctaw Nation** | | | **Choctaw Roll** (Not Including Freedmen) | CARD No. FIELD No. 602 | |

Dawes' Roll No.	NAME	Relationship to Person First Named	AGE	SEX	BLOOD	TRIBAL ENROLLMENT Year	County	No.
1385	1 Maytobe, Armstead 43		40	M	Full	1896	Red River	8669
	2							
	3							
	4							
	5							
	6	ENROLLMENT OF NOS. 1 HEREON						
	7	APPROVED BY THE SECRETARY						
	8	OF INTERIOR DEC 12 1902						
	9							
	10							
	11	On 1896 Choctaw Roll as Armstead Maytube						
	12							
	13							
	14							
	15							
	16							
	17							

TRIBAL ENROLLMENT OF PARENTS

Name of Father	Year	County	Name of Mother	Year	County
1 May-tobe	Dead	Red River	Amy	Dead	Red River
2					
3					
4					
5					
6					
7					
8					
9					
10					
11					
12					
13					
14					
15					
16			Date of Application for Enrollment		April 20/99
17					

2

Choctaw By Blood Enrollment Cards 1898-1914

RESIDENCE: Towson   COUNTY.   **Choctaw Nation**   **Choctaw Roll**   CARD NO.
POST OFFICE: Doaksville, I.T.   *(Not Including Freedmen)*   FIELD NO.   603

Dawes' Roll No.	NAME	Relationship to Person	AGE	SEX	BLOOD	TRIBAL ENROLLMENT		
						Year	County	No.
1386	1 James, Thomas ²⁵	First Named	23	M	Full	1896	Cedar	6740
	2							
	3							
	4	ENROLLMENT						
	5	OF NOS. 1 HEREON APPROVED BY THE SECRETARY						
	6	OF INTERIOR DEC 12 1902						
	7							
	8							
	9							
	10	Nº 1 was husband of Rhoda Mishaia, Choctaw card #652						
	11							
	12							
	13							
	14							
	15							
	16							
	17							

TRIBAL ENROLLMENT OF PARENTS

Name of Father	Year	County	Name of Mother	Year	County
1 Thomas James	Dead	Towson	Silen James	1896	Towson
2					
3					
4					
5					
6					
7					
8					
9					
10					
11					
12					
13					
14					
15					
16			Date of Application for Enrollment	April 20/99	
17					

Choctaw By Blood Enrollment Cards 1898-1914

RESIDENCE: Towson COUNTY.
POST OFFICE: Doaksville, I.T.

Choctaw Nation

Choctaw Roll
(Not Including Freedmen)

CARD NO.
FIELD NO. 604

Dawes' Roll No.	NAME	Relationship to Person	AGE	SEX	BLOOD	TRIBAL ENROLLMENT Year	County	No.
1387	1 Milton, Silon 45	First Named	42	F	Full	1896	Cedar	8594
1388	2 James, Frances ~~DIED PRIOR TO SEPTEMBER 25 1902~~	Dau	14	"	"	1896	"	6741
1389	3 " Rhoda 16	"	13	"	"	1896	"	6742
1390	4 Frazier, Minnie 19	Sister	16	"	"	1896	"	4121
15934	5 Jackson, Learner	Dau of No4	2	"	"			
6								
7	ENROLLMENT							
8	OF NOS. 1 2 3 and 4 HEREON APPROVED BY THE SECRETARY							
9	OF INTERIOR DEC 12 1902							
10								
11								
12	ENROLLMENT							
13	OF NOS. 5 HEREON APPROVED BY THE SECRETARY							
14	OF INTERIOR NOV 24 1905							
15								
16								
17								

TRIBAL ENROLLMENT OF PARENTS

	Name of Father	Year	County	Name of Mother	Year	County
1	Pa-to-bee	Dead	Towson	Jinsey Patobee	Dead	Towson
2	~~Thompson James~~	"	"	~~No 1~~		
3	" "	"	"	No 1		
4	Pa-to-bee	"	"	Margaret Patobee	Dead	Towson
5	Thomas James			No.4		
6						
7						
8						
9						
10	No2 died Feb 10/99 – Evidence of death filed Dec 3 1902					
11	No2 died Feb 10-1899: Enrollment cancelled [remainder illegible]					
12	No.5 born Aug. 19, 1900: application received and No.5 listed on this card March 27, 1905, under Act of Congress approved March 3, 1905					
13	For child of No.4, see N.B. (Apr. 26, 1906) card No. 202					
14						
15				Date of Application for Enrollment.	For Nos.1 to 4 incl.	
16					April 20/99	
17						

4

Choctaw By Blood Enrollment Cards 1898-1914

RESIDENCE: Red River   COUNTY.   **Choctaw Nation**   **Choctaw Roll**   CARD NO.
POST OFFICE: Kullituklo, I.T.   *(Not Including Freedmen)*   FIELD NO. **605**

Dawes' Roll No.	NAME	Relationship to Person First Named	AGE	SEX	BLOOD	TRIBAL ENROLLMENT Year	County	No.
1391	1 Sampson, William ³⁷		34	M	Full	1896	Red River	4433
14920	2 " , Marsill ²⁰	Ward	17	"	"	1896	" "	6997
	3							
	4							
	5							
	6							
	7	ENROLLMENT						
	8	OF NOS. 1 HEREON APPROVED BY THE SECRETARY						
	9	OF INTERIOR Dec 12, 1902						
	10							
	11							
	12	ENROLLMENT						
	13	OF NOS. 2 HEREON APPROVED BY THE SECRETARY						
	14	OF INTERIOR Oct 15, 1903						
	15							
	16							
	17							

TRIBAL ENROLLMENT OF PARENTS

	Name of Father	Year	County	Name of Mother	Year	County
1	Sampson Yokahtubbee	Dead	Eagle	Una tama	1896	Red River
2	Eba-ha-tabee	"	"	Susan	Dead	Eagle
3						
4						
5						
6						
7	No2 on 1896 roll as Marsill Johnson, also as (Marsell Sampson)					
8						
9						
10						
11						
12						
13						
14						
15					Date of Application for Enrollment.	
16						
17					April 20/99	

Choctaw By Blood Enrollment Cards 1898-1914

RESIDENCE: Red River   COUNTY.   **Choctaw Nation**   Choctaw Roll   CARD NO.
POST OFFICE: Kullituklo, I.T.   *(Not Including Freedmen)*   FIELD NO.   606

Dawes' Roll No.	NAME	Relationship to Person First Named	AGE	SEX	BLOOD	TRIBAL ENROLLMENT Year	County	No.
1392	₁ Johnson, Willis ²⁷	First Named	24	M	Full	1896	Red River	6993
1393	₂ " Anthony ²⁴	brother	21	"	"	1896	" "	6994
~~1394~~	~~₃ Fisher, Kitsy ²⁰~~ DIED PRIOR TO SEPTEMBER 25, 1902	~~sister~~	~~17~~	~~F~~	~~"~~	~~1896~~	~~" "~~	~~6995~~
1395	₄ Johnson, Hilton ¹⁹	brother	16	M	"	1896	" "	6996
1396	₅ Fisher, Anias [?] ³	Nephew	5mo	M	"			
	₆							
	₇							
	₈							
	₉							
	₁₀							
	₁₁ ENROLLMENT OF NOS. 1 2 3 4 and 5 HEREON							
	₁₂ APPROVED BY THE SECRETARY							
	₁₃ OF INTERIOR DEC 12 1902							
	₁₄							
	₁₅							
	₁₆							
	₁₇							

TRIBAL ENROLLMENT OF PARENTS

	Name of Father	Year	County	Name of Mother	Year	County
₁	William Johnson	Dead	Red River	Ho-ta-hema	Dead	Red River
₂	" "	"	" "	"	"	" "
₃	" "	"	" "	"	"	" "
₄	" "	"	" "	"	"	" "
₅	Thomas Fisher			No.3		
₆						
₇						
₈						
₉	No3 on 1896 roll as Patsy Johnson					
₁₀	No.3 is now the wife of Thomas Fisher on ~~Choctaw card #589; Copy of letter attached, March 1st, 1900~~					
₁₁	No.3 is now the husband of Weley Thomas on Choctaw card #1209 as Elsie Thomas					
₁₂	Evidence of marriage filed July 21ˢᵗ 1902 filed on Card #1209					
₁₃	No3 died Feb 19-1902; Evidence of death filed Dec 3, 1902					
₁₄	~~No.3 died Feb. 19, 1902. Enrollment cancelled by Department~~				Date of Application for Enrollment.	
₁₅	No.5 Enrolled May 24, 1900.					
₁₆					April 20/99	
₁₇						

6

Choctaw By Blood Enrollment Cards 1898-1914

RESIDENCE: Red River   COUNTY. **Choctaw Nation**   **Choctaw Roll**   CARD NO.
POST OFFICE: Kullituklo, I.T.   *(Not Including Freedmen)*   FIELD NO. 607

Dawes' Roll No.	NAME	Relationship to Person First Named	AGE	SEX	BLOOD	TRIBAL ENROLLMENT Year	County	No.
14573	1 On-na-ti-ma		70	F	Full	1896	Eagle	9933
	2							
	3	ENROLLMENT OF NOS. 1 HEREON APPROVED BY THE SECRETARY OF INTERIOR MAY 20 1903						
	4							
	5							
	6							
	7							
	8							
	9							
	10							
	11							
	12							
	13							
	14							
	15							
	16							
	17							

TRIBAL ENROLLMENT OF PARENTS

	Name of Father	Year	County	Name of Mother	Year	County
1	Yak-nuh-tubbee	Dead	Eagle	Ou-ka-yo	Dead	Eagle
2						
3						
4						
5						
6						
7						
8						
9						
10						
11						
12						
13						
14						
15						
16						April 20/99
17						

7

Choctaw By Blood Enrollment Cards 1898-1914

RESIDENCE: Red River COUNTY.
POST OFFICE: Kullituklo, I.T.

Choctaw Nation

Choctaw Roll
(Not Including Freedmen)

CARD NO.
FIELD NO. 608

Dawes' Roll No.	NAME	Relationship to Person First Named	AGE	SEX	BLOOD	TRIBAL ENROLLMENT Year	County	No.
1397	1 Robert, Mollie 78	First Named	75	F	Full	1896	Red River	10808
	2							
	3							
	4							
	5							
	6							
	7							
	8	ENROLLMENT						
	9	OF NOS. 1 HEREON APPROVED BY THE SECRETARY						
	10	OF INTERIOR DEC 12 1902						
	11							
	12							
	13							
	14							
	15							
	16							
	17							

TRIBAL ENROLLMENT OF PARENTS

	Name of Father	Year	County	Name of Mother	Year	County
1	Nashoba	Dead	Kiamitia			
2						
3						
4						
5						
6	On 1896 roll as Molley Robert					
7	" 1893 Pay Roll Red River do page 65 No 559.					
8	Mother of No1 has removed to Miss. Name unknown.					
9						
10						
11						
12						
13						
14						
15						
16				Date of Application for Enrollment	April 20/99	
17	P.O. Garvin I.T. 11/27/02					

8

Choctaw By Blood Enrollment Cards 1898-1914

RESIDENCE: Towson   COUNTY.   **Choctaw Nation**   **Choctaw Roll**   CARD NO.
POST OFFICE: Doaksville, I.T.   *(Not Including Freedmen)*   FIELD NO.   609

Dawes' Roll No.	NAME		Relationship to Person First Named	AGE	SEX	BLOOD	TRIBAL ENROLLMENT		
							Year	County	No.
1398	1 James, Williamson	24		21	M	Full	1893	Towson	P.R. 254
1399	2 " Sibbie	19	Wife	16	F	"	1896	"	6766
	3								
	4								
	5								
	6								
	7								
	8								
	9								
	10								
	11								
	12								
	13								
	14								
	15								
	16								
	17								

ENROLLMENT
OF NOS. 1 and 2 HEREON
APPROVED BY THE SECRETARY
OF INTERIOR DEC 12 1902

TRIBAL ENROLLMENT OF PARENTS

	Name of Father	Year	County	Name of Mother	Year	County
1	Thompson James	Dead	Towson	Silon Milton	1896	Towson
2	Pleasant Jacob	"	"	Ilen Bob	1896	"
3						
4						
5						
6						
7						
8	No2 on 1896 roll as Sibbie Jacobb.					
9						
10	No1 also on 1896 roll Page 166, No 6739					
11	as William James, Cedar Co					
12						
13						
14						
15						
16				Date of Application for Enrollment	April 20/99	
17						

9

Choctaw By Blood Enrollment Cards 1898-1914

RESIDENCE: Red River COUNTY.	**Choctaw Nation**	Choctaw Roll	CARD NO.
POST OFFICE: Kullituklo, I.T.		(Not Including Freedmen)	FIELD NO. 610

Dawes' Roll No.	NAME	Relationship to Person First Named	AGE	SEX	BLOOD	TRIBAL ENROLLMENT Year	County	No.
1400	1 A-pe-sa-ho-na ~~DIED PRIOR TO SEPTEMBER 25, 1902~~ 86	First Named	83	F	Full	1896	Red River	316
	2							
	3							
	4							
	5							
	6							
	7							
	8							
	9							
	10							
	11	ENROLLMENT						
	12	OF NOS. 1 HEREON APPROVED BY THE SECRETARY						
	13	OF INTERIOR DEC 12 1902						
	14							
	15							
	16							
	17							

TRIBAL ENROLLMENT OF PARENTS

Name of Father	Year	County	Name of Mother	Year	County
1 Ish-tan-tubbee	Dead	Red River	Noah-iuna	Dead	Red River
2					
3					
4					
5					
6					
7					
8					
9					
10					
11					
12					
13					
14					
15					
16			Date of Application for Enrollment.		April 20/99
17					

10

Choctaw By Blood Enrollment Cards 1898-1914

RESIDENCE: Red River   COUNTY.
POST OFFICE: Kullituklo, Ind. Ter.

Choctaw Nation

Choctaw Roll *(Not Including Freedmen)*

CARD NO.
FIELD NO. 611

Dawes' Roll No.		NAME		Relationship to Person Named	AGE	SEX	BLOOD	TRIBAL ENROLLMENT Year	County	No.
1401	1	Burnitt, William	45	First	42	M	Full	1893	Red River	P.R. 47
1402	2	Chubby		S.Son	12	"	1/2	1893	" "	49
14574	3	" Frances	7	Dau	6	F	Full			
Dead	4	" Larless	DEAD.	"	9mo	"	"			
I.W. 1553	5	" Alice		Wife	16	"	I.W.			
	6	No. 4 HEREON DISMISSED UNDER								
	7	ORDER OF THE COMMISSION TO THE FIVE CIVILIZED TRIBES OF MARCH 31, 1905.								
	8									
	9	ENROLLMENT OF NOS. 1 and 2 HEREON								
	10	APPROVED BY THE SECRETARY OF INTERIOR DEC 12 1902						ENROLLMENT OF NOS. ~~~ 5 ~~~ HEREON		
	11							APPROVED BY THE SECRETARY OF INTERIOR AUG 2- 1906		
	12	ENROLLMENT OF NOS. 3 HEREON								
	13	APPROVED BY THE SECRETARY OF INTERIOR MAY 20 1903								
	14									
	15							No		
	16	No2 died July 15, 1902: Enrollment								
	17	cancelled by Department Sept 16, 1904								

TRIBAL ENROLLMENT OF PARENTS

	Name of Father	Year	County	Name of Mother	Year	County
1	Barnatubbee	Dead	Red River	3iney	Dead	Red River
2	Anderson Franklin	1896	Non Citz	Ista Franklin	"	" "
3	No 1			" "	"	" "
4	No 1			" "	"	" "
5	Sam Ball		non citizen	Minnie Ball		non citizen
6						
7						
8	No. 5 transferred from Choctaw card D-9406 to this card May 1, 1906 See decision of April 16,1906					
9	Nos 1 and 5 were married May 26, 1901					
10	No2 on 1893 Pay roll as Kirbie Bonnett					
11	No1 " 1893 " " " Williams " also on 1896 roll as William Burney Page 34					
12	No 1357, Red River Co					
13	No4 Died August 17, 1899. Evidence of death filed March 22, 1901					
14	correct spelling of surname of No1 is Burnitt. See his letter filed 8/7/01.					
15	No3 Notation as to death is an error: should have been No2 instead					
16	See copy of letter of GD Rogers of Nov 25, 1902 filed herein					
17	No2 died July 15, 1902: proof of death filed Dec 4 1902.					

Date of Application for Enrollment: April 20/99

↘ 1 to 4

11

Choctaw By Blood Enrollment Cards 1898-1914

RESIDENCE: Towson COUNTY.
POST OFFICE: Alikchi, I.T.

Choctaw Nation

Choctaw Roll *(Not Including Freedmen)*

CARD NO.
FIELD NO. **612**

Dawes' Roll No.	NAME	Relationship to Person	AGE	SEX	BLOOD	TRIBAL ENROLLMENT Year	County	No.
1403	1 Christie, Moses 28	First Named	25	M	Full	1896	Towson	2463
1404	2 " , Blance 30	Wife	27	F	1/2	1896	"	2464
1405	3 " , Michael 6	Son	3	M	3/4			
1406	4 " , Walter ~PRIOR TO SEPTEMBER 25, 1902~	"	3mo	"	3/4			
1407	5 " , Kate ~DIED PRIOR TO SEPTEMBER 25, 1902~	Dau	3mo	F	3/4			
1408	6 Watkins, Gustava 9	S.Dau	6	"	1/4	1896	Nashoba	13327
1409	7 " , Dukes 2	Son	1mo	M	3/4			
15935	8 " , Annie	Dau	1	F	3/4			
	9							
	10	ENROLLMENT OF NOS. 1 2 3 4 5 6 and 7 HEREON APPROVED BY THE SECRETARY OF INTERIOR Dec 12, 1902						
	11							
	12							
	13							
	14	ENROLLMENT OF NOS. ~8~ HEREON APPROVED BY THE SECRETARY OF INTERIOR Nov. 24, 1905						
	15							
	16							

No4 died April-1900: No5 died April-1900: Enrollment cancelled by Department July 8-1904

TRIBAL ENROLLMENT OF PARENTS

	Name of Father	Year	County	Name of Mother	Year	County
1	Michael Christie	Dead	Towson	Agnes Christie	Dead	Cedar
2	Ben Watkins	1896	Nashoba	Viney Watkins	"	Bok Tulko
3	No 1			No 2		
4	No 1			No 2		
5	No 1			No 2		
6				No 2		
7	No 1			No 2		
8	No 1			No 2		
9						
10	No8 Application made for enrollment of this child and placed					
11	hereon under act of Congress of March 3, 1905.					
12	No6 is illegimate Name of Father unknown					
13	No4 died April 1900: Proof of death filed Dec. 3, 1902.					
	No5 " April 1900: " " " " " " "					
14	No7 Enrolled June 25th 1900.					
15					#1 to 6 inc	
16					Date of Application for Enrollment. April 20/99	
17					No.6 May 3/99	

12

Choctaw By Blood Enrollment Cards 1898-1914

RESIDENCE: Red River   COUNTY.   **Choctaw Nation**   **Choctaw Roll** *(Not Including Freedmen)*   CARD No.
POST OFFICE: Janis, I.T.   FIELD No. 613

Dawes' Roll No.	NAME	Relationship to Person First Named	AGE	SEX	BLOOD	TRIBAL ENROLLMENT Year	County	No.
~~1410~~	1 Barney, Isabelle ⁴⁰	First Named	~~37~~	~~F~~	~~Full~~	~~1896~~	~~Red River~~	~~1347~~
1414	2 " Joseph ¹⁶	Son	13	M	"	1896	" "	1349
~~1412~~	3 " Humphrey ¹¹	"	~~8~~	"	"	~~1896~~	" "	~~1350~~
	4							
	5							
	6							
	7							
	8							
	9							
	10							

DIED PRIOR TO SEPTEMBER 25, 1902 (lines 1 and 3)

ENROLLMENT OF NOS. 1 – 2 and 3 HEREON APPROVED BY THE SECRETARY OF INTERIOR DEC 12 1902

TRIBAL ENROLLMENT OF PARENTS

Name of Father	Year	County	Name of Mother	Year	County
1 Alam[sic] Luke	Dead	Red River	Nancy Luke	Dead	Red River
2 Ellis Barney	"	" "	No 1		
3 " "	"	" "	No 1		

No1 died April 20, 1900; proof of death filed Dec. 3, 1902.
No3 " March 6, 1900; " " " " " " "
No.1 died April 20, 1900; No.3 died March 6, 1900. Enrollment cancelled by Department Sept. 16, 1904.

Date of Application for Enrollment. April 20/99

13

Choctaw By Blood Enrollment Cards 1898-1914

RESIDENCE: Red River   COUNTY.   **Choctaw Nation**   **Choctaw Roll**   CARD NO.
POST OFFICE: Kullituklo, I.T.   *(Not Including Freedmen)*   FIELD NO.   614

Dawes' Roll No.	NAME	Relationship to Person	AGE	SEX	BLOOD	TRIBAL ENROLLMENT Year	County	No.
1413	1 Thomas, Silwie ⁴⁸	First Named	45	F	Full	1896	Red River	12287
1414	2 " Sopha ¹⁶	Dau	13	"	"	1896	" "	12290
1415	3 " Charley ¹³	Son	10	M	"	1896	" "	12291
1416	4 " Moses ¹¹	"	8	"	"	1896	" "	12292
	5							
	6							
	7							
	8							
	9							
	10							
	11	ENROLLMENT						
	12	OF NOS. 1 2 3 and 4 HEREON APPROVED BY THE SECRETARY						
	13	OF INTERIOR DEC 12 1902						
	14							
	15							
	16							
	17							

TRIBAL ENROLLMENT OF PARENTS

	Name of Father	Year	County	Name of Mother	Year	County
1	Johnson LeFlore	Dead	Bok Tuklo	Man-che-huna	Dead	Bok Tuklo
2	Don Ellis	1896	Red River	No 1		
3	" "	1896	" "	No 1		
4	" "	1896	" "	No 1		
5						
6						
7						
8						
9						
10						
11						
12						
13						
14				Date of Application for Enrollment.		
15						
16				April 20/99		
17						

14

Choctaw By Blood Enrollment Cards 1898-1914

RESIDENCE: Towson   COUNTY.

POST OFFICE: Doaksville, I.T.

Choctaw Nation

Choctaw Roll *(Not Including Freedmen)*

CARD NO.

FIELD NO. **615**

Dawes' Roll No.	NAME	Relationship to Person First Named	AGE	SEX	BLOOD	TRIBAL ENROLLMENT Year	TRIBAL ENROLLMENT County	TRIBAL ENROLLMENT No.
1417	1 Ben, John ⁶¹	First Named	58	M	Full	1896	Towson	1107
1418	2 " Emily ²⁹	Wife	26	F	"	1896	"	1108
	3							
	4							
	5							
	6							
	7							
	8							
	9							
	10							
	11							
	12							
	13							
	14							
	15							
	16							
	17							

ENROLLMENT
OF NOS. 1 and 2 HEREON
APPROVED BY THE SECRETARY
OF INTERIOR Dec 12 1902

No1 on 1896 roll as Johnson Ben

TRIBAL ENROLLMENT OF PARENTS

	Name of Father	Year	County	Name of Mother	Year	County
1	Pe-hich-sah	Dead		Fa-le-he-ma	Dead	Towson
2	Mike Cobb	"	Towson	Siney Cobb	"	"
3						
4						
5						
6						
7						
8						
9						
10						
11						
12						
13						
14						
15						
16						
17						

Date of Application for Enrollment.

April 20/99

15

Choctaw By Blood Enrollment Cards 1898-1914

Choctaw Nation

Choctaw Roll
(Not Including Freedmen)

CARD NO.
FIELD NO. 616

Dawes' Roll No.		NAME		Relationship to Person	AGE	SEX	BLOOD	TRIBAL ENROLLMENT		
								Year	County	No.
1419	1	Hickaby, Eli	59	First Named	56	M	Full	1896	Towson	5485
1420	2	" Litie	48	Wife	45	F	"	1896	"	5486
1421	3	" Emiline	15	Dau	12	"	"	1896	"	5487
1422	4	" Adeline	13	"	10	"	"	1896	"	5488
	5									
	6	ENROLLMENT								
	7	OF NOS. 1 2 3 and 4 HEREON APPROVED BY THE SECRETARY								
	8	OF INTERIOR DEC 12 1902								
	9									
	10									
	11									
	12									
	13									
	14									
	15									
	16									
	17									

TRIBAL ENROLLMENT OF PARENTS

	Name of Father	Year	County	Name of Mother	Year	County
1		Died	in Mississippi	Atoka	Dead	Towson
2	Pisa-he-la-by	Dead	Bok Tuklo	Sho-a-huna	"	"
3	No 1			No 2		
4	No 1			No 2		
5						
6						
7	No1 on 1896 roll as Eli Hickby					
8	No2 " 1896 " " Leadie "					
9	No3 " 1896 " " Emeline "					
	No4 " 1896 " " Adaline "					
10						
11						
12						
13						
14						
15						
16				Date of Application for Enrollment		April 20/99
17						

16

Choctaw By Blood Enrollment Cards 1898-1914

RESIDENCE: Eagle COUNTY.
POST OFFICE: Eagletown, I.T.

Choctaw Nation

Choctaw Roll
(Not Including Freedmen)

CARD NO.
FIELD NO. **617**

Dawes' Roll No.	NAME	Relationship to Person	AGE	SEX	BLOOD	TRIBAL ENROLLMENT Year	County	No.
~~1423~~	1 ~~M°Clure, Etsy~~ DIED PRIOR TO SEPTEMBER 25, 1902 63	First Named	~~60~~	~~F~~	~~Full~~	~~1896~~	~~Eagle~~	~~9310~~
	2							
	3							
	4							
	5							
	6							
	7							
	8							
	9							
	10							
	11							
	12							
	13							
	14							
	15							
	16							
	17							

ENROLLMENT
OF NOS. 1 HEREON
APPROVED BY THE SECRETARY
OF INTERIOR DEC 12 1902

On roll as Elsie M°Clure

No1 died April 7, 1902; proof of death filed Dec 13, 1902

TRIBAL ENROLLMENT OF PARENTS

Name of Father	Year	County	Name of Mother	Year	County
1 ~~Charlison Harllson~~	Dead	Nashoba	O-na-chc-ma	Dead	Eagle
2					
3					
4					
5					
6					
7					
8					
9					
10					
11					
12					
13					
14					
15					
16			Date of Application for Enrollment		April 20/99
17					

RESIDENCE: Eagle   COUNTY.

POST OFFICE: Eagletown, I.T.

Choctaw Nation

Choctaw Roll *(Not Including Freedmen)*

CARD NO.

FIELD NO. 618

Dawes' Roll No.	NAME		Relationship to Person First Named	AGE	SEX	BLOOD	TRIBAL ENROLLMENT		
							Year	County	No.
1424	1 Ishteka, Elizabeth	37	First Named	34	F	Full	1896	Eagle	6291
1425	2 ~~Susan~~ DIED PRIOR TO SEPTEMBER 25, 1902		~~Dau~~	~~16~~	"	"	~~1896~~	"	~~6296~~
1426	3 " Watkin	15	Son	12	M	"	1896	"	6297
1427	4 " Sillin	13	Dau	10	F	"	1896	"	6293
	5								
	6								
	7								
	8								
	9								
	10								
	11	ENROLLMENT							
	12	OF NOS. 1 2 3 and 4 HEREON APPROVED BY THE SECRETARY							
	13	OF INTERIOR DEC 12 1902							
	14								
	15								
	16								
	17								

TRIBAL ENROLLMENT OF PARENTS

	Name of Father	Year	County	Name of Mother	Year	County
1	To-an-tubbee	Dead	Eagle	Pike Toantubbee	Dead	Eagle
2	Isaac Ishteka	"	"	No 1		
3	" "	"	"	No 1		
4	" "	"	"	No 1		
5						
6						
7	No4 on 1896 roll as Sillen Ishteka					
8	Nº2 Died July 20, 1900, proof of death filed Dec. 24, 1902.					
9						
10	For child of No.4 see N.B. (Apr. 26, 1906) Card No. 255.					
11						
12						
13						
14				Date of Application for Enrollment.		
15						
16				April 20/99		
17	Lukfata I.T.					

Choctaw By Blood Enrollment Cards 1898-1914

RESIDENCE: Eagle   COUNTY.   **Choctaw Nation**   **Choctaw Roll**   CARD NO.
POST OFFICE: Eagletown, I.T.   *(Not Including Freedmen)*   FIELD NO.   619

Dawes' Roll No.	NAME	Relationship to Person First Named	AGE	SEX	BLOOD	TRIBAL ENROLLMENT Year	County	No.
1428	1 Tonihka, Sinie 24	First Named	21	F	Full	1896	Eagle	5647
1429	2 " Bitty 15	S. Dau	12	"	"	1896	"	12218
1430	3 " Adeline 13	"	10	"	"	1896	"	12214
1431	4 " Artie 11	"	8	"	"	1896	"	12220
	5							
	6							
	7							
	8							
	9							
	10							
	11	ENROLLMENT						
	12	OF NOS. 1 2 3 and 4 HEREON APPROVED BY THE SECRETARY						
	13	OF INTERIOR DEC 12 1902						
	14							
	15							
	16							
	17							

TRIBAL ENROLLMENT OF PARENTS

	Name of Father	Year	County	Name of Mother	Year	County
1	Hickman Hayakonabee	Dead	Eagle	Lihe Hayakonabee	Dead	Eagle
2	Nelson Tonihka	"	"	Jincy Tonihka	"	"
3	" "	"	"	" "	"	"
4	" "	"	"	" "	"	"
5						
6	No1 on 1896 roll as Siney Hayakonubbi					
7	No3 " 1896 " " Atlan Tonihka					
8						
9	No1 on 1896 roll as Siney Haykohaonubbi					
10	Page 137, No. 5647, Eagle Co.					
11						
12						
13						
14						
15						
16				Date of Application for Enrollment	April 20/99	
17						

19

Choctaw By Blood Enrollment Cards 1898-1914

RESIDENCE: Eagle COUNTY. **Choctaw Nation** Choctaw Roll CARD NO.
POST OFFICE: Eagletown, I.T. (Not Including Freedmen) FIELD NO. 620

Dawes' Roll No.	NAME	Relationship to Person	AGE	SEX	BLOOD	TRIBAL ENROLLMENT		
						Year	County	No.
1432	1 Tushka Laisa 19	First Named	16	F	Full	1896	Eagle	5633
1433	2 Hayakonubbi Osborn 15	brother	12	M	"	1896	"	5648
1434	3 " Elizabeth 13	sister	10	F	"	1896	"	5651
1435	4 DIED PRIOR TO SEPTEMBER 25, 1902 10 Solomon	brother	7	M	"	1896	"	5638
1436	5 Tushka, Lena 1	Dau	1mo	F	"			
	6							
	7							
	8							
	9							
	10							
	11	ENROLLMENT OF NOS. 1 2 3 4 and 5 HEREON						
	12	APPROVED BY THE SECRETARY						
	13	OF INTERIOR DEC 12 1902						
	14							
	15							
	16							
	17							

TRIBAL ENROLLMENT OF PARENTS

	Name of Father	Year	County	Name of Mother	Year	County
1	Edmund Hayakonubbi	Dead	Eagle	Lilie Hayakonubbi	Dead	Eagle
2	" "	"	"	" "	"	"
3	" "	"	"	" "	"	"
4	" "	"	"	" "	"	"
5	Levi Tushka	1896	"	No. 1		
6						
7	For child of No1 See NB (Apr 26-06) Card #583					
8	No3 on 1896 roll as Eliz Hayakonubbi on Choctaw Card 7005					
9	No.1 is now wife of Levi Tushka May17,1901. Evidence marriage to be supplied. Filed 6/4/01					
10	No.5 Enrolled May 17, 1901. No.4 died January, 1900: Evidence of death filed Dec 3, 1902.					
11	Nos 2and 3 now living close to Kullytuklo[sic] with Hamplin Hayokainubbi on 7-12-24					
12	No.4 died Jan 1900: Enrollment cancelled by Department (remainder illegible)					
13	For child of No.1 see NB (March 3, 1905) #1146.					
14						
15					Date of Application for Enrollment.	
16				Date of Application for Enrollment	April 20/99	
17						

20

Choctaw By Blood Enrollment Cards 1898-1914

RESIDENCE: Bok Tuklo
POST OFFICE: Lukfata, I.T.
COUNTY. **Choctaw Nation**
Choctaw Roll *(Not Including Freedmen)*
CARD No.
FIELD No. 621

Dawes' Roll No.	NAME	Relationship to Person First Named	AGE	SEX	BLOOD	TRIBAL ENROLLMENT Year	County	No.
1437	1 Hol-ba-ti-ma 49		46	F	Full	1896	Bok Tuklo	5555
	2							
	3							
	4	ENROLLMENT						
	5	OF NOS. 1 HEREON APPROVED BY THE SECRETARY						
	6	OF INTERIOR DEC 12 1902						
	7							
	8							
	9							
	10							
	11							
	12							
	13							
	14							
	15							
	16							
	17							

TRIBAL ENROLLMENT OF PARENTS

	Name of Father	Year	County	Name of Mother	Year	County
1	Ish-to-na-ke	Dead	Bok Tuklo	Ba-che-hu-na	Dead	Bok Tuklo
2						
3						
4						
5						
6						
7						
8						
9						
10						
11						
12						
13						
14						
15				Date of Application for Enrollment.		
16				April 20/99		
17						

Choctaw By Blood Enrollment Cards 1898-1914

RESIDENCE: Eagle   COUNTY.   **Choctaw Nation**   **Choctaw Roll**   CARD NO.
POST OFFICE: Eagletown, I.T.   *(Not Including Freedmen)*   FIELD NO. **622**

Dawes' Roll No.	NAME		Relationship to Person First Named	AGE	SEX	BLOOD	TRIBAL ENROLLMENT		
							Year	County	No.
1438	₁ Stephen, Louis	23	First Named	20	M	Full	1896	Bok Tuklo	11421
1439	₂ " Agnes	27	Wife	24	F	"	1896	" "	11422
	3								
	4								
	5								
	6	ENROLLMENT							
	7	OF NOS. 1 and 2 HEREON APPROVED BY THE SECRETARY							
	8	OF INTERIOR Dec 12, 1902							
	9								
	10								
	11								
	12								
	13								
	14								
	15								
	16								
	17								

TRIBAL ENROLLMENT OF PARENTS

	Name of Father	Year	County	Name of Mother	Year	County
1	Stephen Untahalby	1896	Eagle	Bitsie Untahalby	1896	Eagle
2	Ish-to-na-ke	Dead	Bok Tuklo	Ba-che-hu-na	Dead	Bok Tuklo
3						
4						
5						
6	No.2 on 1896 roll as Iknes Stephen					
7	No.1 is said to have died in Jail at So M^c̲Alester, Ind. Ter. in 1901.					
8	~~Above notation is in error. No.1 died in Ft. Smith, Ark Jail in Dec, 1902.~~					
9						
10						
11	~~No.1 died prior to September 25, 1902; not entitled to land or money~~					
12	See Indian Office Letter April 20, 1908. (I.T. 19827-1908)					
13						
14						
15						
16				Date of Application for Enrollment		April 20/99
17						

Choctaw By Blood Enrollment Cards 1898-1914

RESIDENCE: Eagle   COUNTY.   **Choctaw Nation**   **Choctaw Roll**   CARD NO.

POST OFFICE: Eagletown, I.T.   *(Not Including Freedmen)*   FIELD NO. **623**

Dawes' Roll No.	NAME		Relationship to Person First Named	AGE	SEX	BLOOD	TRIBAL ENROLLMENT		
							Year	County	No.
1440	1	Going, William ~~DIED PRIOR TO SEPTEMBER 25, 1902~~		30	M	Full	1896	Eagle	4795
1441	2	" , Imahoke 41	Wife	38	F	"	1896	"	4790
1442	3	Tonihka, Phoebe 10	S. Dau	7	"	"	1896	"	12225
	4								
	5	ENROLLMENT							
	6	OF NOS. 1 – 2 and 3 HEREON							
	7	APPROVED BY THE SECRETARY OF INTERIOR Dec 12 – 1902							
	8								
	9								
	10	No.1 Died December _ 1900: Enrollment cancelled by Department May 2, 1906.							
	11								
	12								
	13								
	14								
	15								
	16								
	17								

TRIBAL ENROLLMENT OF PARENTS

	Name of Father	Year	County	Name of Mother	Year	County
1	~~Alfred Going~~	1896	~~Red River~~	~~Sophia Going~~	Dead	Eagle
2	Ish-mi-ya-ubbee	Dead	" "	Okla-he-ma	"	Red River
3	Albert Tonihka	"	Eagle	No.2		
4						
5						
6						
7						
8						
9						
10						
11						
12						
13						
14						
15						
16				Date of Application for Enrollment		April 21/99
17						

Choctaw By Blood Enrollment Cards 1898-1914

RESIDENCE: COUNTY.
POST OFFICE:

Choctaw Nation

Choctaw Roll *(Not Including Freedmen)*

CARD NO.
FIELD NO. **624**

Dawes' Roll No.	NAME	Relationship to Person	AGE	SEX	BLOOD	TRIBAL ENROLLMENT		
						Year	County	No.
1443	1 Tonihka, Dickson ³⁴	First Named	31	M	Full	1896	Eagle	12216
1444	2 " Lina ⁴⁹	Wife	46	F	"	1896	"	P.R. 578
1445	3 Going, Jim ~~DIED PRIOR TO SEPTEMBER 25, 1902~~	S.Son	18	M	"	1896	"	4791
1446	4 Ishtechi, Selah ~~DIED PRIOR TO SEPTEMBER 25, 1902~~	Ward	15	F	"	1896	"	6295
	5							
	6							
	7							
	8							
	9							
	10							
	11							
	12							
	13							
	14							
	15							
	16							
	17							

ENROLLMENT
OF NOS. 1 2 3 and 4 HEREON
APPROVED BY THE SECRETARY
OF INTERIOR Dec 12, 1902

TRIBAL ENROLLMENT OF PARENTS

	Name of Father	Year	County	Name of Mother	Year	County
1	Tonihka	Dead	Eagle	E-la-pin-to-la	Dead	Eagle
2	Thompson Anson	"	Red River	Bilsey Anson	1896	"
3	~~Newton Going~~	"	~~Eagle~~	~~No 2~~		
4	~~Anel Ishtechi~~	"	"	~~Sosin Ishtechi~~	~~Dead~~	~~Eagle~~
5						
6						
7			No1 on 1896 roll as Dixon Tonikha			
8			No2 " 1893 Payroll Eagle Co. Page 62 #578 as Lena Toneka.			
9						
10			No.3 died March 4, 1902: Proof of death filed Dec. 3, 1902.			
11			No 4 " in 1901: Evidence as to death filed Dec. 3, 1902.			
12			~~No3 died March 4,1902: No4 died - - 1901: Enrollment cancelled by Department July 8, 1904.~~			
13						
14						
15						
16			Date of Application for Enrollment	April 21/99		
17						

24

Choctaw By Blood Enrollment Cards 1898-1914

RESIDENCE: Eagle   COUNTY. **Choctaw Nation**   **Choctaw Roll**   CARD No.
POST OFFICE: Eagletown, I.T.   *(Not Including Freedmen)*   FIELD No. **625**

Dawes' Roll No.	NAME		Relationship to Person	AGE	SEX	BLOOD	TRIBAL ENROLLMENT		
							Year	County	No.
1447	₁ A-la-ho-nubbi	48	First Named	45	M	Full	1896	Eagle	269
1448	₂ " Louisianna	41	Wife	38	F	"	1896	"	292
DEAD	₃ Tonihka, Lucin DEAD		Ward	11	"	"	1896	"	12224
1449	₄ Homma, Simeon	20	"	17	M	"	1896	"	P.R. 347
	₅								
	₆								
	₇	ENROLLMENT							
	₈	OF NOS. 1 – 2 and 4 HEREON APPROVED BY THE SECRETARY							
	₉	OF INTERIOR Dec 12 1902							
	₁₀								
	₁₁								
	₁₂	No 3 hereon dismissed under order of							
	₁₃	the Commission to the Five Civilized							
	₁₄	Tribes of March 31, 1905.							
	₁₅								
	₁₆								
	₁₇								

TRIBAL ENROLLMENT OF PARENTS

	Name of Father	Year	County	Name of Mother	Year	County
₁	James Othletaby	1896	Eagle	No-ha-ma	Dead	Eagle
₂	To-nih-ka	Dead	"	E-la-pin-to-na	"	"
₃	Lawston Tonihka	"	"	Sis Tonihka	"	"
₄	Lewis Fobb	"	"	Winnie Fobb	"	"
₅						
₆						
₇	No3 on 1896 roll as Lawson Tonihka					
₈						
₉	No2 also on 1896 roll as Simon Homa					
₁₀	Page 137, No 2655, Eagle Co					
₁₁	N⁰3 Died in March 1900: proof of death filed March 13, 1902.					
₁₂	No4 is also known as Simeon Fobb; he is now husband of Jincy Carnes					
₁₃	on Choctaw card #1317					
₁₄						
₁₅					Date of Application for Enrollment.	
₁₆						
₁₇					April 21/99	

Choctaw By Blood Enrollment Cards 1898-1914

RESIDENCE: Nashoba   COUNTY.   **Choctaw Nation**   Choctaw Roll   CARD NO.
POST OFFICE: Alikchi, I.T.   *(Not Including Freedmen)*   FIELD NO. **626**

Dawes' Roll No.	NAME	Relationship to Person	AGE	SEX	BLOOD	TRIBAL ENROLLMENT Year	County	No.
1450	1 Watson, Ben J. 43	First Named	40	M	Full	1896	Nashoba	13336
1451	2 " Margaret 31	Wife	28	F	"	1896	"	13337
~~1452~~	3 ~~DIED PRIOR TO SEPTEMBER 25, 1902 Ellen~~	~~S.Dau~~	~~11~~	~~"~~	~~"~~	~~1896~~	~~"~~	~~13338~~
1453	4 " Lorin 11	S.Son	8	M	"	1896	"	13339
	5							
	6							
	7							
	8							
	9 ENROLLMENT							
	10 OF NOS. 1 2 3 and 4 HEREON ~~APPROVED BY THE SECRETARY~~				No2 on 1896 roll as Margrett Watson			
	11 OF INTERIOR Dec 12 1902							
	12							
	13							
	14							
	15							
	16							
	17							

TRIBAL ENROLLMENT OF PARENTS

	Name of Father	Year	County	Name of Mother	Year	County
1	Jonas Watson	Dead	Nashoba	Hon-te-ma	Dead	Nashoba
2	Edmund Gardner	1896	"	Liza Gardner	1896	"
3	Timothy Cephus	1896	"	No 2		
4	" "	1896	"	No 2		
5						
6						
7	No.3 died May, 1901: Enrollment cancelled by Department July 8 – 1904					
8	No3 died May – 1901: proof of death filed Dec 16, 1902.					
9	See affidavits relative to death of No3 filed Dec. 24, 1902.					
10						
11						
12						
13						
14						
15						
16				Date of Application for Enrollment	April 21/99	
17						

26

Choctaw By Blood Enrollment Cards 1898-1914

RESIDENCE: Nashoba
POST OFFICE: Alikchi, I.T.

COUNTY. **Choctaw Nation**

Choctaw Roll
(Not Including Freedmen)

CARD NO.
FIELD NO. **627**

Dawes' Roll No.	NAME	Relationship to Person	AGE	SEX	BLOOD	TRIBAL ENROLLMENT		
						Year	County	No.
1454	1 Hardy, Laisie 53	First Named	50	F	Full	1896	Nashoba	5551
	2							
	3							
	4							
	5	ENROLLMENT						
	6	OF NOS. 1 HEREON APPROVED BY THE SECRETARY						
	7	OF INTERIOR Dec 12, 1902						
	8							
	9							
	10							
	11							
	12							
	13							
	14							
	15							
	16							
	17							

TRIBAL ENROLLMENT OF PARENTS

	Name of Father	Year	County	Name of Mother	Year	County
1	Hardy	Dead	Nashoba	Pekie Hardy	Dead	Nashoba
2						
3						
4						
5						
6						
7						
8						
9						
10						
11						
12						
13						
14						
15						
16				Date of Application for Enrollment		April 21/99
17						

27

Choctaw By Blood Enrollment Cards 1898-1914

RESIDENCE: Nashoba
POST OFFICE: Alikchi, I.T.
COUNTY. **Choctaw Nation**
Choctaw Roll *(Not Including Freedmen)*
CARD NO.
FIELD NO. **628**

Dawes' Roll No.	NAME		Relationship to Person	AGE	SEX	BLOOD	TRIBAL ENROLLMENT		
							Year	County	No.
1455	1 Brewer, Ellis	46	First Named	43	M	Full	1896	Nashoba	1215
1456	2 " Agnes	41	Wife	38	F	"	1896	"	1216
1457	3 " Annie	11	Dau	8	"	"	1896	"	1217
1458	4 " Raymus	5	Son	1	M	"			
1459	5 Battiest, Selin	19	Ward	16	F	"	1896	"	1214
14575	6 Jefferson, Sissie	1	Dau of No2	3mo	F	"			
	7								
	8		ENROLLMENT						
	9		OF NOS. 1 2 3 4 and 5 HEREON APPROVED BY THE SECRETARY						
	10		OF INTERIOR Dec 12 1902						
	11								
	12								
	13		ENROLLMENT						
	14		OF NOS. 6 HEREON APPROVED BY THE SECRETARY						
	15		OF INTERIOR May 20 1903						
	16								
	17								

TRIBAL ENROLLMENT OF PARENTS

	Name of Father	Year	County	Name of Mother	Year	County
1	Elijah Brewer	Dead	Nashoba		Dead	Nashoba
2	Ish-te-a-tubbee	"	"	An-thle-hu-na	"	"
3	No. 1			No. 2		
4	No. 1			No. 2		
5	William Battiest	Dead	Nashoba	Josie Battiest	1896	Nashoba
6	Austin Jefferson			No. 2		
7						
8						
9	No.5 on 1896 roll as Cillian Battiest					
10	No.4 Affidavit of birth to be supplied. Recd April 21/99					
11	No 6 born Sept. 6, 1902; enrolled Dec 15, 1902					
12	Nos 1 and 2 have been divorced. No.2 now the wife of Austin Jefferson					
13	Choc. #497. No.2 has child named Sissie Jefferson. Evidence of birth to be supplied 12/10/02					
14	For child of No.2 see NB (March 3, 1905) #924					
15					#1 to 5 inc	
16				Date of Application for Enrollment	April 21/99	
17	P.O. Bethel I.T 4/6/05					

RESIDENCE: Nashoba
POST OFFICE: Alikchi, I.T.
COUNTY. **Choctaw Nation**
Choctaw Roll *(Not Including Freedmen)*
CARD No.
FIELD No. 629

Dawes' Roll No.		NAME		Relationship to Person	AGE	SEX	BLOOD	TRIBAL ENROLLMENT		
								Year	County	No.
1460	1	Watson, Ananias	27	First Named	24	M	Full	1896	Nashoba	13309
1461	2	" Semie	24	Wife	21	F	"	1896	"	13310
1462	3	" John	8	Son	5	M	"	1896	"	13311
1463	4	" Jennie		Dau	2	F	"			
1464	5	" Robert	2	Son	8mo	M	"			
1465	6	" Billy	1	Son	2mo	M	"			
	7									
	8									
	9									
	10									
	11									
	12									
	13									
	14									
	15									
	16									
	17									

(Row 4: DIED PRIOR TO SEPTEMBER 25, 1902)

ENROLLMENT
OF NOS. 12345and6 HEREON
APPROVED BY THE SECRETARY
OF INTERIOR Dec 12 1902

TRIBAL ENROLLMENT OF PARENTS

	Name of Father	Year	County	Name of Mother	Year	County
1	Jonas Watson	Dead	Nashoba	Honey Watson	Dead	Nashoba
2	Colone	"	"	La-kie	"	"
3	No 1			No 2		
4	No 1			No 2		
5	No 1			No 2		
6	No 1			No 2		
7	No4 Affidavit of birth to be supplied Rec'd April 21/99					
8	No.5 Enrolled January 3, 1901					
9	No.6 Born April 20, 1901: enrolled June 2, 1902					
10	Not on 1896 Roll as Annanias Watson					
	No4 died Oct. 25, 1900: proof of death filed Dec. 13, 1902.					
11	No.4 died Oct. 25-1900: Enrollment cancelled by Department July 8 – 1904					
12	For child of Nos. 1&2 see NB (March 3, 1905) #936					
13						
14						
15					Date of Application for Enrollment.	
16	Present P.O. Address Bethel I.T. Jany 3. 1901.				April 21/99	
17	P.O. Noah I.T. 4/6/05					

29

Choctaw By Blood Enrollment Cards 1898-1914

RESIDENCE: Nashoba   COUNTY. **Choctaw Nation**   **Choctaw Roll**   CARD NO.
POST OFFICE: Alikchi, I.T.   *(Not Including Freedmen)*   FIELD NO. 630

Dawes' Roll No.	NAME	Relationship to Person	AGE	SEX	BLOOD	TRIBAL ENROLLMENT Year	County	No.
1466	1 Williams, Morris ⁵⁶	First Named	53	M	Full	1896	Nashoba	13364
DEAD.	2 " Tennessee DEAD.	Wife	53	F	"	1896	"	13365
	3							
	4							
	5	ENROLLMENT						
	6	OF NOS. 1 HEREON APPROVED BY THE SECRETARY						
	7	OF INTERIOR DEC 12 1902						
	8							
	9							
	10							
	11	No. 2 HEREON DISMISSED UNDER ORDER OF THE COMMISSION TO THE FIVE						
	12	CIVILIZED TRIBES OF MARCH 31, 1905.						
	13							
	14							
	15							
	16							
	17							

TRIBAL ENROLLMENT OF PARENTS

Name of Father	Year	County	Name of Mother	Year	County
1 A-lo-ma-tubbee	Dead	Nashoba	Pollie	Dead	Nashoba
2 E-la-pin-tubbee	"	Jacks Fork	I-ma-lo-na	"	"
3					
4					
5	N°2 Died May 26, 1901; proof of death filed June 3, 1902.				
6	N°1 is now the husband of Adeline Cephus on Choctaw card #860, June 3, 1902.				
7					
8					
9					
10					
11					
12					
13					
14					
15				Date of Application for Enrollment.	
16				April 21/99	
17					

30

Choctaw By Blood Enrollment Cards 1898-1914

RESIDENCE: Nashoba   COUNTY.   **Choctaw Nation**   **Choctaw Roll**   CARD NO.
POST OFFICE: Alikchi, I.T.   *(Not Including Freedmen)*   FIELD NO. 631

Dawes' Roll No.	NAME		Relationship to Person Named	AGE	SEX	BLOOD	TRIBAL ENROLLMENT		
							Year	County	No.
1467	1	Carterby, Siglon ³⁰	First Named	27	M	Full	1896	Nashoba	2505
1468	2	" Tillis ³⁰	Wife	27	F	"	1896	"	2506
1469	3	" Moses ¹⁰	Son	7	M	"	1896	"	2507
1470	4	" Maleum[?] ⁶	Dau	3	F	"	1896	"	2508
DEAD.	5	" ~~Silas~~ DEAD.	~~Son~~	~~2~~	~~M~~	"			
1471	6	" John ²	Son	8m	M	"			
	7								
	8								
	9	ENROLLMENT							
	10	OF NOS. 1 2 3 4 and 6 HEREON APPROVED BY THE SECRETARY							
	11	OF INTERIOR DEC 12 1902							
	12								
	13	No. 5 HEREON DISMISSED UNDER							
	14	ORDER OF THE COMMISSION TO THE FIVE							
	15	CIVILIZED TRIBES OF MARCH 31, 1905.							
	16								
	17								

TRIBAL ENROLLMENT OF PARENTS

	Name of Father	Year	County	Name of Mother	Year	County
1	Tillie Carterby	Dead	Nashoba	Emeline Carterby	1896	Nashoba
2	Sha-la-tuby	"	"	Millie	1896	"
3	No 1			No 2		
4	No 1			No 2		
5	~~No 1~~			~~No 2~~		
6	No 1			No 2		
7						
8	No1 on 1896 roll as Siglynn Carterby					
9	No.6 Enrolled January 24, 1901.					
10	~~N⁰5 Died Sept. 30, 1900: proof of death filed June 2, 1902~~ ~~For children of Nos 1&2 see NB (March 3, 1905) #952~~					
11						
12						
13						
14				Date of Application for Enrollment.		
15						
16				April 21/99		
17						

Choctaw By Blood Enrollment Cards 1898-1914

RESIDENCE: Nashoba   COUNTY.   **Choctaw Nation**   **Choctaw Roll**   CARD No.
POST OFFICE: Alikchi, I.T.   *(Not Including Freedmen)*   FIELD No.   632

Dawes' Roll No.		NAME		Relationship to Person First Named	AGE	SEX	BLOOD	TRIBAL ENROLLMENT Year	County	No.
1472	1	Baker, Elsie			40	F	Full	1896	Nashoba	1198
1473	2	" Isham	22	Son	19	M	"	1896	"	1199
1474	3	" Davis	20	"	17	"	"	1896	"	1200
1475	4	" Robinson	17	"	14	"	"	1896	"	1201
1476	5	" Charles	12	"	9	"	"	1896	"	1202
1477	6	" Emma	6	Dau	3	F	"	1896	"	1203
	7									
	8	ENROLLMENT								
	9	OF NOS. 12345and6 HEREON APPROVED BY THE SECRETARY								
	10	OF INTERIOR DEC 12 1902								
	11									
	12									
	13									
	14									
	15									
	16									
	17									

TRIBAL ENROLLMENT OF PARENTS

	Name of Father	Year	County	Name of Mother	Year	County
1	Ta-nich-cha	1896	Nashoba	A-pa-sa-tema	Dead	Nashoba
2	John Baker	Dead	"	No 1		
3	" "	"	"	No 1		
4	" "	"	"	No 1		
5	" "	"	"	No 1		
6	Alman Carterby	1896	Nashoba	No 1		
7						
8	No1 died Nov. – 1901; proof of death filed Dec 12, 1902					
9	No2 is now husband of Minnie Cephus on Choc card #923					
10	Marriage certificate recd 12/9/02					
11	Not died Nov. – 1901. Enrollment cancelled by Department					
12	For child of No.4 see NB (March 3, 1905) #855					
13	" " " No.2 " " " " " #940					
	" " " " " " " " " #605					
14						
15						
16				Date of Application for Enrollment	April 21/99	
17	Beebe I.T. 12/9/02					

Choctaw By Blood Enrollment Cards 1898-1914

RESIDENCE: Towson   COUNTY.   **Choctaw Nation**   **Choctaw Roll**   CARD NO.

POST OFFICE: Alikchi, I.T.   *(Not Including Freedmen)*   FIELD NO. **633**

Dawes' Roll No.	NAME		Relationship to Person First Named	AGE	SEX	BLOOD	TRIBAL ENROLLMENT		
							Year	County	No.
1478	1 Daniel, John	31		28	M	Full	1896	Towson	3376
1479	2 " Mary	41	Wife	38	F	"	1896	"	3377
~~1480~~	~~3 " Annie~~ *Died prior to September 25, 1902*		~~Dau~~	~~8~~	~~"~~	~~"~~	~~1896~~	~~"~~	~~P.R. 95~~
1481	4 " Sillian	5	"	1½	"	"			
	5								
	6								
	7								
	8								
	9								
	10								
	11	ENROLLMENT OF NOS. 1 2 3 and 4 HEREON APPROVED BY THE SECRETARY OF INTERIOR Dec 12 1902							
	12								
	13								
	14								
	15								
	16								
	17								

TRIBAL ENROLLMENT OF PARENTS

	Name of Father	Year	County	Name of Mother	Year	County
1	Tush-kia	Dead	Towson	Mary Tushkia	Dead	Towson
2		"	"	Tek-ho-you	"	"
3	~~No.1~~			~~No.2~~		
4	No.1			No.2		
5						
6						
7			No.4 Affidavit of birth to be supplied. Recd Apr 29/99			
8						
9			~~No.3 on 1893 Payroll as Anni Daniel.~~			
10			No.3 died Sept – 1899: Enrollment cancelled by Department July 8 – 1904			
11						
12						
13						
14					Date of Application for Enrollment.	
15						
16					April 21/99	
17						

33

Choctaw By Blood Enrollment Cards 1898-1914

RESIDENCE: Bok Tuklo COUNTY.
POST OFFICE: Fowlerville, I.T.

Choctaw Nation

Choctaw Roll *(Not Including Freedmen)*

CARD NO.
FIELD NO. **634**

Dawes' Roll No.	NAME	Relationship to Person First Named	AGE	SEX	BLOOD	TRIBAL ENROLLMENT Year	County	No.
1482	1 Willis, Joe ~~DIED PRIOR TO SEPTEMBER 25, 1902~~		38	M	Full	1896	Bok Tuklo	13401
1483	2 " Tahobbe 53	Wife	50	F	"	1893	" "	P.R. 290
1484	3 " Sampson ~~DIED PRIOR TO SEPTEMBER 25, 1902~~	Son	24	M	"	1896	" "	13402
	4							
	5							
	6							
	7							
	8							
	9							
	10							
	11	ENROLLMENT						
	12	OF NOS. 1 – 2 and 3 HEREON APPROVED BY THE SECRETARY						
	13	OF INTERIOR Dec 12 1902						
	14							
	15							
	16							
	17							

TRIBAL ENROLLMENT OF PARENTS

	Name of Father	Year	County	Name of Mother	Year	County
1	Su-illis	Dead	Kiamitia	Sissie	Dead	Kiamitia
2	Moses Homma	"	Cedar	I-ye-ah	"	Towson
3	No 1			Phoebe Willis	"	"
4						
5						
6		No2 appears on 1893 Pay Roll as a male				
7		No2 also on 1896 roll Bok Tuklo Co, Page				
8		53, No 6281 as "Itahobbe"				
		No1 died April, 1899. proof of death filed Dec 16, 1902.				
9		No3 " Nov. 20 1901: Proof of death filed Dec. 30, 1902				
10	No.1 died April - 1899: No.3 died Nov. 20 - 1901: Enrollment cancelled by Department July 8 - 1904					
11						
12						
13						
14						
15						
16				Date of Application for Enrollment.	April 21/99	
17						

Choctaw By Blood Enrollment Cards 1898-1914

RESIDENCE: Bok Tuklo   COUNTY. **Choctaw Nation**   **Choctaw Roll**   CARD NO.
POST OFFICE: Lukfata, I.T.   *(Not Including Freedmen)*   FIELD NO.   635

Dawes' Roll No.	NAME	Relationship to Person First Named	AGE	SEX	BLOOD	TRIBAL ENROLLMENT		
						Year	County	No.
1485	1 Anderson, William 39		36	M	Full	1896	Bok Tuklo	256
	2							
	3							
	4							
	5							
	6							
	7	ENROLLMENT						
	8	OF NOS. 1 HEREON APPROVED BY THE SECRETARY						
	9	OF INTERIOR DEC 12 1902						
	10							
	11							
	12							
	13							
	14							
	15	On 1896 roll as Willy Anderson. Page 6 № 256						
	16							
	17							

TRIBAL ENROLLMENT OF PARENTS

	Name of Father	Year	County	Name of Mother	Year	County
1	Po-an-tubbee	Dead	Bok Tuklo	Lucy Poantubbee	Dead	Bok Tuklo
2						
3						
4						
5						
6						
7						
8						
9						
10						
11						
12						
13						
14						
15						
16				Date of Application for Enrollment		April 21/99
17						

35

Choctaw By Blood Enrollment Cards 1898-1914

RESIDENCE: Red River   COUNTY.

POST OFFICE: Garvin, I.T.

Choctaw Nation

Choctaw Roll
(Not Including Freedmen)

CARD NO.

FIELD NO. 636

Dawes' Roll No.	NAME	Relationship to Person	AGE	SEX	BLOOD	TRIBAL ENROLLMENT		
						Year	County	No.
1486	1 Henderson, Martha 56	First Named	53	F	Full	1896	Red River	5684
	2							
	3							
	4							
	5							
	6							
	7							
	8							
	9							
	10							
	11							
	12							
	13							
	14							
	15							
	16							
	17							

ENROLLMENT
OF NOS. 1 HEREON
APPROVED BY THE SECRETARY
OF INTERIOR DEC 12 1902

TRIBAL ENROLLMENT OF PARENTS

	Name of Father	Year	County	Name of Mother	Year	County
1	Chas. B. Anderson	Dead	Sugar Loaf	Sallie Anderson	Dead	Towson
2						
3						
4						
5						
6						
7						
8						
9						
10						
11						
12						
13						
14						
15						
16					Date of Application for Enrollment	April 21/99
17						

Choctaw By Blood Enrollment Cards 1898-1914

RESIDENCE: Towson COUNTY.
POST OFFICE: Fowlerville, I.T.

Choctaw Nation

Choctaw Roll
(Not Including Freedmen)

CARD NO.
FIELD NO. 637

Dawes' Roll No.	NAME	Relationship to Person Named	AGE	SEX	BLOOD	Year	TRIBAL ENROLLMENT County	No.
1487	1 Garland, John A 35	First	32	M	1/2	1896	Towson	4729
I.W. 628	2 " Quay 19	Wife	16	F	I.W.			
1488	3 " Garrett Arthur 2	Son	2mo	M	1/4			
1489	4 " John Spencer 1	Son	3mo	M	1/4			
	5							
	6							
	7	ENROLLMENT OF NOS. 1 3 and 4 HEREON						
	8	APPROVED BY THE SECRETARY OF INTERIOR DEC 12 1902						
	9							
	10							
	11	ENROLLMENT OF NOS. 2 HEREON						
	12	APPROVED BY THE SECRETARY OF INTERIOR MAR 26 1904						
	13							
	14							
	15							
	16							
	17							

TRIBAL ENROLLMENT OF PARENTS

	Name of Father	Year	County	Name of Mother	Year	County
1	Cornelius Garland	Dead	Towson	Sarah Garland	1896	Towson
2	Tilman Whitten	1896	Non Citz	Corrie Whitten	1896	Non Citz
3	No. 1			No. 2		
4	No. 1			No. 2		
5						
6						
7						
8	No 1 on 1896 roll as John Garland.					
9						
10	No. 3 Enrolled June 23d 1900					
11	No.4 born Oct. 25, 1901: Enrolled Jany. 27, 1902.					
12	For child of No 1&2 see N.B. (Apr 26, 1906) Card No 173.					
13	" " " " " " " (March 3, 1905) " " 713					
14					Date of Application for Enrollment.	
15						
16					April 21/99	
17	Chula I.T. 11/28/02					

P.O. [Illegible] I.T. 7/8/03

37

Choctaw By Blood Enrollment Cards 1898-1914

RESIDENCE: Towson   COUNTY.

POST OFFICE: Fowlerville, I.T.

Choctaw Nation

Choctaw Roll
(Not Including Freedmen)

CARD NO.

FIELD NO. **638**

Dawes' Roll No.	NAME		Relationship to Person First Named	AGE	SEX	BLOOD	TRIBAL ENROLLMENT		
							Year	County	No.
1490	1 Pebsworth, Sam	24	First Named	21	M	1/4	1896	Towson	10331
1491	2 " Robert L	17	brother	14	"	1/4	1896	"	10332
1492	3 " Hugh	15	"	12	"	1/4	1896	"	10333
1493	4 " James	12	"	9	"	1/4	1896	"	10334
1495	5 " John	10	"	7	"	1/4	1896	"	10335
1495	6 " Louis	8	"	5	"	1/4	1896	"	10336
	7								
	8			Further action in connection with allotment to Nos. 1 to 6					
	9			inclusive is pending under protest of Attorneys for					
	10			Choctaw and Chickasaw Nations Jan 23-04. Protest					
	11	ENROLLMENT		withdrawn by Attys Mch 24, 1904					
	12	OF NOS. 1 2 3 4 5 and 6 HEREON APPROVED BY THE SECRETARY								
	13	OF INTERIOR Dec 12 1902								
	14								
	15								
	16								
	17								

TRIBAL ENROLLMENT OF PARENTS

	Name of Father	Year	County	Name of Mother	Year	County
1	John Pebsworth	Dead	Towson	Mary Pebsworth	Dead	Non Citz
2	" "	"	"	" "	"	" "
3	" "	"	"	" "	"	" "
4	" "	"	"	" "	"	" "
5	" "	"	"	" "	"	" "
6	" "	"	"	" "	"	" "
7						
8						
9						
10			No2 on 1896 roll as Robt. Lee Pebsworth			
11						
12			Dec. 8/99. See Dawes Commission			
13			record 1896, Case 1376			
14						
15					Date of Application for Enrollment.	
16					April 21/99	
17						

Choctaw By Blood Enrollment Cards 1898-1914

RESIDENCE: Towson   COUNTY.   **Choctaw Nation**   **Choctaw Roll**   CARD No.
POST OFFICE: Fowlerville, I.T.   (Not Including Freedmen)   FIELD No.   639

Dawes' Roll No.	NAME	Relationship to Person First Named	AGE	SEX	BLOOD	TRIBAL ENROLLMENT Year	County	No.
1496	1 Garland, Sarah ⁵⁸	First Named	55	F	1/2	1896	Towson	4727
1497	2 " Mary J ⁴¹	Dau	38	"	1/2	1896	"	4728
	3							
	4							
	5							
	6							
	7							
	8							
	9							
	10							
	11							
	12							
	13							
	14							
	15							
	16							
	17							

ENROLLMENT
OF NOS. 1 and 2 HEREON
APPROVED BY THE SECRETARY
OF INTERIOR DEC 12 1902

TRIBAL ENROLLMENT OF PARENTS

	Name of Father	Year	County	Name of Mother	Year	County
1	Thomas LeFlore	Dead	Towson	Sukey LeFlore	Dead	Towson
2	Cornelius Garland	"	"	No 1		
3						
4						
5						
6						
7						
8						
9						
10						
11						
12						
13						
14						
15						
16						
17						

Date of Application for Enrollment.
April 21/99

39

Choctaw By Blood Enrollment Cards 1898-1914

				RESIDENCE: Red River COUNTY.	POST OFFICE: Shawneetown, I.T.

RESIDENCE: Red River COUNTY. **Choctaw Nation** **Choctaw Roll** *(Not Including Freedmen)* CARD NO.
POST OFFICE: Shawneetown, I.T. FIELD NO. 640

Dawes' Roll No.	NAME	Relationship to Person	AGE	SEX	BLOOD	TRIBAL ENROLLMENT		
						Year	County	No.
1498	1 Battiest, Nicy 48	First Named	45	F	Full	1896	Red River	1351
	2							
	3							
	4							
	5	ENROLLMENT						
	6	OF NOS. 1 HEREON APPROVED BY THE SECRETARY						
	7	OF INTERIOR DEC 12 1902						
	8							
	9							
	10							
	11							
	12	On 1896 roll as Bisey Battiest						
	13							
	14							
	15							
	16							
	17							

TRIBAL ENROLLMENT OF PARENTS

	Name of Father	Year	County	Name of Mother	Year	County
1	Nicholas Battiest	Dead	Red River		Dead	Red River
2						
3						
4						
5						
6						
7						
8						
9						
10						
11						
12						
13						
14						
15						
16				Date of Application for Enrollment		April 21/99
17						

Choctaw By Blood Enrollment Cards 1898-1914

RESIDENCE: Red River COUNTY.
POST OFFICE: Kullituklo, I.T.

Choctaw Nation

Choctaw Roll (Not Including Freedmen)

CARD NO.
FIELD NO. **641**

Dawes' Roll No.	NAME		Relationship to Person	AGE	SEX	BLOOD	TRIBAL ENROLLMENT		
							Year	County	No.
1499	1 Makatobe, Sarly	61	First Named	58	F	Full	1896	Red River	8670
1500	2 " Seely	20	Niece	17	"	"	1896	" "	8671
1501	3 " David	15	Nephew	12	M	"	1896	" "	8672
4									
5									
6									
7	ENROLLMENT								
8	OF NOS. 1 – 2 and 3 HEREON APPROVED BY THE SECRETARY								
9	OF INTERIOR DEC 12 1902								
10									
11									
12	Surnames of Nos 1 2 and 3 on Choc Roll as Makotube								
13									
14									
15									
16									
17									

TRIBAL ENROLLMENT OF PARENTS

	Name of Father	Year	County	Name of Mother	Year	County
1	Ish-ta-la-by	Dead	Eagle	E-ma lo-ba	Dead	Eagle
2	Ka-non-te-koby	"	"	Ma-yee	"	"
3	"	"	"	"	"	"
4						
5						
6						
7						
8						
9						
10						
11						
12						
13						
14						
15					Date of Application for Enrollment	
16					April 21/99	
17	Shawneetown I.T. 11/26/02					

41

RESIDENCE: Eagle   COUNTY.   **Choctaw Nation**   Choctaw Roll   CARD NO.
POST OFFICE: Eagletown, I.T.   (Not Including Freedmen)   FIELD NO.   642

Dawes' Roll No.	NAME	Relationship to Person First Named	AGE	SEX	BLOOD	TRIBAL ENROLLMENT Year	County	No.
1502	1 Loman, Simpson	Named	39	M	Full	1896	Eagle	8021
1503	2 " Bessie ³⁸	Wife	35	F	"	1896	"	2595
1504	3 " Samuell ¹⁸	Son	13	M	"	1896	"	8022
1505	4 " Lowina ¹⁴	Dau	11	F	"	1896	"	8023
1506	5 Cornelius, John ¹⁵	S.Son	12	M	"	1896	"	2619
1507	6 " Elum ¹³	"	10	"	"	1896	"	2604
1508	7 " Elizabeth ¹¹	S.Dau	8	F	"	1896	"	2605
	8							
	9							
	10							
	11	ENROLLMENT						
	12	OF NOS. 1 2 3 4 5 6 and 7 HEREON APPROVED BY THE SECRETARY						
	13	OF INTERIOR DEC 12 1902						
	14							
	15							
	16							
	17							

DIED PRIOR TO SEPTEMBER 25, 190[?]

TRIBAL ENROLLMENT OF PARENTS

	Name of Father	Year	County	Name of Mother	Year	County
1	Eastman Loman	Dead	Red River	Ou-te-a-hona	Dead	Red River
2	Gilbert Louis	"	Eagle	Betsey Louis	"	Eagle
3	No 1			Sealy Loman	1896	"
4	No 1			Sealy Loman	1896	"
5	Lewis Cornelius	Dead	Eagle	No 2		
6	" "	"	"	No 2		
7	" "	"	"	No 2		
8	No2 on 1896 roll as Bessie Cornelius					
9	No1 died July 1902; proof of death filed Dec 12, 1902					
10	No1 died July - 1902; Enrollment cancelled by Department [remainder illegible]					
11	No.2 Died prior to September 25, 1902; not entitled to land or money See Indian Office letter of June 1, 1911					
12						
13						
14						
15					Date of Application for Enrollment.	
16					April 21/99	
17						

Choctaw By Blood Enrollment Cards 1898-1914

RESIDENCE: Eagle   COUNTY. **Choctaw Nation**   **Choctaw Roll** *(Not Including Freedmen)* CARD NO.
POST OFFICE: Eagletown, I.T.   FIELD NO. 643

Dawes' Roll No.	NAME	Relationship to Person First Named	AGE	SEX	BLOOD	TRIBAL ENROLLMENT Year	County	No.
1509	1 Ward, Morris 71	Named	68	M	Full	1896	Nashoba	13234
1510	2 " Beckie 41	Wife	38	F	"	1896	"	13235
1511	3 " Bensie 13	Dau	10	"	"	1896	"	13236
	4							
	5							
	6							
	7							
	8							
	9							
	10							
	11	ENROLLMENT						
	12	OF NOS. 1- 2 and 3 HEREON APPROVED BY THE SECRETARY						
	13	OF INTERIOR DEC 12 1902						
	14							
	15							
	16							
	17							

TRIBAL ENROLLMENT OF PARENTS

	Name of Father	Year	County	Name of Mother	Year	County
1	A-fa-mun-taby	Dead	Nashoba	Da la le-huna	Dead	Nashoba
2	Ellis Morgan	"	Skullyville	Beckie Morgan	"	Eagle
3	No 1			No 2		
4						
5						
6						
7						
8						
9						
10						
11						
12						
13						
14						
15						
16						
17						

Date of Application for Enrollment April 21/99

43

Choctaw By Blood Enrollment Cards 1898-1914

RESIDENCE: Eagle   COUNTY.   **Choctaw Nation**   **Choctaw Roll**   CARD NO.

POST OFFICE: Eagletown, I.T.   *(Not Including Freedmen)*   FIELD NO. 644

Dawes' Roll No.	NAME	Relationship to Person First Named	AGE	SEX	BLOOD	TRIBAL ENROLLMENT Year	County	No.
1512	1 Battiest, Phoebe *DIED PRIOR TO SEPTEMBER 25 190* 53	Named	50	F	Full	1896	Eagle	1265
	2							
	3							
	4							
	5							
	6							
	7							
	8							
	9							
	10							
	11							
	12							
	13							
	14							
	15							
	16							
	17							

ENROLLMENT
OF NOS. 1 HEREON
APPROVED BY THE SECRETARY
OF INTERIOR DEC 12 1902

N° 1 Died April 28, 1901, proof of death filed Dec. 24, 1902

No. 1 died April 28, 1901: Enrollment cancelled by Department [remainder illegible]

TRIBAL ENROLLMENT OF PARENTS

	Name of Father	Year	County	Name of Mother	Year	County
1	Edmund Battiest	Dead	Eagle	Bitsie Battiest	Dead	Eagle
2						
3						
4						
5						
6						
7						
8						
9						
10						
11						
12						
13						
14						
15						
16					Date of Application for Enrollment	April 21/99
17						

Choctaw By Blood Enrollment Cards 1898-1914

RESIDENCE: Towson COUNTY.
POST OFFICE: Fowlerville, I.T.

Choctaw Nation

Choctaw Roll
(Not Including Freedmen)

CARD NO.
FIELD NO. 645

Dawes' Roll No.	NAME	Relationship to Person Named	AGE	SEX	BLOOD	TRIBAL ENROLLMENT Year	County	No.
1513	1 Simpson, Henry	DIED PRIOR TO SEPTEMBER 25, 1902 First	24	M	Full	1896	Towson	11375
1514	2 " Siney 23	Wife	20	F	"	1896	"	11376
1515	3 " Standley	DIED PRIOR TO SEPTEMBER 25, 1902 Son	2	M	"			
	4							
	5							
	6							
	7							
	8							
	9							
	10							
	11	ENROLLMENT OF NOS. 1-2 and 3 HEREON						
	12	APPROVED BY THE SECRETARY						
	13	OF INTERIOR DEC 12 1902						
	14							
	15							
	16							
	17							

TRIBAL ENROLLMENT OF PARENTS

	Name of Father	Year	County	Name of Mother	Year	County
1	Simpson	Dead	Towson	Ellen Simpson	1896	Towson
2	Foster Cobb	"	"		Dead	"
3	No 1			No 2		
4						
5						
6						
7						
8		No3 Affidavit of birth to be supplied				
9		No1 died April, 1900; proof of death filed Dec 3, 1902				
10		No3 " April 1899; " " " " " " "				
11						
12	No1 died April 1900; No3 died April 1899. Enrollment cancelled by Department					
13						
14						
15						
16			Date of Application for Enrollment April 21/99			
17						

45

Choctaw By Blood Enrollment Cards 1898-1914

RESIDENCE: Eagle COUNTY.
POST OFFICE: Eagletown, I.T.

Choctaw Nation

Choctaw Roll *(Not Including Freedmen)*

CARD NO.
FIELD NO. **646**

Dawes' Roll No.	NAME		Relationship to Person	AGE	SEX	BLOOD	TRIBAL ENROLLMENT		
							Year	County	No.
1516	1 Mambi, Williamson	45	First Named	42	M	Full	1896	Eagle	8645
1517	2 " Ellen	49	Wife	46	F	"	1896	"	8646
1518	3 " Stile	18	Son	15	M	"	1896	"	8648
1519	4 " Wattis	13	"	10	"	"	1896	"	8653
1520	5 " Norman	6	"	3	"	"	1896	"	8651
~~1521~~	~~6 Billy, Maley~~ DIED PRIOR TO SEPTEMBER 25, 1902		~~Ward~~	~~16~~	~~F~~	~~"~~	~~1896~~	~~"~~	~~1296~~
1522	7 " Witson	15	"	12	M	"	1896	"	1329
~~1523~~	~~8 " Lucy~~ DIED PRIOR TO SEPTEMBER 25, 1902		~~"~~	~~10~~	~~F~~	~~"~~	~~1896~~	~~"~~	~~1288~~
1524	9 " James	10	"	7	M	"	1896	"	1279
	10								
	11								
	12								
	13								
	14								
	15								
	16								
	17								

ENROLLMENT
OF NOS. 123456789 HEREON
APPROVED BY THE SECRETARY
OF INTERIOR Dec 12 1902

TRIBAL ENROLLMENT OF PARENTS

	Name of Father	Year	County	Name of Mother	Year	County
1	Mambi	Dead	Eagle	Pollie Mambi	Dead	Eagle
2	Joel Lewis	"	"	Liney Lewis	"	"
3	No 1			No 2		
4	No 1			No 2		
5	No 1			No 2		
6	~~Fisher Billy~~	~~Dead~~	~~Eagle~~	~~Sophia Billy~~	~~Dead~~	~~Eagle~~
7	" "	"	"	" "	"	"
8	" "	"	"	" "	"	"
9	" "	"	"	" "	"	"
10			No 1 on 1896 roll as William Mambi			
11			No 7 on 1896 " " Wilson Billy			
12			No 6 died April 1900: proof of death filed Dec 12, 1902			
13			No 8 " April 1900: " " " " " " "			
14	No 6 died April-1900: No 8 died April-1900: Enrollment cancelled by Department July 8-1904					
15						Date of Application for Enrollment.
16						
17						April 21/99

46

Choctaw By Blood Enrollment Cards 1898-1914

RESIDENCE: Eagle COUNTY.
POST OFFICE: Eagletown, I.T.

Choctaw Nation

Choctaw Roll
(Not Including Freedmen)

CARD No.
FIELD NO. 647

Dawes' Roll No.	NAME	Relationship to Person First Named	AGE	SEX	BLOOD	TRIBAL ENROLLMENT Year	County	No.
1525	1 Jones, Quitman 29		26	M	Full	1896	Eagle	6946
	2							
	3							
	4							
	5							
	6	ENROLLMENT						
	7	OF NOS. 1 HEREON APPROVED BY THE SECRETARY						
	8	OF INTERIOR DEC 12 1902						
	9							
	10							
	11							
	12							
	13							
	14							
	15							
	16							
	17							

TRIBAL ENROLLMENT OF PARENTS

	Name of Father	Year	County	Name of Mother	Year	County
1	Jones Jones	Dead	Eagle	Niccy Jones	Dead	Eagle
2						
3						
4						
5						
6						
7						
8						
9						
10						
11						
12						
13						
14						
15						
16						
17						

Date of Application for Enrollment April 21/99

47

Choctaw By Blood Enrollment Cards 1898-1914

RESIDENCE: Eagle   COUNTY.
POST OFFICE: Eagletown, I.T.

Choctaw Nation

Choctaw Roll
(Not Including Freedmen)

CARD NO.
FIELD NO. **648**

Dawes' Roll No.	NAME		Relationship to Person	AGE	SEX	BLOOD	TRIBAL ENROLLMENT		
							Year	County	No.
1526	1 Bohanan, Sampson	58	First Named	55	M	Full	1896	Eagle	1313
1527	2 ~~Annie~~ DIED PRIOR TO SEPTEMBER 25, 190?		~~Wife~~	~~52~~	~~F~~	~~"~~	~~1896~~	~~"~~	P.R. 94
1528 ✓	3 " John	19	Son	16	M	"	1896	"	1285
1529	4 " Elsey	12	Dau	9	F	"	1896	"	1268
1530	5 " Emily	10	"	7	"	"	1896	"	1269
1531	6 " Lena	21	"	18	"	"	1896	"	P.R. 69
	7								
	8	ENROLLMENT							
	9	OF NOS. 1 2 3 4 5 and 6 HEREON APPROVED BY THE SECRETARY							
	10	OF INTERIOR Dec 12 1902							
	11								
	12								
	13								
	14								
	15								
	16								
	17								

TRIBAL ENROLLMENT OF PARENTS

	Name of Father	Year	County	Name of Mother	Year	County
1	Joshua Bohanan	Dead	Kiamitia	Ish-te-mi-ah	Dead	Eagle
2	~~Pen-tubbee~~	"	~~Eagle~~	~~Cha-lo-ma~~	"	~~Nashoba~~
3	No 1			No 2		
4	No 1			No 2		
5	No 1			No 2		
6	No 1			No 2		
7						
8						
9		For child of No1 see NB (Apr 26 '06) Card #599.				
10		No3 is now husband of Artie Dyer Choctaw Card #670 Jany 20, 1903.				
11		No2 on 1893 Pay roll as Ebahotima No6 " 1893 " " " Leny Bohanan				
12		For child of No6 see NB (Apr 26 '06) Card No 711				
13		No6 also on 1896 roll as Linny Bohanan				
14		Page 32, No 1290, Eagle Co.				
15						
16		No2 also on 1896 roll as Ebahotima Page 91, No 3764, Eagle Co.		Date of Application for Enrollment	April 21/99	
17		No2 Died in 1899 Enrollment cancelled by Department May 2 1906.				

48

Choctaw By Blood Enrollment Cards 1898-1914

RESIDENCE: Cedar COUNTY. **Choctaw Nation** **Choctaw Roll** CARD NO.
POST OFFICE: Doaksville, I.T. (Not Including Freedmen) FIELD NO. **649**

Dawes' Roll No.	NAME	Relationship to Person First Named	AGE	SEX	BLOOD	TRIBAL ENROLLMENT Year	County	No.
1532	1 Jefferson, Stewart 43	Named	40	M	Full	1896	Eagle	6734
1533	2 " Betsy 32	Wife	29	F	"	1896	"	6735
1534	3 " Sarah 11	Dau	8	"	"	1896	"	6736
1535	4 " Nancy 9	"	6	"	"	1896	"	6737
	5							
	6							
	7							
	8	ENROLLMENT						
	9	OF NOS. 1 2 3 and 4 HEREON APPROVED BY THE SECRETARY						
	10	OF INTERIOR Dec 12 1902						
	11							
	12	No 3 on 1896 roll as Sarah Jefferson						
	13							
	14							
	15							
	16							
	17							

TRIBAL ENROLLMENT OF PARENTS

	Name of Father	Year	County	Name of Mother	Year	County
1	The-eh-nubbi	Dead	Cedar	Okla-huma	Dead	Cedar
2	A-pis-ta-ken-by	1896	Towson	Ho-te-na	"	Towson
3	No 1			No 2		
4	No 1			No 2		
5						
6						
7						
8						
9						
10						
11						
12						
13						
14						
15				Date of Application for Enrollment.		
16				April 21/99		
17						

RESIDENCE: Cedar   COUNTY. **Choctaw Nation**   **Choctaw Roll**   CARD NO.
POST OFFICE: Doaksville, I.T.   *(Not Including Freedmen)*   FIELD NO. 650

Dawes' Roll No.	NAME		Relationship to Person	AGE	SEX	BLOOD	TRIBAL ENROLLMENT		
							Year	County	No.
1536	1 Tillis, Jim	68	First Named	65	M	Full	1896	Cedar	12071
1537	2 " Mila	37	Wife	34	F	"	1893	"	P.R. 343
	3								
	4								
	5								
	6								
	7								
	8								
	9								
	10								
	11								
	12								
	13								
	14								
	15								
	16								
	17								

ENROLLMENT
OF NOS. 1 and 2 HEREON
APPROVED BY THE SECRETARY
OF INTERIOR DEC 12 1902

No1 is deaf. Could not ascertain name of his mother
No2 on 1893 Pay roll as Molly Nakishuehabe, also on
1896 roll as Mollie Page 214, No 858, Cedar Co

TRIBAL ENROLLMENT OF PARENTS

	Name of Father	Year	County	Name of Mother	Year	County
1	Na-ka-stu-na	Dead	in Mississippi		Dead	Cedar
2	Ha-ne-ubbee	"	Nashoba	Kon-chee	"	Towson
3						
4						
5						
6						
7						
8						
9						
10						
11						
12						
13						
14						
15						
16						
17						

Date of Application
for Enrollment.

April 21/99

Choctaw By Blood Enrollment Cards 1898-1914

RESIDENCE: Bok Tuklo
POST OFFICE: Lukfata, I.T.

COUNTY. **Choctaw Nation**

Choctaw Roll
(Not Including Freedmen)

CARD NO.
FIELD NO. **651**

Dawes' Roll No.	NAME			Relationship to Person First Named	AGE	SEX	BLOOD	TRIBAL ENROLLMENT		
								Year	County	No.
1538	Ward, Wilmon	1	31		28	M	Full	1896	Bok Tuklo	13410
1539	" Siwen	2	21	Wife	18	F	"	1896	" "	6286
1540	" Winney	3	10	Dau	7	"	"	1896	" "	13412
1541	" Henry	4	9	Son	6	M	"	1896	" "	13413
1542	" Cillin	5	2	Dau	6mo	F	"			
		6								
		7								
		8								
		9								
		10								
		11	ENROLLMENT OF NOS. 1 2 3 4 and 5 HEREON							
		12	APPROVED BY THE SECRETARY OF INTERIOR Dec 12 1902							
		13								
		14								
		15								
		16								
		17								

TRIBAL ENROLLMENT OF PARENTS

	Name of Father	Year	County	Name of Mother	Year	County
1	Caston Ward	1896	Bok Tuklo	Pikey Ward	Dead	Bok Tuklo
2	Sias Ishtiahonobbe	Dead	" "	Wesey Ishtiahonobbe	"	" "
3	No 1			Sarah Ward	"	" "
4	No 1			" "	"	" "
5	No.1			No.2		
6						
7						
8						
9	No1 on 1896 roll as Wilborn Ward					
10	No2 " 1896 " " Siwen Ishtiahonobee					
11	No3 " 1896 " " Wenney Ward					
12	No.5 Enrolled June 3, 1901					
13	No2 died -- 1899. Enrollment cancelled by Department July 8, 1904					
14	Name of No.2 restored to roll under Departmental authority of June 1, 1905. (I.T.D. 5568 – 1905) she being alive on Sept 20, 1902.			June 9, 1905.	#1 to 4 inc	
15				Date of Application for Enrollment.		
16				April 21/99		
17						

51

Choctaw By Blood Enrollment Cards 1898-1914

RESIDENCE: Kiamitia   COUNTY.   **Choctaw Nation**   Choctaw Roll   CARD NO.
POST OFFICE: Grant, I.T.   *(Not Including Freedmen)*   FIELD NO. **652**

Dawes' Roll No.	NAME	Relationship to Person First Named	AGE	SEX	BLOOD	TRIBAL ENROLLMENT Year	County	No.
1543	₁ Mishaia, Mary DIED PRIOR TO SEPTEMBER 25, 1902	First Named	45	F	Full	1896	Kiamitia	8713
1544	₂ Ahekatubby, John ²²	Son	19	M	"	1896	"	348
1545 Ⓧ	₃ " Simeon ¹⁸	Ward	15	"	"	1896	"	349
1546	₄ Mishaia, Ellen DIED PRIOR TO SEPTEMBER 25, 1902	"	14	F	"	1896	"	8605
1547	₅ " Rhoda ¹⁶	"	13	"	"	1896	"	8714
15823	₆ James, Sillian ²	Dau of No 5	2	F	"			

Ⓧ 6/7/1917- No3 hereon reported to be a duplicate of No.4 on Choctaw card No. 1953 under investigation

No1 died Dec-1901: No4 died Nov-1901: Enrollment cancelled by Department July 8-1904   W.H.A

₉ No4 also on 1896 Choctaw census roll page 215: No 8607 as Ellen Mishaya.

₁₀ ENROLLMENT OF NOS. 1 2 3 4 and 5 HEREON
₁₁ APPROVED BY THE SECRETARY
₁₂ OF INTERIOR Dec 12 1902

For child of No.2 see NB (April 26, 1906) #87
No.6 born Sept.4,1900: application received Apr 17, 1905, under Act of Congress of Mar. 3'05
₁₆ No3 at Antlers I.T with
₁₇ Daniel Robert

N°3 is 22 years old. See his testimony and that of Daniel Roberts of May 16, 1903.
For child of No5 see NB (March 3, 1905) #1105
" " " No2 " " " " " #1191
The notation relative to the death of N°5 on this card is an error: See testimony of Thomas James and others of April 30, 1903.

TRIBAL ENROLLMENT OF PARENTS

	Name of Father	Year	County	Name of Mother	Year	County
₁	Mishaia	Dead	Towson	Mary Mishaia	Dead	Towson
₂	Alex Ahekoubbi	"	"	No 1		
₃	Ben "	"	"	Bicey Ahekoubbi	1896	Jacks Fork
₄	Connie Mishaia	"	Kiamitia	Selina Mishaia	Dead	Towson
₅	Hicks "	"	Towson	Lottie Mishaia	"	"
₆	Thomas James			No.5		
₇			No3 on 1896 roll as Simon Ahekotubbi			
₈			No1 " 1896 " " Mary Mishaya			
₉			No5 " 1896 " " Rhoda "			
₁₀			No4 " 1896 " " Ellen "			
			No2 " 1896 " " John Ahekotubbi			
₁₁	No2 is now the husband of Emma Robertson Choctaw Card #1609 March 27, 1902					
₁₂	No1 died Dec – 1901: proof of death filed Dec. 5, 1902.					
₁₃	No4 " Nov – 1901:	" " " " "				
	No5 " Oct – 1901:	" " " " " "				
₁₄						#1 to 5

₁₅	ENROLLMENT	Date of Application for Enrollment.
₁₆	OF NOS. ~~~ 6 ~~~ HEREON 12/2/02 APPROVED BY THE SECRETARY	April 21/99
₁₇	P.O. Doaksville I.T. OF INTERIOR Jun 12 - 1905	

N°5 was wife of Thomas James Choctaw Card #603 at time of her death See certificate of marriage filed Jany 20 1903

Choctaw By Blood Enrollment Cards 1898-1914

RESIDENCE: Nashoba   COUNTY. **Choctaw Nation**   **Choctaw Roll**   CARD NO.
POST OFFICE: Alikchi, I.T.   *(Not Including Freedmen)*   FIELD NO. 653

Dawes' Roll No.	NAME		Relationship to Person	AGE	SEX	BLOOD	TRIBAL ENROLLMENT		
							Year	County	No.
1548	1 Johnson, Elsie	45	First Named	42	F	Full	1896	Nashoba	6854
1549	2 " Edmond	17	Son	14	M	"	1896	"	6856
	3								
	4								
	5	ENROLLMENT OF NOS. 1 and 2 HEREON							
	6	APPROVED BY THE SECRETARY							
	7	OF INTERIOR DEC 12 1902							
	8								
	9								
	10	Name of No1's mother waived by Commissioner McKennon							
	11	No2 on 1896 roll as Edmund Johnson							
	12								
	13								
	14								
	15								
	16								
	17								

TRIBAL ENROLLMENT OF PARENTS

	Name of Father	Year	County	Name of Mother	Year	County
1	Me-a-sho-tubbee	Dead	Eagle		Dead	Eagle
2	Mormon Johnson	"	Nashoba	No 1		
3						
4						
5						
6						
7						
8						
9						
10						
11						
12						
13						
14						
15						
16				DATE OF APPLICATION FOR ENROLLMENT.		April 21/99
17						

53

Choctaw By Blood Enrollment Cards 1898-1914

RESIDENCE: Nashoba   COUNTY.   **Choctaw Nation**   Choctaw Roll   CARD NO.
POST OFFICE: Smithville, I.T.   (Not Including Freedmen)   FIELD NO. 654

Dawes' Roll No.	NAME	Relationship to Person	AGE	SEX	BLOOD	TRIBAL ENROLLMENT		
						Year	County	No.
1550	1 Samuel, Nellie 33	First Named	30	F	Full	1896	Nashoba	11403
1551	2 " Noel 18	Son	15	M	"	1896	"	11404
15936	3 Stechi, Eliza	Dau	2	F	"			
	4							
	5							
	6	ENROLLMENT OF NOS. 1 and 2 HEREON APPROVED BY THE SECRETARY OF INTERIOR Dec 12, 1902						
	7							
	8							
	9	ENROLLMENT OF NOS. ~~3~~ HEREON APPROVED BY THE SECRETARY OF INTERIOR Nov. 24 1905						
	10							
	11							
	12							
	13							
	14							
	15							
	16							
	17							

TRIBAL ENROLLMENT OF PARENTS

	Name of Father	Year	County	Name of Mother	Year	County
1	Bob James	Dead	Nashoba	E-la-he-ma	Dead	Eagle
2	Johnson Samuel	"	"	No. 1		
3	Solomon Stechi		Choctaw R1707	No. 1		
4						
5			No1 is the wife of Soloman Stechi said to be a full blood			
6			Choctaw and brother Iston McCoy on Choctaw card #531			
7			See statement of Edmund M. Wilson Dec 23/02			
8			These parties have a child but its name or sex could not be ascertained by Wilson			
9						
10			No3 application made for the enrollment of this child			
11			under act of March 3 1905			
12						
13						
14						#1&2 inc
15						Date of Application for Enrollment.
16						April 21/99
17	P.O. Beach I.T.					

54

Choctaw By Blood Enrollment Cards 1898-1914

Dawes' Roll No.	NAME		Relationship to Person Named	AGE	SEX	BLOOD	TRIBAL ENROLLMENT		
							Year	County	No.
1552	1 Clay, Wilsey	61	First Named	58	F	Full	1896	Bok Tuklo	2573
1553	2 " Ida	21	Dau	18	"	1/2	1896	" "	2576
DEAD	3 Durant, Ben DEAD		G.Son	18	M	3/4	1896	Blue	3569
1554	4 " Licey	17	G.Dau	14	F	1/2	1896	Bok Tuklo	3405
	5								
	6								
	7								
	8								
	9								
	10								
	11								
	12								
	13								
	14								
	15								
	16								
	17								

ENROLLMENT
OF NOS. 1 – 2 and 4 HEREON
APPROVED BY THE SECRETARY
OF INTERIOR Dec 12 1902

No.3 hereon dismissed under order of
the Commission to the Five Civilized
Tribes of March 31, 1905.

TRIBAL ENROLLMENT OF PARENTS

	Name of Father	Year	County	Name of Mother	Year	County
1	Joe Cahn	Dead	Eagle	Patsey Cahn	Dead	Eagle
2	Charles Gavner	1896	Non Citz	No 1		
3	Peter Durant	Dead	Bok Tuklo	Ellen Durant	Dead	Bok Tuklo
4	Thomas Durant	"	" "	Melinda Durant	"	Nashoba

No4 is duplicate of Lizzie Durant No1 n Choctaw card #966 Enroll-
ment hereon cancelled by Departmental authority of Sept. 19, 1906
(I.T.D. #17730-1906) D.C. 41530-1906
No3 also on 1896 roll page 82, No 3404
as Benj. Durant, Bok Tuklo Co.
No.3 Died Sept. 28, 1901; proof of death filed March 25 1902.
For child of No.2 see N.B (Apr 26, 1906) Card No.1.

Date of Application
for Enrollment.

April 21/99

55

Choctaw By Blood Enrollment Cards 1898-1914

RESIDENCE: Red River   COUNTY.   **Choctaw Nation**   Choctaw Roll   CARD NO.
POST OFFICE: Garvin, I.T.   *(Not Including Freedmen)*   FIELD NO. **656**

Dawes' Roll No.	NAME		Relationship to Person	AGE	SEX	BLOOD	TRIBAL ENROLLMENT		
							Year	County	No.
1555	1 Durant, William A.	32	First Named	29	M	1/2	1896	Nashoba	3382
1556	2 " Laura	22	Wife	19	F	1/2	1896	Bok Tuklo	2575
1557	3 " Gibby	11	Son	8	M	1/2	1896	Nashoba	3383
1558	4 " Eddie	9	"	6	"	1/2	1896	"	3384
1559	5 " Louis	8	"	5	"	1/2	1896	"	3385
	6								
	7								
	8	ENROLLMENT OF NOS. 1 2 3 4 and 5 HEREON							
	9	APPROVED BY THE SECRETARY OF INTERIOR Dec 12 1902							
	10								
	11								
	12								
	13								
	14								
	15	No1 on 1896 roll as Wm. A. Durant							
	16	No2 " 1896 " " Laura Clay							
	17								

TRIBAL ENROLLMENT OF PARENTS

	Name of Father	Year	County	Name of Mother	Year	County
1	Allington Durant	Dead	Red River	Mary Durant	Dead	Red River
2	Charles Gavener	1896	Non Citz	Wilsey Clay	1896	Bok Tuklo
3	No 1			Sarah Durant	Dead	Red River
4	No 1			" "	"	" " "
5	No 1			" "	"	" " "
6						
7						
8						
9						
10						
11						
12						
13						
14						
15					Date of Application for Enrollment.	
16					April 21/99	
17						

Choctaw By Blood Enrollment Cards 1898-1914

RESIDENCE: Nashoba
POST OFFICE: Alikchi, I.T.

COUNTY.

Choctaw Nation

Choctaw Roll
(Not Including Freedmen)

CARD NO.
FIELD NO. **657**

Dawes' Roll No.	NAME		Relationship to Person	AGE	SEX	BLOOD	TRIBAL ENROLLMENT		
							Year	County	No.
1560	1 Ya-to-ner	59	First Named	56	F	Full	1896	Nashoba	14229
1561	2 Noahobi, Liksi	24	Dau	21	F	"	1893	"	P.R. 907
	3 Williams, Osborne		Son	18	M	"	1896	"	13328
1562	4 Noahobi, Mila	6	Dau	3	F	"	1896	"	9703
14576	5 Bond, Sampson	1	Son of N°2	9mo	M	"			
	6								
	7		No1 died Dec 30, 1901: Enrollment cancelled by Department Dec 17, 1906.						
	8	No. 3 hereon dismissed under order of the Commissioner to the Five Civilized Tribes of July 18, 1905.							
	9								
	10	ENROLLMENT							
	11	OF NOS. 1 – 2 and 4 HEREON APPROVED BY THE SECRETARY							
	12	OF INTERIOR Dec 12 1902							
	13								
	14	ENROLLMENT							
	15	OF NOS. 5 HEREON APPROVED BY THE SECRETARY							
	16	OF INTERIOR May 20 1903							
	17								

TRIBAL ENROLLMENT OF PARENTS

	Name of Father	Year	County	Name of Mother	Year	County
1	Phillie Carterby	Dead	Nashoba	Ma-ho-na	Dead	Nashoba
2	Morris Baker	1896	"	No 1		
3	Morris Williams	1896	"	No 1		
4	Allington Battiest	1896	"	No 1		
5	Byington Bond	1896	"	No 2		
6						
7	No2 on 1893 Pay roll as "Liksi"					
8	No4 " 1896 roll as Maile Noahobi.					
9	N°2 is the wife of Byington Bond Choctaw card #508. Evidence of marriage requested Dec 23, 1902. Filed Jany 28 1903					
10	N°5 Born March 28, 1902, enrolled Dec. 24, 1902.					
11						
12	No2 is a woman. Sex changed under Departmental authority of January 12, 1905					
13	(I.T.D. 212-1905) D.C. #2543-1905					
14	For child of No.2 see NB (March 3, 1905) #920					
15						
16					Date of Application for Enrollment.	
17	P.O. Bethel I.T. 4/5/05				April 21/99	

Choctaw By Blood Enrollment Cards 1898-1914

RESIDENCE: Nashoba — COUNTY.

POST OFFICE: Alikchi, I.T.

Choctaw Nation

Choctaw Roll *(Not Including Freedmen)*

CARD No.

FIELD No. **658**

Dawes' Roll No.	NAME		Relationship to Person First Named	AGE	SEX	BLOOD	TRIBAL ENROLLMENT Year	County	No.
1563	1 Noahobi, Mitsie	34	First Named	31	F	Full	1896	Nashoba	9702
1564	2 John, Esa	21	Dau	18	F	"	1896	"	7971
1565	3 Lowman, Elias	12	Son	9	M	"	1896	"	7973
1566	4 " Lartie	8	Dau	5	F	"	1896	"	7974
1567	5 John, Annie May		Grand Dau	7mo	F	"			
1568	6 " Wilson	1	Gr Son	4mo	M	"			
	7								
	8								
	9								
	10								
	11								
	12								
	13								
	14								
	15								
	16								
	17								

DIED PRIOR TO SEPTEMBER 25, 1902

ENROLLMENT OF NOS. 1 2 3 4 5 and 6 HEREON APPROVED BY THE SECRETARY OF INTERIOR Dec 12 1902

TRIBAL ENROLLMENT OF PARENTS

	Name of Father	Year	County	Name of Mother	Year	County
1	Noahobi	Dead	Nashoba	Yo-to-na	1896	Nashoba
2	Greeks Lowman	1896	"	No 1		
3	" "	1896	"	No 1		
4	" "	1896	"	No 1		
5	Carney John	1896	"	No 2		
6	" "	1896	"	N°2		
7						
8						
9	No2 is now the wife of Carney John on Choctaw card No.1074.					
10	Evidence of marriage filed February 12, 1901.					
11	As to sex of No2, see letter of Carney John filed February 12, 1901.					
	No5 Enrolled February 12, 1901					
12	N°6 Born Jany 4, 1902: enrolled May 14, 1902					
13	No5 died Oct 7, 1901: proof of death filed Dec 15, 1902					
14	No.5 died Oct.7, 1901: Enrollment cancelled by Department Sept 16, 1904					
15						
16						
17						

#1 to 4
Date of Application for Enrollment.

April 21/99

58

Choctaw By Blood Enrollment Cards 1898-1914

RESIDENCE: Red River COUNTY.
POST OFFICE: Garvin, I.T.

Choctaw Nation

Choctaw Roll
(Not Including Freedmen)

CARD NO.
FIELD NO. 659

Dawes' Roll No.	NAME	Relationship to Person First Named	AGE	SEX	BLOOD	TRIBAL ENROLLMENT Year	County	No.
1569	1 Watson, Rosie 56	First Named	53	F	3/4	1896	Towson	13162
	2							
	3							
	4							
	5							
	6							
	7							
	8							
	9							
	10							
	11							
	12							
	13							
	14							
	15							
	16							
	17							

ENROLLMENT
OF NOS. 1 HEREON
APPROVED BY THE SECRETARY
OF INTERIOR DEC 12 1902

TRIBAL ENROLLMENT OF PARENTS

	Name of Father	Year	County	Name of Mother	Year	County
1	Mitchell LeFlore	Dead	Towson	Bookie Frazier	Dead	Dok Tuklo
2						
3						
4						
5						
6						
7						
8						
9						
10						
11						
12						
13						
14						
15						
16				Date of Application for Enrollment		April 21/99
17						

Choctaw By Blood Enrollment Cards 1898-1914

RESIDENCE: Towson   COUNTY.   **Choctaw Nation**   Choctaw Roll   CARD No.

POST OFFICE: Garvin, I.T.   *(Not Including Freedmen)*   FIELD No.   660

Dawes' Roll No.	NAME	Relationship to Person First Named	AGE	SEX	BLOOD	TRIBAL ENROLLMENT Year	County	No.
1570	1 Harley, Silvey ⁵⁵	First Named	52	F	Full	1896	Towson	5509
1571	2 Washington, Sally ²²	Dau	19	"	"	1896	"	5510
1572	3 Washington, Benson ²	Grand Son	7mo	M	"			
1573	4 " Sarah ¹	Gr Dau	2mo	F	"			
	5							
	6							
	7	ENROLLMENT						
	8	OF NOS. 1 2 3 and 4 HEREON APPROVED BY THE SECRETARY						
	9	OF INTERIOR DEC 12 1902						
	10							
	11							
	12							
	13							
	14							
	15							
	16							
	17							

TRIBAL ENROLLMENT OF PARENTS

	Name of Father	Year	County	Name of Mother	Year	County
1	Yak-na-la	Dead	Red River	Ish-to-lou-ille	Dead	Red River
2	Dixon Harley	"	" "	No 1		
3	George L Washington	1896	Towson	No 2		
4	" " "	1896	"	No 2		
5						
6	No1 on 1896 roll as Silvey Hally					
7	No2 " 1896 " " Sally "					
	No.2 is now the wife of George L. Washington on Choctaw card #663					
8	No3 Enrolled April 25, 1901					
9	N⁰4 Born Feby. 11, 1902, enrolled April 21, 1902.					
10	For child of No.2 see NB (March 3 1905) #957					
11						
12						
13						
14					Date of Application for Enrollment.	
15						
16					April 21/99	
17						

Choctaw By Blood Enrollment Cards 1898-1914

RESIDENCE: Eagle COUNTY.
POST OFFICE: Eagletown, I.T.

Choctaw Nation

Choctaw Roll
(Not Including Freedmen)

CARD NO.
FIELD NO. **661**

Dawes' Roll No.	NAME	Relationship to Person First Named	AGE	SEX	BLOOD	TRIBAL ENROLLMENT Year	County	No.
1574	1 Ward, Elam M ³⁵	First Named	32	M	Full	1896	Nashoba	13250
1575	2 " Sophie ³³	Wife	30	F	"	1896	"	3428
1576	3 " Classy ⁹	Dau	6	"	"	1893	"	P.R. 868
	4							
	5							
	6							
	7	ENROLLMENT						
	8	OF NOS. 1 – 2 and 3 HEREON APPROVED BY THE SECRETARY OF INTERIOR DEC 12 1902						
	9							
	10							
	11							
	12							
	13							
	14							
	15							
	16							
	17							

TRIBAL ENROLLMENT OF PARENTS

	Name of Father	Year	County	Name of Mother	Year	County
1	Morris Ward	1896	Eagle	Mary Ward	Dead	Nashoba
2	Eastman Cornelius	Dead	Bok Tuklo	Con-che-ho-ka	"	Bok Tuklo
3	No 1			Amanda Reuben	"	Nashoba
4						
5						
6						
7	No1 on 1896 roll as Elum M. Ward					
8	No2 " 1896 " " Sophie Davis					
9						
10	No3 on 1896 roll Page 277 No 10785 as					
11	Clarissa Reuben, Nashoba Co.					
12						
13						
14					Date of Application for Enrollment.	
15					April 21/99	
16						
17	Lukfata I.T. 11/28/02					

61

Choctaw By Blood Enrollment Cards 1898-1914

RESIDENCE: Eagle   COUNTY.

POST OFFICE: Eagletown, I.T.

Choctaw Nation

Choctaw Roll (Not Including Freedmen)

CARD NO.

FIELD NO. 662

Dawes' Roll No.	NAME	Relationship to Person	AGE	SEX	BLOOD	TRIBAL ENROLLMENT Year	County	No.
1577	1 Hopayashubbi, Harmon [47]	First Named	44	M	Full	1896	Eagle	5613
1578	2 " Sophie [36]	Wife	33	F	"	1896	"	5614
~~1579~~	3 ~~" Silin~~ Died prior to September 25, 1902 [9]	~~Dau~~	~~6~~	~~"~~	~~"~~	~~1896~~	~~"~~	~~5616~~
~~1580~~	4 ~~" Winnie~~ Died prior to September 25, 1902 [7]	~~"~~	~~4~~	~~"~~	~~"~~	~~1896~~	~~"~~	~~5612~~
1581	5 Wesley, Lizzie [14]	S.Dau	11	"	"	1896	"	13444
1582	6 " Willis [11]	S.Son	8	M	"	1896	"	13445
1583	7 Hopayashubbi, Tamby [20]	brother	17	"	"	1896	"	5611
1584	8 " Eatima [21]	sister	18	F	"	1896	"	5615
	9							
	10							
	11	ENROLLMENT						
	12	OF NOS. 1234567and8 HEREON APPROVED BY THE SECRETARY						
	13	OF INTERIOR Dec 12 1902						
	14							
	15							
	16							
	17							

TRIBAL ENROLLMENT OF PARENTS

	Name of Father	Year	County	Name of Mother	Year	County
1	O-pi-ish-ubbee	Dead	Eagle	A-ma-hoh-ke	Dead	Eagle
2	Abel Cooper	"	"	Emily Cooper	"	"
3	~~No 1~~			~~No 2~~		
4	~~No 1~~			~~No 2~~		
5	Gibson Wesley	Dead	Eagle	No.2		
6	" "	"	"	No.2		
7	O-pi-ish-ubbee	Dead	"	Liza	Dead	Eagle
8	" "	"	"	"	"	"
9						
10	No.3 died Feb 28, 1900: proof of death filed Dec 6, 1902					
11	No.4 " Aug 30, 1900: " " " " " " "					
12	No.3 died Feb 28-1900: No4 died Aug 30-1900: Enrollment cancelled by Department July 8-1904					
13						
14						
15						
16				Date of Application for Enrollment		April 21/99
17						

Choctaw By Blood Enrollment Cards 1898-1914

RESIDENCE: Towson
POST OFFICE: Garvin, I.T.

COUNTY. **Choctaw Nation**

Choctaw Roll (Not Including Freedmen)

CARD NO.
FIELD NO. **663**

Dawes' Roll No.	NAME	Relationship to Person	AGE	SEX	BLOOD	TRIBAL ENROLLMENT		
						Year	County	No.
1585	1 Washington, George L 31	First Named	28	M	Full	1896	Towson	13217
14577	2 Forbes, Nellie Ida 28	Wife	25	F	"	1896	"	13218
3								
4								
5	ENROLLMENT OF NOS. ~~1~~ HEREON APPROVED BY THE SECRETARY OF INTERIOR Dec 12 1902							
6								
7								
8								
9	ENROLLMENT OF NOS. ~2~ HEREON APPROVED BY THE SECRETARY OF INTERIOR May 20 1903							
10								
11								
12								
13								
14								
15								
16								
17								

TRIBAL ENROLLMENT OF PARENTS

	Name of Father	Year	County	Name of Mother	Year	County
1	Levi Washington	Dead	Red River	Sukey Washington	Dead	Red River
2	Frank Victor	"	" "	Sissie Victor	"	" "
3						
4						
5						
6						
7						
8						
9		For child of No.1 see NB (March 3, 1905) #957				
10		No.1 on 1896 roll as Geo. L. Washington.				
11		No.1 is now the husband of Sally Harley on Choctaw card #660				
12		No1 was divorced from No.2 by decree of Choctaw Court for March 7, 1901				
13		2nd Jud Dist C.N. July 6, 1899, Papers filed April 24, 1901				
14		No1 is now the husband of Sally Harley on Choctaw Card #660. See letter of				
15		No.1 dated April 20, 1901, filed with records in this case April 24, 1901				
16		No.2 is now wife of W.E. Forbes; evidence of marriage filed December 5, 190				
17		Her correct name is Nellie Ida Forbes see application for enrollment of William Eddie Forbes Nov. 25, 1902.				

Date of Application for Enrollment.

April 21/99

63

| RESIDENCE: Bok Tuklo | COUNTY. | **Choctaw Nation** | Choctaw Roll | CARD NO. |
| POST OFFICE: Lukfata, I.T. | | | *(Not Including Freedmen)* | FIELD NO. 664 |

Dawes' Roll No.	NAME		Relationship to Person First Named	AGE	SEX	BLOOD	TRIBAL ENROLLMENT		
							Year	County	No.
DEAD	1 Ward, Caston	DEAD		48	M	Full	1896	Bok Tuklo	13403
1586	2 " Casie	48	Wife	45	F	"	1896	" "	13404
DEAD	3 " Elian	DEAD	Dau	26	"	"	1896	" "	13405
DEAD	4 " Isaac	DEAD	Son	12	M	"	1896	" "	13406
DEAD	5 " Mary	DEAD	Dau	4	F	"	1896	" "	13407
15746	6 Ward, Annie	10	Dau	12	F	"	1896	Bok Tuklo	13408
15762	7 Hinson, Nicy	28	"	28	F	"	1896	" "	12194
	8								
	9	ENROLLMENT							
	10	OF NOS. ~2~ HEREON APPROVED BY THE SECRETARY							
	11	OF INTERIOR Dec 12 1902							
	12	No. 1-3-4-5 hereon dismissed under							
	13	order of the Commission to the Five							
	14	Civilized Tribes of March 31, 1905.							
	15	ENROLLMENT					Application for enrollment of No7 was		
	16	OF NOS. ~6~ HEREON APPROVED BY THE SECRETARY					made at Alikchi in 1899. See decision of		
	17	OF INTERIOR Dec 2 1904					Nov 29, 1904		

TRIBAL ENROLLMENT OF PARENTS

	Name of Father	Year	County	Name of Mother	Year	County
1	Yah-ho-ta-by	Dead	Nashoba	Ho-ta-che-hona	Dead	Eagle
2	A-po-an-tubby	"	Bok Tuklo	A-no-le-he-ma	"	"
3	No.1			Pikcy Ward	"	Bok Tuklo
4	No.1			No.2		
5	No.1	ENROLLMENT OF NOS. ~ 7 ~ HEREON		No.2		
6	No.1	APPROVED BY THE SECRETARY OF INTERIOR Dec 28 1904		No.2		
7	No.1			No.2		
8	No7 placed on this card December 15, 1904					
9	No7 on 1896 roll as Nocie Thomas					
10	No1 died May 8, 1900: Evidence of death filed Dec.27,1901 No3 is the wife of David Hinson on Choc card #1011. See letter					
11	of W.N. Anderson filed Dec. 27, 1901.					
12	No3 died June 5,1900: proof of death filed Jany 25, 1902					
13	No4 " Jany 4,1900: " " " " " " "					
14	No5 " Feby 17,1900: " " " " " " " No6 on 1896 Choctaw Census roll as Jannie Ward					
15	No6 transferred from Choctaw card #D865: See testimony of					
16	Sept. 6, 1904 Oct 11, 1904			Date of Application for Enrollment.	April 21/99	
17					1 to 5 inc	

Choctaw By Blood Enrollment Cards 1898-1914

RESIDENCE: Cedar COUNTY.
POST OFFICE: Alikchi, I.T.

Choctaw Nation

Choctaw Roll (Not Including Freedmen)

CARD No.
FIELD No. **665**

Dawes' Roll No.	NAME	Relationship to Person	AGE	SEX	BLOOD	TRIBAL ENROLLMENT Year	County	No.
1587	1 Willis, Marcus ~~Died abt. Sept. 25, 1902~~ 49	First Named	46	M	Full	1896	Cedar	13153
1588	2 Willis, Willie 24	Son	21	"	"	1896	"	13155
1589	3 " Denison 10	"	7	"	"	1896	"	13156
I.W. 1205	4 " Gracie 21	Wife of No.2	21	F	I.W.			
	5							
	6	ENROLLMENT						
	7	OF NOS. 1 – 2 and 3 HEREON APPROVED BY THE SECRETARY						
	8	OF INTERIOR Dec 12 1902						
	9	ENROLLMENT						
	10	OF NOS. ~~4~~ HEREON APPROVED BY THE SECRETARY						
	11	OF INTERIOR Dec 13 1904						
	12							
	13							
	14							
	15							
	16							
	17							

TRIBAL ENROLLMENT OF PARENTS

	Name of Father	Year	County	Name of Mother	Year	County
1	Ste-mo-lich-be	Dead	Towson	Mollie	Dead	Towson
2	No. 1			Nancy Ward	"	Cedar
3	No. 1			Sophila Ward	"	"
4	L.D. Harrington		non citizen	Acy Harrington		non citizen
5						
6			No 1 on 1896 roll as Markus Willis			
7			For children of nos 2 & 4 see NB (Mar 3 1905) #602			
8			No.1 died May 1, 1901: proof of death filed Dec 5, 1902			
9			No2 is now husband of Gracie Willis on Choctaw card D844 Evidence of marriage filed Dec. 1, 1902			
10			No1 died May 1-1901: Enrollment cancelled by Department July 8-1904.			
11			Evidence of marriage of nos. 2 and 4 filed Dec 1, 1902			
12			No.4 originally listed for enrollment on Choctaw card #D-844 Dec. 1, 1902 transferred to this card Nov. 26, 1904: See decision of Nov. 3, 1904.			
13						
14					Date of Application for Enrollment	#1 to 3
15						
16						April 21/99
17	No.2 PO Ft. Towson 3/12/04					

65

Choctaw By Blood Enrollment Cards 1898-1914

RESIDENCE: Eagle   COUNTY.   **Choctaw Nation**   **Choctaw Roll** CARD NO.
POST OFFICE: Eagletown, I.T.   *(Not Including Freedmen)*   FIELD NO. **666**

Dawes' Roll No.	NAME		Relationship to Person	AGE	SEX	BLOOD	TRIBAL ENROLLMENT		
							Year	County	No.
1590	1 Homer, Edmon	30	First Named	27	M	Full	1896	Eagle	5620
1591	2 " Silwe	35	Wife	32	F	"	1896	"	8655
1592	3 Mambi, Jennie	12	S.Dau	9	"	"	1896	"	8654
	4								
	5								
	6								
	7	ENROLLMENT							
	8	OF NOS. 1, 2 and 3 HEREON APPROVED BY THE SECRETARY							
	9	OF INTERIOR Dec. 12, 1902							
	10								
	11								
	12								
	13								
	14								
	15								
	16								
	17								

TRIBAL ENROLLMENT OF PARENTS

	Name of Father	Year	County	Name of Mother	Year	County
1	Pa-lu-me	Dead	Nashoba	Jennie	Dead	Nashoba
2	Maw-bee	"	Eagle	Al-mon-tina	"	Eagle
3	Silas Wilson	1896	"	No 2		
4						
5	No1 on 1896 roll as Edmund Homa					
6	No2 " 1896 " " Silwe Mambi					
7	No3 " 1896 " " Janie "					
	No2 " 1896 " " Silway " , Page 216, No 8652, Eagle Co.					
8	No3 " 1896 " " Jimmie " , " 216, " 8650 " "					
9	For child of Nos 1&3 see NB (Apr. 26, 1906) Card No 39.					
10						
11						
12						
13						
14						
15					Date of Application for Enrollment.	
16					April 21/99	
17						

Choctaw By Blood Enrollment Cards 1898-1914

RESIDENCE: Nashoba   COUNTY.   **Choctaw Nation**   **Choctaw Roll** CARD NO.
POST OFFICE: Smithville, I.T.   *(Not Including Freedmen)*   FIELD NO. **667**

Dawes' Roll No.	NAME	Relationship to Person Named	AGE	SEX	BLOOD	TRIBAL ENROLLMENT Year	County	No.
1593	1 Johnson, Elam J 31	First	28	M	Full	1896	Nashoba	6822
DEAD	2 " Serena DEAD	Wife	21	F	"	1896	"	6823
1594	3 " Annie 8	Dau	5	"	"	1896	"	6824
1595	4 " Dora 6	Dau	3	"	"	1896	"	6825
	5							
	6	ENROLLMENT						
	7	OF NOS. 1 – 3 and 4 HEREON APPROVED BY THE SECRETARY						
	8	OF INTERIOR Dec 12 1902						
	9							
	10							
	11	No.2 hereon dismissed under order of the Commission to the Five Civilized						
	12	Tribes of March 31, 1905.						
	13							
	14							
	15							
	16							
	17							

TRIBAL ENROLLMENT OF PARENTS

	Name of Father	Year	County	Name of Mother	Year	County
1	Joseph Johnson	1896	Nashoba	Cealy Johnson	Dead	Nashoba
2	James Wright	Dead	Wade	Leviney Wright	"	Wade
3	No 1			No 2		
4	No 1			No 2		
5						
6						
7	No1 on 1896 roll as Elum J. Johnson					
8	No2 died June 10, 1899: proof of death filed Dec. 15, 1902					
9	For child of No.1 see N.B (March 3, 1905) #966					
10	No.1 is now the husband of Frances Watson on Choc. Card #486 Nov. 29, 1901					
11						
12						
13						
14						
15						
16				Date of Application for Enrollment April 21/99		
17						

Choctaw By Blood Enrollment Cards 1898-1914

RESIDENCE: Nashoba COUNTY. **Choctaw Nation** **Choctaw Roll** CARD NO.
POST OFFICE: Smithville, I.T. *(Not Including Freedmen)* FIELD NO. 668

Dawes' Roll No.	NAME		Relationship to Person	AGE	SEX	BLOOD	TRIBAL ENROLLMENT		
							Year	County	No.
1596	1 Johnson, Wilmon J	27	First Named	24	M	Full	1896	Nashoba	6827
1597	2 ~~DIED PRIOR TO SEPTEMBER 25, 1902~~ Falisen		Wife	20	F	"	1896	"	6828
1598	3 " Carrie	4	Dau	1	"	"			
1599	4 " Lizzie	1	Dau	4Mo	F	"			
	5								
	6								
	7	ENROLLMENT							.
	8	OF NOS. 1 2 3 and 4 HEREON APPROVED BY THE SECRETARY							
	9	OF INTERIOR DEC 12 1902							
	10								
	11								
	12								
	13								
	14								
	15								
	16								
	17								

TRIBAL ENROLLMENT OF PARENTS

	Name of Father	Year	County	Name of Mother	Year	County
1	Joseph Johnson	1896	Nashoba	Cealy Johnson	Dead	Nashoba
2	~~Calvin Taylor~~	~~Dead~~	"	~~Phoebe McKinney~~	~~1896~~	~~Atoka~~
3	No 1			No 2		
4	Nº 1			Nº 2		
5						
6						
7						
8						
9						
10			~~No1 on 1896 roll as Wm. J. Johnson~~			
11			No2 " 1896 " " Falisen C "			
12			No3 Affidavit of birth to be supplied Recd May 3/99			
13			Nº4 Born Oct. 4, 1901: enrolled Feby. 21, 1902.			
13			~~No2 died Aug. 24, 1902; proof of death filed Dec 5, 1902~~			
14			~~No2 died Aug 24-1902; Enrollment cancelled by Department [remainder illegible]~~			
15			For child of No.1 see NB (March 3 1905) #945			
16				Date of Application for Enrollment		April 21/99
17						

68

Choctaw By Blood Enrollment Cards 1898-1914

RESIDENCE: Eagle   COUNTY.   **Choctaw Nation**   Choctaw Roll *(Not Including Freedmen)*   CARD NO.

POST OFFICE: Eagletown, I.T.   FIELD NO. **669**

Dawes' Roll No.	NAME		Relationship to Person	AGE	SEX	BLOOD	TRIBAL ENROLLMENT		
							Year	County	No.
1600	1 Joseph, William	39	First Named	36	M	Full	1896	Eagle	6952
1601	2 " , Louisa	44	Wife	41	F	"	1896	"	4796
1602	3 " , Inis	7	Dau	4	"	"	1896	"	6954
1603	4 Going, Mima	8	S. Dau	5	"	"	1896	"	4792
	5								
	6								
	7								
	8								
	9								
	10								
	11								
	12								
	13								
	14								
	15								
	16								
	17								

ENROLLMENT
OF NOS. 1 2 3 and 4 HEREON
APPROVED BY THE SECRETARY
OF INTERIOR Dec. 12, 1902

TRIBAL ENROLLMENT OF PARENTS

	Name of Father	Year	County	Name of Mother	Year	County
1	George Joseph	1896	Eagle	Nancy Joseph	Dead	Eagle
2	Joe James	Dead	Red River	Sunday James	"	Red River
3	No 1			Nellie Joseph	Dead	Eagle
4	Alickson Going	Dead	Eagle	Sissy Harley	1896	Eagle
5						
6	No2 on 1896 roll as Louisa Going.					
7	No3 " 1896 " " Amis Joseph.					
8	No4 " 1896 " " Minnie Going.					
9	No4 is daughter of Sissy Harley on Choctaw Card #1200.					
10	See testimony of Sissy and Stiles Harley of Feb. 12, 1904.					
11	See Allotment Jacket of N°4 for copy of above testimony					
	11-14-39 JBF					
12						
13						
14						
15						
16				Date of Application for Enrollment		April 21/99
17						

Choctaw By Blood Enrollment Cards 1898-1914

RESIDENCE: Eagle   COUNTY.   **Choctaw Nation**
POST OFFICE: Eagletown, I.T.

Choctaw Roll
(Not Including Freedmen)

CARD NO.
FIELD NO. 670

Dawes' Roll No.	NAME	Relationship to Person First Named	AGE	SEX	BLOOD	Year	County	No.
						Year	County	No.
1604	₁ Dyer, Collison		29	M	Full	1896	Eagle	3406
1605	₂ " Artie ²⁵	Wife	22	F	"	1896	"	261
14578	₃ Bohanan, Phoebe ²	Dau of No2	2	F	"			
	₄							
	₅							
	₆							
	₇	ENROLLMENT OF NOS. 1 and 2 HEREON						
	₈	APPROVED BY THE SECRETARY						
	₉	OF INTERIOR Dec 12, 1902						
	₁₀							
	₁₁	ENROLLMENT OF NOS. 3 HEREON						
	₁₂	APPROVED BY THE SECRETARY						
	₁₃	OF INTERIOR May 20, 1903						
	₁₄							
	₁₅							
	₁₆							
	₁₇							

DIED PRIOR TO SEPTEMBER 25, 1902

TRIBAL ENROLLMENT OF PARENTS

Name of Father	Year	County	Name of Mother	Year	County
₁ Moses Dyer	Dead	Eagle	Lottie Dyer	Dead	Eagle
₂ Tom Amos	"	"	Harriet Amos	1896	"
₃ John Bohanan	1896	"	No 2		-
₄					
₅					
₆					
₇	No2 on 1896 roll as Artie Amos				
₈	No1 on 1896 roll as Colison Dyer.				
₉	No2 born Jan'y 20, 1901; Enrolled Dec 17, 1902.				
	No2 is wife of John Bohanan Choctaw Card #648. Certificate of				
₁₀	marriage filed Jany 20, 1903.				
₁₁	No1 Died March 23, 1900. Proof filed Jany 20, 1903				
₁₂	No1 died March 23-1900: Enrollment cancelled by Department July 8-1904				
₁₃					
₁₄				#1 to 2	
₁₅				Date of Application for Enrollment.	
₁₆				April 21/99	
₁₇					

Choctaw By Blood Enrollment Cards 1898-1914

RESIDENCE: Eagle   COUNTY.
POST OFFICE: Eagletown, I.T.

Choctaw Nation

Choctaw Roll   CARD No.
(Not Including Freedmen)   FIELD No. **671**

Dawes' Roll No.		NAME		Relationship to Person First Named	AGE	SEX	BLOOD	TRIBAL ENROLLMENT Year	County	No.
1606	1	Amos, Harriet		Named	52	F	Full	1896	Eagle	280
1607	2	" Anthony	23	Son	20	M	"	1896	"	262
1608	3	" Allen	21	"	18	"	"	1896	"	263
1609	4	" Minnie	19	Dau	16	F	"	1896	"	293
1610	5	" Mary J.	17	"	14	"	"	1896	"	294
1611	6	" Evelina	13	"	10	"	"	1896	"	264

DIED PRIOR TO SEPTEMBER 25, 1902

ENROLLMENT
OF NOS. 1 2 3 4 5 and 6 HEREON
APPROVED BY THE SECRETARY
OF INTERIOR Dec 12 1902

TRIBAL ENROLLMENT OF PARENTS

	Name of Father	Year	County	Name of Mother	Year	County
1	James Hudson	Dead	Eagle	O-bi-tc-ma	Dead	Eagle
2	Tom Amos	"	"	No 1		
3	" "	"	"	No 1		
4	" "	"	"	No 1		
5	" "	"	"	No 1		
6	" "	"	"	No 1		

No 2 on 1896 roll as Artinie Amos
No 5 " 1896 " " Mary "
No 6 " 1896 " " Avelina "
No 1 died May or June, 1902: proof of death filed Dec 12, 1902
No 1 died June - 1902: Enrollment cancelled by Department July 8 - 1904.

Date of Application for Enrollment. April 21/99

71

Choctaw By Blood Enrollment Cards 1898-1914

RESIDENCE: Eagle   COUNTY.   **Choctaw Nation**   **Choctaw Roll** CARD NO.
POST OFFICE: Eagletown, I.T.   *(Not Including Freedmen)* FIELD NO. 672

Dawes' Roll No.	NAME	Relationship to Person	AGE	SEX	BLOOD	TRIBAL ENROLLMENT		
						Year	County	No.
1612	1 Fobb, Eaton 27	First Named	24	M	Full	1896	Eagle	4163
	2							
	3							
	4	ENROLLMENT						
	5	OF NOS. 1 HEREON APPROVED BY THE SECRETARY						
	6	OF INTERIOR DEC 12 1902						
	7							
	8							
	9							
	10							
	11							
	12							
	13							
	14							
	15							
	16							
	17							

TRIBAL ENROLLMENT OF PARENTS

	Name of Father	Year	County	Name of Mother	Year	County
1	Joe Fobb	Dead	Eagle	Heat Fobb	1896	Eagle
2						
3						
4						
5						
6						
7						
8						
9						
10						
11						
12						
13						
14						
15						
16				Date of Application for Enrollment		April 21/99
17						

Choctaw By Blood Enrollment Cards 1898-1914

RESIDENCE: Eagle   COUNTY.   **Choctaw Nation**   **Choctaw Roll**   CARD NO.
POST OFFICE: Eagletown, I.T.   *(Not Including Freedmen)*   FIELD NO.   673

Dawes' Roll No.	NAME	Relationship to Person	AGE	SEX	BLOOD	TRIBAL ENROLLMENT		
						Year	County	No.
1613	1 Fobb, Hate 43	First Named	40	F	Full	1896	Eagle	4168
	2							
	3							
	4							
	5							
	6							
	7							
	8							
	9							
	10							
	11							
	12							
	13							
	14							
	15							
	16							
	17							

ENROLLMENT
OF NOS. 1 HEREON
APPROVED BY THE SECRETARY
OF INTERIOR DEC 12 1902

TRIBAL ENROLLMENT OF PARENTS

	Name of Father	Year	County	Name of Mother	Year	County
1	Lowe Jones	Dead	Eagle	Okla-hoh-ka	Dead	Eagle
2						
3						
4						
5						
6						
7						
8						
9						
10						
11						
12						
13						
14						
15						
16						
17						

DATE OF APPLICATION
FOR ENROLLMENT   April 21/99

73

Choctaw By Blood Enrollment Cards 1898-1914

RESIDENCE: Eagle COUNTY.
POST OFFICE: Eagletown, I.T.

Choctaw Nation

Choctaw Roll
(Not Including Freedmen)

CARD NO.
FIELD NO. 674

Dawes' Roll No.	NAME	Relationship to Person	AGE	SEX	BLOOD	TRIBAL ENROLLMENT		
						Year	County	No.
1614	1 Colbert, Noel 26	First Named	23	M	Full	1896	Eagle	2629
	2							
	3							
	4							
	5							
	6							
	7							
	8							
	9							
	10							
	11	ENROLLMENT OF NOS. 1 HEREON APPROVED BY THE SECRETARY OF INTERIOR Dec 12, 1902						
	12							
	13							
	14							
	15							
	16							
	17							

TRIBAL ENROLLMENT OF PARENTS

	Name of Father	Year	County	Name of Mother	Year	County
1	Allington Colbert	Dead	Eagle	Mandy Colbert	Dead	Eagle
2						
3						
4						
5						
6						
7						
8						
9						
10						
11						
12						
13						
14					Date of Application for Enrollment.	
15						
16					April 21/99	
17						

74

Choctaw By Blood Enrollment Cards 1898-1914

RESIDENCE: Eagle

POST OFFICE: Eagletown, I.T

COUNTY.

Choctaw Nation

Choctaw Roll
(Not Including Freedmen)

CARD NO.

FIELD NO. 675

Dawes' Roll No.	NAME		Relationship to Person	AGE	SEX	BLOOD	TRIBAL ENROLLMENT		
							Year	County	No.
1615	1 Thompson, Thomas	DIED PRIOR TO SEPTEMBER 25, 1902	First Named	21	M	Full	1896	Eagle	12248
1616	2 " Frances	42	Wife	39	F	"	1896	"	5582
1617	3 Hudson, Roar	20	S.Son	17	M	"	1896	"	5584
1618	4 " Jimmie	18	"	15	"	"	1896	"	5577
1619	5 " Sophie	15	S.Dau	12	F	"	1896	"	5586
1620	6 " Winnie	DIED PRIOR TO SEPTEMBER 25, 1902	"	10	"	"	1896	"	5590
1621	7 Hudson Adeline	11	"	8	"	"	1896	"	5574
1622	8 Hudson Caroline	8	S.Dau	5	F	"	1896	"	5575
1623	9 " George	6	S.Son	2	M	"			
1624	10 Thompson, Lucy	3	Dau	6mo	F	"			
	11								
	12 No.6 died Aug 16 - 1900: Enrollment cancelled by Department July 8 – 1904 Born Mch2-C6								
	13 No.1 died April 5,1902; Enrollment For children of No.3 see NB(March 3'05) #1069								
	14 cancelled by Department Sept 23, 1904. No.5 in Wheelock Academy								
	15 No6 died Aug 16, 1900: proof of death filed Dec 12, 1902								
	16 For child of No5 see NB(Apr26-06) Card #422								
	17 " " " " " " (Mar3-05) " #961								

ENROLLMENT
OF NOS. 1 2 3 4 5 6 7 8 9 and 10 HEREON
APPROVED BY THE SECRETARY
OF INTERIOR Dec 12 1902

TRIBAL ENROLLMENT OF PARENTS

	Name of Father	Year	County	Name of Mother	Year	County
1	George Thompson	1896	Eagle	Lucy Thompson	1896	Eagle
2	Johua[sic] Bohanan	Dead	"	Louisa Christy	Dead	"
3	Wash Hudson	"	"	No 2		
4	" "	"	"	No 2		
5	" "	"	"	No 2		
6	" "	"	"	No 2		
7	" "	"	"	No 2		
8	" "	"	"	No 2		
9	" "	"	"	No 2		
10	No. 1			No 2		
11	No1 on 1896 roll as Tommie Thompson					
12	No2 " 1896 " " Frances Hudson					
13	No7 " 1896 " " Arteline "					
14	No.10 Enrolled April 7th, 1900					
15	No7 Name is Hudson. Correction authorized by Departmental letter of No.28,1903 (D.C.8292-1903)					
16	Nº1 Died April 5, 1902, proof of death filed Feby.9, 1903					
17						

Date of Application for Enrollment.

April 21/99

No5 P.O. Goodwater I.T. 4/10/05

75

Choctaw By Blood Enrollment Cards 1898-1914

RESIDENCE: Eagle COUNTY.
POST OFFICE: ~~Corrogordo, Ark~~

Choctaw Nation

Choctaw Roll
(Not Including Freedmen)

CARD NO.
FIELD NO. **676**

Dawes' Roll No.	NAME		Relationship to Person First Named	AGE	SEX	BLOOD	TRIBAL ENROLLMENT		
							Year	County	No.
1625	1 Dyer, David	43	First Named	40	M	Full	1896	Eagle	3414
1626	2 " Celia	37	Wife	34	F	"	1896	"	3407
1627	3 " Eliza	15	Dau	12	"	"	1896	"	5600
1628	4 " Smallwood	12	Son	9	M	"	1896	"	3426
1629	5 " Wilsey	7	Dau	4	F	"	1896	"	3429
DEAD	6 ~~" Minnie~~		"	~~1~~	"	"			
1630	7 " Johanna	6	Dau	2mo	F	"			
	8								
	9 No6 hereon dismissed under order of								
	10 the Commission to the Five Civilized								
	11 Tribes of March 31, 1905.								
	12								
	13								
	14								
	15								
	16								
	17								

ENROLLMENT
OF NOS. 1 2 3 4 5 and 7 HEREON
APPROVED BY THE SECRETARY
OF INTERIOR Dec. 12, 1902

TRIBAL ENROLLMENT OF PARENTS

	Name of Father	Year	County	Name of Mother	Year	County
1	James Dyer	1896	Eagle	Eve Dyer	Dead	Eagle
2	Cornelius Homma	1896	"	Isabelle Homma	1896	"
3	No 1			No 2		
4	No 1			No 2		
5	No 1			No 2		
6	~~No 1~~			~~No 2~~		
7	No 1			No 2		
8						
9	For child of No3 see N.B. (Apr. 26,1906) No 599.					
10	No3 on 1896 roll as Eliza Homa.					
11	No5 " 1896 " Milsey Dyer.					
12	~~No5 affidavit of birth to be supplied. Recd May 6/99.~~					
13	~~No6 " " " " " " 6/99.~~					
14	No7 Enrolled April 27, 1901.					
15	No6 Died January 2nd 1901: Evidence of death filed April 27, 1901.				Date of Application for Enrollment.	
16	~~For child of Nos. 1&2 see N.B. (March 3, 1905)#1361.~~					
17	No3 Ultima Thule Ark. 6/1/07.				April 21/99	
	P.O. is now Eagletown I.T.					

Choctaw By Blood Enrollment Cards 1898-1914

RESIDENCE: Eagle   COUNTY.   **Choctaw Nation**   **Choctaw Roll**   CARD NO.
POST OFFICE: Eagletown, I.T.   *(Not Including Freedmen)*   FIELD NO.   **677**

Dawes' Roll No.		NAME	Relationship to Person First Named	AGE	SEX	BLOOD	TRIBAL ENROLLMENT		
							Year	County	No.
1631	1	Homma, Cornelius ~~DIED PRIOR TO SEPTEMBER 25, 1902~~	First Named	53	M	Full	1896	Eagle	5597
1632	2	" Isabel ⁶⁷	Wife	64	F	"	1896	"	5598
	3								
	4								
	5								
	6								
	7	ENROLLMENT OF NOS. 1 and 2 HEREON							
	8	APPROVED BY THE SECRETARY OF INTERIOR Dec 12 1902							
	9								
	10								
	11								
	12								
	13								
	14								
	15								
	16								
	17								

TRIBAL ENROLLMENT OF PARENTS

	Name of Father	Year	County	Name of Mother	Year	County
1	John Homma	Dead	Eagle	Jincey Homma	Dead	Eagle
2		Died	in Mississippi	Ar-chi-hok-ke	"	"
3						
4						
5	Surname of Nos 1 and 2 on 1896 roll as Homa.					
6						
7	Nº 1 Died June 9, 1899. Proof of death filed Jany. 28, 1903					
8	~~No. 1 died June 9, 1899. Enrollment cancelled by Department Sept. 16, 1904~~					
9						
10						
11						
12						
13						
14					Date of Application for Enrollment.	
15						
16					April 21/99	
17						

Choctaw By Blood Enrollment Cards 1898-1914

RESIDENCE: Eagle COUNTY.
POST OFFICE: Eagletown, I.T.

Choctaw Nation

Choctaw Roll
(Not Including Freedmen)

CARD NO.
FIELD NO. 678

Dawes' Roll No.	NAME		Relationship to Person First Named	AGE	SEX	BLOOD	TRIBAL ENROLLMENT		
							Year	County	No.
1633	1 Bohanan, Milwee	28	First Named	25	M	Full	1896	Eagle	1299
1634	2 " Laurina	21	Wife	18	F	1/2	1896	"	3420
1635	3 Bohanan Emma	4	Dau	1	"	3/4			
	4								
	5								
	6								
	7								
	8								
	9								
	10								
	11	ENROLLMENT							
	12	OF NOS. 1 2 and 3 HEREON APPROVED BY THE SECRETARY							
	13	OF INTERIOR DEC 12 1902							
	14								
	15								
	16								
	17								

TRIBAL ENROLLMENT OF PARENTS

	Name of Father	Year	County	Name of Mother	Year	County
1	Sampson Bohanan	1896	Eagle	Annie Bohanan	1896	Eagle
2	James Dyer	1896	"	Malinda Dyer	1896	Non Citz
3	No 1			No 2		
4	For child of No2 see NB (Apr 26-06) Card #647					
5						
6	No2 on 1896 roll as Laurina Dyer.					
7						
8	No3 Affidavit of birth to be supplied. Recd May 4/99					
9	As to marriage of parents of No2, see Card					
10	of father, James Dyer, No 537.					
11						
12	Nos 1 and 2 have seprated[sic]					
13						
14					Date of Application for Enrollment.	
15						
16					April 21/99	
17						

Choctaw By Blood Enrollment Cards 1898-1914

RESIDENCE: Nashoba
POST OFFICE: Alikchi, I.T.

COUNTY.

Choctaw Nation

Choctaw Roll
(Not Including Freedmen)

CARD No.
FIELD No. 679

Dawes' Roll No.	NAME		Relationship to Person Named	AGE	SEX	BLOOD	TRIBAL ENROLLMENT		
							Year	County	No.
1636	₁ Baker, Morris	59	First Named	56	M	Full	1896	Nashoba	1166
1637	₂ " Sissie	20	Dau	17	F	"	1896	"	1169
1638	₃ " Fannie	22	"	19	"	"	1896	"	1168
DEAD.	₄ John, Paio		Ward	14	M	"	1896	"	6854
1639	₅ Noah, Harrison	5	G.Son	2	"	"			
	6								
	7								
	8	ENROLLMENT							
	9	OF NOS. 1 2 3 and 5 HEREON APPROVED BY THE SECRETARY							
	10	OF INTERIOR DEC 12 1902							
	11								
	12	No. 4 HEREON DISMISSED UNDER							
	13	ORDER OF THE COMMISSION TO THE FIVE							
	14	CIVILIZED TRIBES OF MARCH 31, 1905.							
	15								
	16								
	17								

TRIBAL ENROLLMENT OF PARENTS

	Name of Father	Year	County	Name of Mother	Year	County
1	Ak-o-chan-teby	Dead	Nashoba	A-pe-la-hu-na	Dead	Nashoba
2	No 1			Enie Baker	"	"
3	No 1			" "	"	"
4	Lake John	Dead	Nashoba	Iltney John	"	"
5	Simeon Noah	1896	"	No 2		
6						
7						
8						
9	No4 on 1896 roll as Perro John					
10	No4 Died Jan 13ᵗʰ 1902: Proof of Death filed Decʳ 23ʳᵈ 1902					
11						
12						
13						
14					Date of Application for Enrollment.	
15						
16					April 21/99	
17						

Choctaw By Blood Enrollment Cards 1898-1914

RESIDENCE: Nashoba   COUNTY.

POST OFFICE: Alikchi, I.T.

Choctaw Nation

Choctaw Roll
(Not Including Freedmen)

CARD NO.

FIELD NO. 680

Dawes' Roll No.	NAME		Relationship to Person First Named	AGE	SEX	BLOOD	TRIBAL ENROLLMENT		
							Year	County	No.
1640	1 Noah, Simeon	32	First Named	29	M	Full	1896	Nashoba	9682
1641	2 " Susan	29	Wife	26	F	"	1896	"	9683
	3								
	4								
	5								
	6								
	7								
	8								
	9								
	10								
	11	ENROLLMENT OF NOS. 1 and 2 HEREON APPROVED BY THE SECRETARY OF INTERIOR DEC 12 1902							
	12								
	13								
	14								
	15								
	16								
	17								

TRIBAL ENROLLMENT OF PARENTS

	Name of Father	Year	County	Name of Mother	Year	County
1	Baxter Noah	Dead	Nashoba	Nancy Noah	1896	Nashoba
2	Morris Baker	1896	"	Inie Baker	Dead	"
3						
4						
5						
6						
7						
8						
9						
10						
11						
12						
13						
14						
15						
16					Date of Application for Enrollment	April 21/99
17	P.O. Bethel I.T. 12/18/02					

Choctaw By Blood Enrollment Cards 1898-1914

RESIDENCE: Nashoba
POST OFFICE: Alikchi, I.T.
COUNTY.

Choctaw Nation

Choctaw Roll *(Not Including Freedmen)*

CARD NO.
FIELD NO. 681

Dawes' Roll No.	NAME	Relationship to Person First Named	AGE	SEX	BLOOD	TRIBAL ENROLLMENT Year	County	No.
DEAD.	1 Baker, Mitchell	Named	24	M	Full	1896	Nashoba	1170
1642	2 " Nancy ⁴⁹	Wife	46	F	"	1896	"	1171
1643	3 Winship, Ennittie ¹⁸	Cousin	15	"	"	1896	"	9686
1644	4 Noah, Charles ¹⁶	"	13	M	"	1896	"	9684
1645	5 Winship, Enie	Dau of No.3	7mo	F	3/4			
	6							
	7							
	8							
	9	ENROLLMENT						
	10	OF NOS. 2 3 4 and 5 HEREON APPROVED BY THE SECRETARY						
	11	OF INTERIOR DEC 12 1902						
	12							
	13	No. 1 HEREON DISMISSED UNDER						
	14	ORDER OF THE COMMISSION TO THE FIVE CIVILIZED TRIBES OF MARCH 31, 1905						
	15							
	16							
	17							

TRIBAL ENROLLMENT OF PARENTS

	Name of Father	Year	County	Name of Mother	Year	County
1	John Baker	Dead	Nashoba	Ilsie Baker	1896	Nashoba
2	Gaines	"	"	Pollie	Dead	"
3	Bo-kus-ta	Dead	"	Nancy Bokusta	1896	"
4	"	"	"	" "	1896	"
5	Isaac Winship	1896	"	No 3		
6						
7	No3 is now the wife of Isaac Winship on Choctaw card #5635 Nov. 25, 1901					
8	No.5 born April 25, 1901: Enrolled Nov. 25, 1901					
9	No.1 Died Dec 19" 1901: Proof of Death filed Dec' 23 1902					
	For children of No.3 see NB (March 3, 1905) #925					
10						
11						
12						
13						
14						
15				#1 to 4		
16				Date of Application for Enrollment		April 21/99
17						

81

Choctaw By Blood Enrollment Cards 1898-1914

RESIDENCE: Cedar COUNTY.
POST OFFICE: Alikchi, I.T.

Choctaw Nation

Choctaw Roll
(Not Including Freedmen)

CARD NO.
FIELD NO. 682

Dawes' Roll No.	NAME		Relationship to Person	AGE	SEX	BLOOD	TRIBAL ENROLLMENT		
							Year	County	No.
1646	1 Jacob, Nancy	63	First Named	60	F	Full	1896	Cedar	6738
	2								
	3								
	4								
	5								
	6	ENROLLMENT							
	7	OF NOS. I HEREON APPROVED BY THE SECRETARY							
	8	OF INTERIOR DEC 12 1902							
	9								
	10								
	11								
	12								
	13								
	14								
	15								
	16								
	17								

TRIBAL ENROLLMENT OF PARENTS

	Name of Father	Year	County	Name of Mother	Year	County
1	Po-lis-sobe	Died	in Mississippi	A-me-la	Dead	Kiamitia
2						
3						
4						
5						
6						
7						
8						
9						
10						
11						
12						
13						
14						
15						
16						
17						

Date of Application for Enrollment   April 21/99

82

Choctaw By Blood Enrollment Cards 1898-1914

RESIDENCE: Nashoba   COUNTY.   **Choctaw Nation**   **Choctaw Roll** (Not Including Freedmen)   CARD NO.
POST OFFICE: Smithville, I.T.   FIELD NO. **683**

Dawes' Roll No.	NAME		Relationship to Person First Named	AGE	SEX	BLOOD	TRIBAL ENROLLMENT		
							Year	County	No.
1647	₁ Samuel, Louisa	96	First Named	93	F	Full	1896	Nashoba	11393
1648	₂ " Willie C.	10	Ward	7	M	"	1896	"	11394
3									
4									
5									
6									
7									
8									
9									
10									
11									
12									
13									
14									
15									
16									
17									

ENROLLMENT
OF NOS. 1 and 2 HEREON
APPROVED BY THE SECRETARY
OF INTERIOR Dec. 12, 1902

TRIBAL ENROLLMENT OF PARENTS

Name of Father	Year	County	Name of Mother	Year	County
₁ Jimmie	Died	in Mississippi	O-nan-che-hema	Dead	Sugar Loaf
₂ Wallace Fisher	Dead	Nashoba	Sophia Fisher	"	Nashoba
3					
4					
5					
6					
7					
8					
9					
10					
11					
12					
13					
14					
15					
16			Date of Application for Enrollment		April 21/99
17	No 1 Died Nov. 20, 1911. So reported by letter.				

Choctaw By Blood Enrollment Cards 1898-1914

RESIDENCE: Towson COUNTY.
POST OFFICE: Doaksville, I.T.

Choctaw Nation

Choctaw Roll
(Not Including Freedmen)

CARD NO.
FIELD NO. 684

Dawes' Roll No.	NAME	Relationship to Person	AGE	SEX	BLOOD	TRIBAL ENROLLMENT		
						Year	County	No.
1649	1 Tillis, William ^56	First Named	53	M	Full	1896	Cedar	12069
	2							
	3							
	4							
	5							
	6							
	7							
	8							
	9							
	10							
	11	ENROLLMENT OF NOS. 1 HEREON						
	12	APPROVED BY THE SECRETARY						
	13	OF INTERIOR Dec. 12, 1902						
	14							
	15							
	16							
	17							

TRIBAL ENROLLMENT OF PARENTS

	Name of Father	Year	County	Name of Mother	Year	County
1	William Tillis	Dead	Towson	Ya-le-ho-na	Dead	Towson
2						
3						
4						
5						
6						
7						
8						
9						
10						
11						
12						
13						
14						
15						
16						
17				Date of Application for Enrollment.	April 22/99	

84

Choctaw By Blood Enrollment Cards 1898-1914

RESIDENCE: Towson COUNTY.
POST OFFICE: Fowlerville, I.T.

Choctaw Nation

Choctaw Roll (Not Including Freedmen)

CARD NO.
FIELD NO. 685

Dawes' Roll No.	NAME	Relationship to Person First Named	AGE	SEX	BLOOD	TRIBAL ENROLLMENT Year	County	No.
1650	1 Shotube, Dickson 53	First Named	50	M	Full	1896	Towson	11378
1651	2 " Jane 33	Wife	30	F	"	1896	"	11379
1652	3 DIED PRIOR TO SEPTEMBER 25, 1952 Nelis	Dau	30	"	"	1896	"	11381
1653	4 DIED PRIOR TO SEPTEMBER 25, 17 Johnie	Son	14	M	"	1896	"	11380
1654	5 " Louie 8	"	5	"	"	1896	"	11382
1655	6 " Mina DIED PRIOR TO SEPTEMBER 25,	Dau	3	F	"	1896	"	11383
1656	7 " Ena DIED PRIOR TO SEPTEMBER 25, 4	"	5mo	"	"			
1657	8 Daniel, Frances 12	G.Dau	9	"	"	1896	Towson	3375
1658	9 Austin, Lina 9	"	6	"	"	1896	"	204
1659	10 DIED PRIOR TO SEPTEMBER 25, 2 Shotube, Forbes	Son	2mo	M	"			

No3 died July-1898:No4 died Sept-1898:No6 died Feb 1899:No7 died Feb 1899:No10 died March-1901:
Enrollment cancelled by Department July 8, 1904.
No3 11died July, 1898: Proof of death filed Dec 3, 1901:
No4 13Sept, 1898: " " " " " " "
No6 14Feb, 1899: " " " " " " "
No7 Feb, 1899: " " " " " " "
No10 15March1901: " " " " " " "
16
17 P.O. Chula I.T. 11/26/02

TRIBAL ENROLLMENT OF PARENTS

Name of Father	Year	County	Name of Mother	Year	County
1 Sho-tube	Dead	Towson		Dead	Towson
2 Abel Hoyopatebe	"	"	Isabelle Hoyopatebe	"	Red River
3 No 1			Ilsie Shotube	"	Towson
4 No 1			" "	"	"
5 No 1			No 2		
6 No 1			No 2		
7 No 1			No 2		
8 Umpsion Daniel	Dead	Towson	No 3		
9 Willis Austin	1896	"	No.3		
10 No 1			No 2		
11					
12 No3 on 1896 roll as Nebus Shotube					
13 No6 " 1896 " " Susan "					
14 No9 " 1896 " " Lainie Austin					
15 No10 Enrolled July 9, 1900					
No1 on 1896 roll as Dixon Shotube					
16 No8 " " " " Francis Daniel					
17 For child of Nos 1&2 see N.B. (March 3, 1905) #1123.					

ENROLLMENT
OF NOS. 123456789and10 HEREON
APPROVED BY THE SECRETARY
OF INTERIOR Dec 12, 1902

#1 to 9

Date of Application
for Enrollment.
April 22/99

Choctaw By Blood Enrollment Cards 1898-1914

RESIDENCE: Nashoba COUNTY.
POST OFFICE: Smithville, I.T.

Choctaw Nation

Choctaw Roll
(Not Including Freedmen)

CARD NO.
FIELD NO. **686**

Dawes' Roll No.	NAME		Relationship to Person	AGE	SEX	BLOOD	TRIBAL ENROLLMENT		
							Year	County	No.
1660	1 Gibson, Thomas	46	First Named	43	M	Full	1896	Nashoba	4749
1661	2 " Amanda	51	Wife	48	F	"	1896	"	4759
1662	3 " Wilmon	18	Son	15	M	"	1896	"	4777
	4								
	5								
	6								
	7								
	8								
	9								
	10								
	11								
	12								
	13								
	14								
	15								
	16								
	17								

ENROLLMENT
OF NOS. 1 2 and 3 HEREON
APPROVED BY THE SECRETARY
OF INTERIOR Dec 12, 1902

For child of No 3 see NB. (March 3, 1905) #979

TRIBAL ENROLLMENT OF PARENTS

	Name of Father	Year	County	Name of Mother	Year	County
1	Solomon Gibson	Dead	Jacks Fork	Salema Gibson	Dead	Kiamitia
2	Isaac Watson	"	Nashoba	Viney Watson	"	Nashoba
3	No 1			No 2		
4						
5						
6						
7						
8						
9						
10						
11						
12						
13						
14						
15						
16						
17						

Date of Application for Enrollment April 22/99

Choctaw By Blood Enrollment Cards 1898-1914

RESIDENCE: Red River   COUNTY.

POST OFFICE: Kullituklo, I.T.

Choctaw Nation

Choctaw Roll
(Not Including Freedmen)

CARD NO.

FIELD NO. **687**

Dawes' Roll No.	NAME		Relationship to Person First Named	AGE	SEX	BLOOD	TRIBAL ENROLLMENT		
							Year	County	No.
1663	₁ Nelson, Eliza	40		37	F	Full	1896	Red River	9729
1664	₂ ~~Annie~~ DIED PRIOR TO SEPTEMBER 25, 1902		Dau	13	"	"	1896	" "	9731
1665	₃ " Alvin	13	Son	10	M	"	1896	" "	9732
1666	₄ " Abel	10	"	7	"	"	1896	" "	9733
1667	₅ ~~Napoleon~~ DIED PRIOR TO SEPTEMBER 25, 1902		"	4	"	"	1896	" "	9734
	6								
	7								
	8								
	9								
	10								
	11								
	12								
	13								
	14								
	15								
	16								
	17								

ENROLLMENT
OF NOS. 1 2 3 4 and 5 HEREON
APPROVED BY THE SECRETARY
OF INTERIOR Dec 12, 1902

TRIBAL ENROLLMENT OF PARENTS

	Name of Father	Year	County	Name of Mother	Year	County
1	Rich Walker	Dead	Red River	Betsy Walker	1896	Red River
2	~~Elliston Nelson~~	"	" "	~~No 1~~		
3	" "	"	" "	No 1		
4	" "	"	" "	No 1		
5	" "	"	" "	No 1		
6						
7			No1 on 1896 roll as Bicey Nelson			
8			No2 " 1896 " " Ann "			
9			~~No2 died March, 1902: Evidence of death filed Dec. 3, 1902.~~			
10			No5 " July - 1900: " " " " " "			
11	No2 died March-1902: No5 died July-1900: Enrollment cancelled by Department Sept 16, 1904.					
12						
13						
14					Date of Application for Enrollment.	
15					April 22/99	
16						
17						

Choctaw By Blood Enrollment Cards 1898-1914

RESIDENCE: Red River   COUNTY.   **Choctaw Nation**   **Choctaw Roll**   CARD No.
POST OFFICE: Kullituklo, I.T.   *(Not Including Freedmen)*   FIELD No. 688

Dawes' Roll No.	NAME	Relationship to Person	AGE	SEX	BLOOD	TRIBAL ENROLLMENT		
						Year	County	No.
1668	1 Boyd, Roca 48	First Named	45	F	Full	1893	Red River	P.R. 248
	2							
	3							
	4							
	5							
	6							
	7	ENROLLMENT						
	8	OF NOS. I HEREON APPROVED BY THE SECRETARY						
	9	OF INTERIOR DEC 12 1902						
	10							
	11							
	12							
	13							
	14	On 1893 Payroll as Hotatona Haner.						
	15							
	16							
	17							

TRIBAL ENROLLMENT OF PARENTS

	Name of Father	Year	County	Name of Mother	Year	County
1	Me-hah-le-ka	Dead	Eagle	Ta-la-watchee	Dead	Eagle
2						
3						
4						
5						
6						
7						
8						
9						
10						
11						
12						
13						
14						
15						
16						Date of Application for Enrollment April 22/99
17						

88

Choctaw By Blood Enrollment Cards 1898-1914

RESIDENCE: Eagle   COUNTY.

POST OFFICE: Eagletown, I.T.   **Choctaw Nation**   **Choctaw Roll** *(Not Including Freedmen)*

CARD NO.

FIELD NO. 689

Dawes' Roll No.	NAME	Relationship to Person	AGE	SEX	BLOOD	TRIBAL ENROLLMENT Year	County	No.
1669	1 Lewis, Silvy 33	First Named	30	F	Full	1893	Eagle	P.R 505
	2							
	3							
	4							
	5							
	6							
	7	ENROLLMENT OF NOS. 1 HEREON						
	8	APPROVED BY THE SECRETARY OF INTERIOR DEC 12 1902						
	9							
	10							
	11							
	12	On 1893 Payroll as Sidney Louis						
	13							
	14							
	15							
	16							
	17							

TRIBAL ENROLLMENT OF PARENTS

	Name of Father	Year	County	Name of Mother	Year	County
1	Gilbert Lewis	Dead	Eagle	Ah-took-lan-tema	Dead	Eagle
2						
3						
4						
5						
6						
7						
8						
9						
10						
11						
12						
13						
14						
15						
16				Date of Application for Enrollment	April 22/99	
17						

89

Choctaw By Blood Enrollment Cards 1898-1914

RESIDENCE: Red River   COUNTY.   **Choctaw Nation**   Choctaw Roll   CARD No.
POST OFFICE: Kullituklo, I.T.   *(Not Including Freedmen)*   FIELD No. **690**

Dawes' Roll No.	NAME	Relationship to Person First Named	AGE	SEX	BLOOD	TRIBAL ENROLLMENT		
						Year	County	No.
1670	1 Williston, Louisa	DIED PRIOR TO SEPTEMBER 25, 1902	48	F	Full	1896	Red River	13624
1671	2 " Silas 21	Son	18	M	"	1896	" "	13626
	3							
	4							
	5							
	6							
	7							
	8	ENROLLMENT						
	9	OF NOS. 1 and 2 HEREON APPROVED BY THE SECRETARY						
	10	OF INTERIOR Dec 12, 1902						
	11							
	12							
	13							
	14	No1 died January 5, 1900: Evidence of death filed Dec. 3, 1902.						
	15	No1 died Jan 5, 1900: Enrollment cancelled by Department July 8, 1904.						
	16							
	17							

TRIBAL ENROLLMENT OF PARENTS

	Name of Father	Year	County	Name of Mother	Year	County
1	Willis Covatte	Dead	Bok Tuklo	Kiasa Covatte	Dead	Bok Tuklo
2	Chas. Williston	"	Red River	No.1		
3						
4						
5						
6						
7						
8						
9						
10						
11						
12						
13						
14					Date of Application for Enrollment.	
15						
16					April 22/99	
17						

90

Choctaw By Blood Enrollment Cards 1898-1914

RESIDENCE: Nashoba COUNTY.
POST OFFICE: Smithville, I.T.

Choctaw Nation

Choctaw Roll
(Not Including Freedmen)

CARD NO.

FIELD NO. 691

Dawes' Roll No.	NAME		Relationship to Person First Named	AGE	SEX	BLOOD	TRIBAL ENROLLMENT		
							Year	County	No.
1672	₁ Gibson, Hettie	45		42	F	Full	1893	Nashoba	P.R. 229
1673	₂ " Liza Ann	12	Dau	9	"	"	1893	"	231
3									
4	ENROLLMENT								
5	OF NOS. 1 and 2 HEREON APPROVED BY THE SECRETARY								
6	OF INTERIOR DEC 12 1902								
7									
8									
9									
10									
11									
12									
13									
14									
15									
16									
17									

TRIBAL ENROLLMENT OF PARENTS

	Name of Father	Year	County	Name of Mother	Year	County
1	James Wall	1896	Eagle	Pisa-ho-le-ma	Dead	Eagle
2	Willie Gibson	1896	Kiamitia	No 1		
3						
4						
5	No1 on 1893 Pay roll as Hide Gibson					
6	No2 " 1893 " " " Lasen "					
7						
8	No2 on 1896 roll, Page 349, No 13275 as Losan Waul, Nashoba Co					
9	No1 " 1896 " " 349, " 13274 " Hitty Waul, " "					
10						
11						
12						
13						
14						
15						
16					Date of Application for Enrollment	April 22/99
17						

91

Choctaw By Blood Enrollment Cards 1898-1914

RESIDENCE: Red River   COUNTY.
POST OFFICE: Kullituklo, I.T.

Choctaw Nation

Choctaw Roll
(Not Including Freedmen)

CARD No.
FIELD No. 692

Dawes' Roll No.	NAME	Relationship to Person	AGE	SEX	BLOOD	Year	County	No.
1674	1 Filemontubbee, Joel 51	First Named	48	M	Full	1896	Red River	4207
1675	2 Sallie	Wife	67	F	"	1896	" "	4208
1676	3 Johnson, Lucy Ann 23	Ward	20	"	"	1896	" "	4209
	4							
	5							
	6							
	7							
	8							
	9							
	10							
	11	ENROLLMENT OF NOS. 1 2 and 3 HEREON						
	12	APPROVED BY THE SECRETARY						
	13	OF INTERIOR DEC 12 1902						
	14							
	15							
	16							
	17							

TRIBAL ENROLLMENT OF PARENTS

	Name of Father	Year	County	Name of Mother	Year	County
1	File-mon-tubbee	Dead	Red River	Pisa-ho-tema	Dead	Eagle
2	Julius Homa	"	" "	Mi-ho-te-kona	"	Red River
3	Joe Johnson	"	Bok Tuklo	Sarah Johnson	"	" "

No3 on 1896 roll as Lucy Ann Filemontubbee

No2 died Sept. 5, 1902: Evidence of death filed Dec 3, 1902.
No2 died Sept 5, 1902: Enrollment cancelled by Department

For child of No3 see NB (Mar 3-05) Card #904
      "   "   "   " NB (Apr 26-06) " #476

Date of Application for Enrollment.
April 22/99

92

Choctaw By Blood Enrollment Cards 1898-1914

RESIDENCE: Red River   COUNTY.   **Choctaw Nation**   **Choctaw Roll**   CARD NO.
POST OFFICE: Kullituklo, I.T.   (Not Including Freedmen)   FIELD NO.   693

Dawes' Roll No.		NAME		Relationship to Person	AGE	SEX	BLOOD	TRIBAL ENROLLMENT		
								Year	County	No.
1677	1	Suckky, Abel	33	First Named	30	M	Full	1896	Red River	11444
1678	2	" Julia	58	Wife	55	F	"	1896	" "	11445
1679	3	" Harrison	DIED PRIOR TO SEPTEMBER 25, 1902	Son	18	M	"	1896	" "	11446
1680	4	" Bettie	15	Dau	12	F	"	1896	" "	11447
1681	5	" Cillissie	9	"	6	"	"	1896	" "	11449
	6									
	7									
	8									
	9									
	10									
	11									
	12									
	13									
	14									
	15									
	16									
	17									

ENROLLMENT
OF NOS. 1 2 3 4 and 5 HEREON
APPROVED BY THE SECRETARY
OF INTERIOR DEC 12 1902

TRIBAL ENROLLMENT OF PARENTS

	Name of Father	Year	County	Name of Mother	Year	County
1	Jimmie Suckky	Dead	Red River	Pa-e-hah	Dead	Red River
2	[Illegible]	"	Eagle	Nah-see	"	" "
3	No 1			No 2		
4	No 1			No 2		
5	No 1			No 2		
6						
7			No3 died July 7, 1900: Evidence of death filed Dec 3, 1902			
8			No3 died July 7, 1900: Enrollment cancelled by Department [remainder illegible]			
9			No1 now husband of Siney Hall, #13513 Card #7-5326			
10						
11						
12						
13						
14					Date of Application for Enrollment.	
15						
16					April 22/99	
17	Haworth Okla.					

93

Choctaw By Blood Enrollment Cards 1898-1914

RESIDENCE: Eagle   COUNTY.   **Choctaw Nation**   **Choctaw Roll**   CARD NO.
POST OFFICE: Eagletown, I.T.   *(Not Including Freedmen)*   FIELD NO. **694**

Dawes' Roll No.	NAME	Relationship to Person First Named	AGE	SEX	BLOOD	TRIBAL ENROLLMENT		
						Year	County	No.
1682	₁ Wade, Emiline ²²	First Named	19	F	Full	1896	Eagle	1271
1683	₂ Wade, Sylvania ²	Dau	9mo	F	"			
	3							
	4							
	5	ENROLLMENT						
	6	OF NOS. 1 and 2 HEREON						
	7	APPROVED BY THE SECRETARY OF INTERIOR Dec 12, 1902						
	8							
	9							
	10							
	11							
	12							
	13							
	14							
	15							
	16							
	17							

TRIBAL ENROLLMENT OF PARENTS

	Name of Father	Year	County	Name of Mother	Year	County
1	Tushka Billy	Dead	Eagle	Amy Billy	1896	Eagle
2	Barnett Wade	1896	"	No 1		
3						
4						
5						
6	On 1896 roll as Emeline Billy					
7	No1 now he wife of Barnet Wade on Choctaw Card No. 1250. Evidence of marriage filed August 30, 1901.					
8	No2 Enrolled August 30, 1901.					
9	For child of No1 see NB (March 3, 1905) #909.					
10						
11						
12						
13						
14						
15						
16				Date of Application for Enrollment	of No.1	
17				April 22/99		

Choctaw By Blood Enrollment Cards 1898-1914

RESIDENCE: Red River   COUNTY.   **Choctaw Nation**   **Choctaw Roll**   CARD NO.
POST OFFICE: Kullituklo, I.T.   *(Not Including Freedmen)*   FIELD NO. **695**

Dawes' Roll No.	NAME	Relationship to Person First Named	AGE	SEX	BLOOD	TRIBAL ENROLLMENT Year	County	No.
1684	1 Williston, Jacob 23	First Named	20	M	Full	1896	Red River	13625
1685	2 ~~Selay~~ DIED PRIOR TO SEPTEMBER 25, 1902	Wife	30	F	"	1896	" "	12206
1686	3 " Impson 6	Son	3	M	"			
	4							
	5							
	6							
	7							
	8							
	9							
	10							
	11							
	12							
	13							
	14							
	15							
	16							
	17							

ENROLLMENT
OF NOS. 1 2 and 3 HEREON
APPROVED BY THE SECRETARY
OF INTERIOR Dec 12 1902

TRIBAL ENROLLMENT OF PARENTS

Name of Father	Year	County	Name of Mother	Year	County
1 Chas. Williston	Dead	Red River	Louisa Williston	1896	Red River
2 ~~Thompson Showona~~	"	~~Cedar~~	~~Pisa-ho-tema~~	Dead	Towson
3 No. 1			No. 2		
4					
5					
6			No. 2 on 1896 roll as Selay Thompson		
7					
8					
9			No. 2 died July 27, 1899; Evidence of death filed Dec. 3, 1902		
10	No2 died July 27-1899; Enrollment cancelled by Department July 8-1904				
11					
12					
13					
14			Date of Application for Enrollment.		
15					
16			April 22/99		
17					

95

Choctaw By Blood Enrollment Cards 1898-1914

RESIDENCE: Nashoba COUNTY.

POST OFFICE: Smithville

Choctaw Nation

Choctaw Roll
(Not Including Freedmen)

CARD NO.

FIELD NO. **696**

Dawes' Roll No.	NAME		Relationship to Person	AGE	SEX	BLOOD	TRIBAL ENROLLMENT		
							Year	County	No.
1687	1 Taylor, Sarah	39	First Named	36	F	Full	1896	Nashoba	12142
1688	2 Amos, Kelisin	13	Nephew	10	M	"	1893	Eagle	P.R. 51
1689	3 " , Eni	10	Niece	7	F	"	1893	"	52
	4								
	5								
	6								
	7								
	8								
	9								
	10								
	11	ENROLLMENT OF NOS. 1, 2 and 3 HEREON							
	12	APPROVED BY THE SECRETARY							
	13	OF INTERIOR Dec. 12, 1902							
	14								
	15								
	16								
	17								

TRIBAL ENROLLMENT OF PARENTS

	Name of Father	Year	County	Name of Mother	Year	County
1	Lus-so	Dead	Eagle	Ellen Lusso	Dead	Eagle
2	Anderson Amos	"	"	Sail Amos	"	"
3	" "	"	"	" "	"	"
4						
5						
6						
7	No3 on 1893 Payroll Emi Amos					
8						
9	No 2 also on 1896 roll as Gleason Amos					
10	Page 7, No. 279, Eagle Co.					
11						
12						
13						
14						
15						
16				Date of Application for Enrollment April 22/99		
17						

RESIDENCE: Red River COUNTY.
POST OFFICE: Garvin, I.T.

Choctaw Nation

Choctaw Roll
(Not Including Freedmen)

CARD No.
FIELD No. 697

Dawes' Roll No.	NAME		Relationship to Person First Named	AGE	SEX	BLOOD	TRIBAL ENROLLMENT		
							Year	County	No.
									P.R.
1690	1 Jackson, Louina	45	First Named	42	F	Full	1893	Red River	416
1691	2 Washington, Ben	21	Son	18	M	"	1896	" "	13581
1692	3 " , Salis	20	"	17	"	"	1896	" "	13582
1693	4 " , Esias	7	"	14	"	"	1896	" "	13583
1694	5 Mitchell, Annie	13	Dau	10	F	"	1896	" "	8656
	6								
	7								
	8								
	9								
	10								
	11	ENROLLMENT							
	12	OF NOS. 1,2,3,4 and 5 HEREON APPROVED BY THE SECRETARY OF INTERIOR Dec 12, 1902							
	13								
	14								
	15								
	16								
	17								

TRIBAL ENROLLMENT OF PARENTS

	Name of Father	Year	County	Name of Mother	Year	County
1	Noah-tambe	Dead	Red River	Ho-ta-wa-che	Dead	Red River
2	Sampson Washington	"	" " "	No.1		
3	" "	"	" " "	No.1		
4	" "	"	" " "	No.1		
5	Albert Mitchell	"	" " "	No1		
6						
7	No1 on 1893 Pay roll as Louina Lomon.					
8	No.4 " 1896 roll as Esar Washington					
9	No1 also on 1896 roll, Page 172, No 6999					
10	as Lowinah Jackson					
11	No2 is now husband of Acy Colbert on Choctaw Card #1048.					
12	For child of No2 see N.B. (March 3, 1905) #964					
13	" " " " 3 " " (Apr 26-06) #421					
14						
15					Date of Application for Enrollment.	
16					April 22/99	
17	No2 Garvin I.T. 12/12/02					

Choctaw By Blood Enrollment Cards 1898-1914

RESIDENCE: Nashoba
POST OFFICE: Alikchi, I.T.

COUNTY.

Choctaw Nation

Choctaw Roll
(Not Including Freedmen)

CARD NO.

FIELD NO. **698**

Dawes' Roll No.	NAME	Relationship to Person	AGE	SEX	BLOOD	TRIBAL ENROLLMENT		
						Year	County	No.
1695	1 Noah, Elizabeth 73	First Named	70	F	Full	1893	Nashoba	P.R. 607
	2							
	3							
	4							
	5							
	6							
	7							
	8							
	9							
	10							
	11							
	12							
	13							
	14							
	15							
	16							
	17							

ENROLLMENT
OF NOS. 1 HEREON
APPROVED BY THE SECRETARY
OF INTERIOR Dec 12, 1902.

Also on 1896 roll page 245, No. 9689
as Kanyotema Noah.

TRIBAL ENROLLMENT OF PARENTS

	Name of Father	Year	County	Name of Mother	Year	County
1	E-man-tubbee	Dead	Skullyville	Clok-ma-hona	Dead	Nashoba
2						
3						
4						
5						
6						
7						
8						
9						
10						
11						
12						
13						
14						
15						
16						
17						

Date of Application for Enrollment. April 22/99

98

Choctaw By Blood Enrollment Cards 1898-1914

RESIDENCE: Nashoba
POST OFFICE: Alikchi, I.T.

COUNTY. **Choctaw Nation**

Choctaw Roll (Not Including Freedmen)

CARD NO.
FIELD NO. **699**

Dawes' Roll No.	NAME		Relationship to Person	AGE	SEX	BLOOD	TRIBAL ENROLLMENT		
							Year	County	No.
1696	1 Morrison, Alens	42	First Named	39	F	Full	1896	Nashoba	8622
1697	2 " Lizzie	21	Dau	18	"	"	1896	"	8623
1698	3 " Paul St.	12	Son	9	M	"	1896	"	8625
14579	4 Jefferson, Laura	1	Dau of No.2	7mo	F	"			
	5								
	6								
	7	ENROLLMENT OF NOS. 1 2 and 3 HEREON APPROVED BY THE SECRETARY OF INTERIOR Dec 12 1902							
	8								
	9								
	10								
	11								
	12	ENROLLMENT OF NOS. 4 HEREON APPROVED BY THE SECRETARY OF INTERIOR May 20 1903							
	13								
	14								
	15								
	16								
	17								

TRIBAL ENROLLMENT OF PARENTS

	Name of Father	Year	County	Name of Mother	Year	County
1	Willis Hoyabee	Dead	Atoka	Liza Hoyabee	Dead	Nashoba
2	Thompson Morrison	"	Nashoba	No. 1		
3	" "	"	"	No. 1		
4	Ellis Jefferson		Choctaw Roll	No. 2		
5						
6						

7   No 1 on 1896 roll as Elies Morrison
8   No.2 is now wife of Ellis Jefferson on Choc Card #1000
    No.4 born April 9, 1902: enrolled Dec 2-1902
9

10   For child of No 2 see N.B. (Apr 26-06) Card #483
11   "   "   "   "   " (Mar3-05)   " #934.
12

13   #1 to 3
14   Date of Application for Enrollment.
15
16   April 22/99
17   P.O. Garvin, I.T. 4/10/05

Choctaw By Blood Enrollment Cards 1898-1914

| RESIDENCE: Nashoba | | COUNTY. | | | | | Choctaw Roll | | CARD No. |
| POST OFFICE: Alikchi, I.T. | | **Choctaw Nation** | | | | | *(Not Including Freedmen)* | | FIELD No. **700** |

Dawes' Roll No.	NAME	Relationship to Person First Named	AGE	SEX	BLOOD	TRIBAL ENROLLMENT		
						Year	County	No.
1699	1 Noah, Frances ⁴¹		38	F	Full	1893	Cedar	P.R. 320
1700	2 LeFlore, Joel ⁸	Son	5	M	"	1896	Nashoba	4143
1701	3 Jefferson, Minie Ranet ²	Dau	2m	F	"			
	4							
	5							
	6							
	7							
	8							
	9							
	10							
	11	ENROLLMENT OF NOS. 1, 2 and 3 HEREON						
	12	APPROVED BY THE SECRETARY						
	13	OF INTERIOR Dec 12 1902						
	14							
	15							
	16							
	17							

TRIBAL ENROLLMENT OF PARENTS

Name of Father	Year	County	Name of Mother	Year	County
1 Philip Noah	Dead	Cedar	Kittie Noah	Dead	Nashoba
2 Henry LeFlore	1896	"	No.1		
3 Austin Jefferson	1896	Nashoba	No.1		
4					
5					
6	No.1 on 1893 Payroll as Francis LeFlore.				
7	No.2 on 1896 roll as Joel Floore page 100. #4143.				
8					
9	No.1 also on 1896 roll Page 245 No. 9688				
10	as Fonsil Noah.				
11	No.3 Born June 13, 1900; enrolled June 2, 1902.				
	No.3 is illegitimate				
12					
13					
14					
15				#1&2	
16				Date of Application for Enrollment	April 22/99
17					

Choctaw By Blood Enrollment Cards 1898-1914

RESIDENCE: Eagle   COUNTY.
POST OFFICE: Eagletown, I.T.

Choctaw Nation

Choctaw Roll
(Not Including Freedmen)

CARD NO.

FIELD NO. **701**

Dawes' Roll No.	NAME	Relationship to Person	AGE	SEX	BLOOD	TRIBAL ENROLLMENT		
						Year	County	No.
1702	DIED PRIOR TO SEPTEMBER 25, 1902 1 Jefferson, Sallie	First Named	41	F	Full	1896	Eagle	6968
2								
3								
4								
5	ENROLLMENT							
6	OF NOS. 1 HEREON							
7	APPROVED BY THE SECRETARY OF INTERIOR Dec 12 1902							
8								
9								
10								
11	No.1 died Dec. 27, 1901. Evidence of death filed Dec. 3, 1902.							
12	No.1 died Dec. 27-1901: Enrollment cancelled by Department July 8, 1904.							
13								
14								
15								
16								
17								

TRIBAL ENROLLMENT OF PARENTS

	Name of Father	Year	County	Name of Mother	Year	County
1	Tulekee Bobb	Dead	Eagle	Na-ne-ma-nohke	Dead	Eagle
2						
3						
4						
5						
6						
7						
8						
9						
10						
11						
12						
13						
14						
15						
16				Date of Application for Enrollment		April 22/99
17						

101

Choctaw By Blood Enrollment Cards 1898-1914

RESIDENCE: Red River   COUNTY.
POST OFFICE: Kullituklo, I.T.

Choctaw Nation

Choctaw Roll   CARD NO.
(Not Including Freedmen)   FIELD NO.   702

Dawes' Roll No.	NAME		Relationship to Person	AGE	SEX	BLOOD	TRIBAL ENROLLMENT		
							Year	County	No.
1703	1 Tohkubbi, Cephus	26	First Named	23	M	Full	1896	Red River	12296
1704	2 " Seon	25	Wife	22	F	"	1896	" "	12289
1705	3 " Marina	4	Dau	6mo	"	"			
1706	4 " Alphus	1	Son	7mo	M	"			
	5								
	6								
	7								
	8	ENROLLMENT							
	9	OF NOS. 1, 2, 3 and 4 HEREON APPROVED BY THE SECRETARY							
	10	OF INTERIOR DEC 12 1902							
	11								
	12								
	13								
	14								
	15								
	16								
	17								

TRIBAL ENROLLMENT OF PARENTS

	Name of Father	Year	County	Name of Mother	Year	County
1	William Tohkubbi	Dead	Bok Tuklo	Sealie Tohkubbi	Dead	Red River
2	Josiah Thomas	"	" " "	Silway Thomas	1896	" "
3	No 1			No 2		
4	Nº1			Nº2		
5						
6						
7						
8						
9						
10			No1 on 1896 roll as Sephus Tohkubbi			
11			No2 " 1896 " " Seon Thomas			
12			Nº4 Born Feby 8, 1902: enrolled Aug. 26, 1902.			
13						
14						
15		For child of Nos 1&2 see N B (Apr 26-06) Card #465		#1 to 3 inc		
16		" " " " " " " (Mar 3-05) " #683		Date of Application for Enrollment April 22/99		
17						

102

Choctaw By Blood Enrollment Cards 1898-1914

RESIDENCE: Nashoba COUNTY.

POST OFFICE: Smithville, I.T.

Choctaw Nation

Choctaw Roll
(Not Including Freedmen)

CARD NO.

FIELD NO. 703

Dawes' Roll No.	NAME	Relationship to Person First Named	AGE	SEX	BLOOD	TRIBAL ENROLLMENT Year	County	No.
1707	1 Stechi, Solomon 48		45	M	Full	1896	Nashoba	11395
	2							
	3							
	4	ENROLLMENT						
	5	OF NOS. 1 HEREON APPROVED BY THE SECRETARY						
	6	OF INTERIOR DEC 12 1902						
	7							
	8							
	9							
	10							
	11							
	12							
	13							
	14							
	15							
	16							
	17							

TRIBAL ENROLLMENT OF PARENTS

	Name of Father	Year	County	Name of Mother	Year	County
1	Stechi	Dead	Nashoba	Al-mo-tona	Dead	Eagle
2						
3						
4						
5						
6						
7						
8						
9						
10						
11						
12						
13						
14						
15				Date of Application for Enrollment. April 22/99		
16						
17						

103

Choctaw By Blood Enrollment Cards 1898-1914

RESIDENCE: Red River   COUNTY.
POST OFFICE: Kullituklo, I.T.

Choctaw Nation

Choctaw Roll CARD NO.
(Not Including Freedmen) FIELD NO. 704

Dawes' Roll No.		NAME		Relationship to Person First Named	AGE	SEX	BLOOD	TRIBAL ENROLLMENT		
								Year	County	No.
DEAD	1	Allen, Solomon DEAD			37	M	Full	1896	Red River	317
1708	2	" Nicey	23	Wife	20	F	"	1896	" "	1381
1709	3	" Salina	4	Dau	1mo	"	"			
1710	4	" Tensey	1	Dau	4mo	F	"			
	5									
	6	ENROLLMENT								
	7	OF NOS. 2, 3 and 4 HEREON APPROVED BY THE SECRETARY								
	8	OF INTERIOR DEC 12 1902								
	9									
	10	No. 1 HEREON DISMISSED UNDER								
	11	ORDER OF THE COMMISSION TO THE FIVE								
	12	CIVILIZED TRIBES OF MARCH 31, 1905.								
	13									
	14									
	15									
	16									
	17									

TRIBAL ENROLLMENT OF PARENTS

	Name of Father	Year	County	Name of Mother	Year	County
1	John Allen	1896	Wade	Sukkie Hard	1896	Red River
2	La-wa-chubbee	Dead	Red River	Viney Hote	1896	" "
3	No 1			No 2		
4	No 1			No 2		
5						
6	No2 on 1896 roll as Nancy Belvin					
7	No.4 Born July 6-1901: Enrolled Nov. 9, 1901.					
8	No.1 Died March 20, 1901: Evidence of death filed Nov. 9, 1901.					
	No2 is now wife of Willis Tushka on Choctaw card #1149					
9	No2 on 1893 payroll Red River Co page 6 No 41 as Nisey Balfin					
10						
11						
12						
13						
14						
15						
16				Date of Application for Enrollment	April 22/99	
17						

104

Choctaw By Blood Enrollment Cards 1898-1914

RESIDENCE: Red River COUNTY. POST OFFICE: Goodwater, I.T.								

Choctaw Nation — Choctaw Roll (Not Including Freedmen) — CARD NO. FIELD NO. **705**

Dawes' Roll No.	NAME	Relationship to Person	AGE	SEX	BLOOD	TRIBAL ENROLLMENT		
						Year	County	No.
14312	1 Clover, R. L.	50 First Named	47	M	1/4			
I.W. 1522	2 " , Mary F.	Wife	44	F	I.W.			
3								
4	ENROLLMENT							
5	OF NOS. 1 HEREON APPROVED BY THE SECRETARY							
6	OF INTERIOR Apr 11 1903							
7								
8	ENROLLMENT							
9	OF NOS. ~~2~~ HEREON APPROVED BY THE SECRETARY							
10	OF INTERIOR Mar 14 1906							
11								
12	Further action in connection with allotment to No.1 suspended under protest of attorney							
13	for Choctaw and Chickasaw Nation Jan 23-1904 – Protest overruled by Dept March 31,1904							
14								
15								
16								
17								

TRIBAL ENROLLMENT OF PARENTS

	Name of Father	Year	County	Name of Mother	Year	County
1	Eli Cover[sic]	Dead	Non Citz.	Matilda Clover	1896	Non Citz
2	Wᵐ Rickets	Dead	Non Citz.	Nancy Johnson	Dead	" "
3						
4						
5	Admitted by the Dawes Commission Case No. 725.					
6						
7	See Choctaw memorandum, under act of May 31, 1900;					
8	Case No. 38, for refusal of four children Sept. 28th, 1900.					
9	No.1 is now husband of Mary F. Clover on Choctaw card D.846. Evidence					
	of marriage filed Nov. 28, 1902.					
10	No.2 transferred to this card from 7-D-846, January 13, 1906; see decision					
11	of December 28, 1905					
12						
13						
14						
15						
16						
17						

#1 Date of Application for Enrollment April 22/99

Choctaw By Blood Enrollment Cards 1898-1914

RESIDENCE: Nashoba
POST OFFICE: Alikchi, I.T.

COUNTY. **Choctaw Nation**

Choctaw Roll
(Not Including Freedmen)

CARD No.
FIELD No. 706

Dawes' Roll No.	NAME		Relationship to Person	AGE	SEX	BLOOD	TRIBAL ENROLLMENT		
							Year	County	No.
1711	1 Wallace, Loston	22	First Named	19	M	Full	1896	Nashoba	13341
1712	2 " Enissa	27	Wife	24	F	"	1896	"	1167
	3								
	4	ENROLLMENT OF NOS. 1 and 2 HEREON							
	5	APPROVED BY THE SECRETARY OF INTERIOR DEC 12 1902							
	6								
	7								
	8								
	9								
	10								
	11								
	12								
	13	No1 on 1896 roll as Liston Wallace							
	14	No2 " 1896 " " Susie Baker							
	15	For child of No.1 see NB (March 3, 1905) #953							
	16								
	17								

TRIBAL ENROLLMENT OF PARENTS

	Name of Father	Year	County	Name of Mother	Year	County
1	Johnson Wallace	Dead	Nashoba	Hinnie Wallace	Dead	Nashoba
2	Morris Baker	1896	"	Annie Baker	"	"
3						
4						
5						
6						
7						
8						
9						
10						
11						
12						
13						
14						
15						
16					Date of Application for Enrollment	April 22/99
17						

106

Choctaw By Blood Enrollment Cards 1898-1914

RESIDENCE: Nashoba   COUNTY.   **Choctaw Nation**

POST OFFICE: Smithville, I.T.

Choctaw Roll _(Not Including Freedmen)_

CARD NO.

FIELD NO. 707

Dawes' Roll No.	NAME	Relationship to Person	AGE	SEX	BLOOD	TRIBAL ENROLLMENT		
						Year	County	No.
1713	1 James, Geon ²⁶	First Named	23	M	Full	1896	Nashoba	6808
1714	2 " Lita ³⁴	Wife	31	F	"	1893	Eagle	P.R. 75
1715	3 " Davis ⁵	Son	1	M	"			
	4							
	5							
	6	ENROLLMENT						
	7	OF NOS. 1 2 and 3 HEREON APPROVED BY THE SECRETARY						
	8	OF INTERIOR DEC 12 1902						
	9							
	10							
	11							
	12							
	13							
	14							
	15							
	16							
	17							

TRIBAL ENROLLMENT OF PARENTS

	Name of Father	Year	County	Name of Mother	Year	County
1	Bob James	Dead	Nashoba	Motsey James	1896	Nashoba
2	Jerry Barnes	1896	Eagle	Bessie Barnes	1896	Red River
3	No 1			No 2		
4						
5						
6	No 1 on 1896 roll as Gaines James					
7	No2 " 1893 Pay roll as Laitie Bunce					
8	No2 is now wife of Coleman Baker Choctaw #539					
9	No2 also on 1896 roll Page 348, No 13251 as Laitey Ward, Nashoba Co.					
10						
11						
12						
13						
14						
15						
16					DATE OF APPLICATION FOR ENROLLMENT	April 22/99
17						

107

Choctaw By Blood Enrollment Cards 1898-1914

RESIDENCE: Nashoba   COUNTY.   **Choctaw Nation**   Choctaw Roll   CARD NO.
POST OFFICE: Alikchi, I.T.   (Not Including Freedmen)   FIELD NO. **708**

Dawes' Roll No.	NAME		Relationship to Person	AGE	SEX	BLOOD	TRIBAL ENROLLMENT		
							Year	County	No.
1716	1 Cobb, Sampson	41	First Named	38	M	Full	1896	Nashoba	2509
1717	2 " , Sophie	35	Wife	32	F	"	1896	"	2537
1718	3 " , Simon	14	Son	11	M	"	1896	"	2510
*1719	4 " , Aaron	10	Dau	7	F	"	1896	"	2511
1720	5 " , Sillan	6	Son	1	F	"			
1722	6 Noah, John	17	S.Son	14	M	"	1896	Nashoba	9681
1721	7 Cobb, Albert	3	Son	4mo	M	"			
14580	8 " , Rosie	1	Dau	6mo	F	"			
	9								
	10								
	11								
	12								
	13								
	14								
	15								
	16								
	17								

ENROLLMENT
OF NOS. 1,2,3,4,5,6 and 7 HEREON
APPROVED BY THE SECRETARY
OF INTERIOR Dec. 12, 1902
4/22/36. Sex of Nº5 changed by Dept. Authy. April 6, 1936. (D 6427-36).DF
1-16-31

No3 on Choctaw roll as Simmon Cobb
No8 born July 25,1902: enrolled Dec. 15, 1902
For child of Nos1&2 see N.B. (March3, 1905) '990

ENROLLMENT
OF NOS. 8 HEREON
APPROVED BY THE SECRETARY
OF INTERIOR May 20, 1903

TRIBAL ENROLLMENT OF PARENTS

	Name of Father	Year	County	Name of Mother	Year	County
1	Gaines Cobb	Dead	Sugar Loaf	Sarah Cobb	Dead	Sugar Loaf
2	Elijah Stephen	"	Nashoba	Ale-on	"	Nashoba
3	No 1			No 2		
4	No 1			No 2		
5	No 1			No 2		
6	Nellis Noah	1896	Nashoba	No 2		
7	No 1			No 2		
8	No 1			No 2		
9						
10						
11	Sex of No4 changed from "M" to "F"					
12	by authority of December 17, 1930-109					
13						
14					Date of Application for Enrollment.	
15					No.7 Enrolled Nov 24/99	
16	P.O. [Illegible] I.T. 4/27/07				April 22/99	
17	Bethel I.T. 12/15/02					

Choctaw By Blood Enrollment Cards 1898-1914

RESIDENCE: Nashoba
POST OFFICE: Alikchi, I.T.

COUNTY. **Choctaw Nation**

Choctaw Roll *(Not Including Freedmen)*

CARD No.
FIELD No. 709

Dawes' Roll No.		NAME	Relationship to Person First Named	AGE	SEX	BLOOD	TRIBAL ENROLLMENT		
							Year	County	No.
1723	1	Stephen, Paul		47	M	Full	1896	Nashoba	11418
1724	2	" Bicey	Wife	46	F	"	1896	"	11409
1725	3	" Arion	Ward	12	"	"	1893	Skullyville	P.R. 527
	4								
	5								
	6								
	7								
	8	ENROLLMENT OF NOS. 1, 2 and 3 HEREON							
	9	APPROVED BY THE SECRETARY							
	10	OF INTERIOR DEC 12 1902							
	11								
	12								
	13								
	14								
	15								
	16								
	17								

TRIBAL ENROLLMENT OF PARENTS

	Name of Father	Year	County	Name of Mother	Year	County
1	Lu Stephen	Dead	Nashoba	Ileann Stephen	Dead	Nashoba
2	Wash Hudson	"	Eagle	Nanaomatona	"	Eagle
3	Andy Williams	"	Skullyville	Tennessee Stephens	"	Skullyville
4						
5						
6	No1 on 1893 pay roll Nashoba Co page 57 No 667					
7	No2 " " " " " " 59 " 686					
8	No2 on 1896 roll as Baisy Stephen					
9	No3 " 1894 Pay roll as Arion Stephens also on					
10	1896 roll, Page 392, No 11322, Wade Co. as					
11	Arion Stephens					
12						
13	No3 on 1896 Choctaw Roll, Page 211,					
14	No 8473, Skullyville Co, as Aian Meaders.					
15	Sheriff of Skullyville Co says that No1					
16	has always been recognized as a Negro. Dec 15/99.					
17	For child of No.3 see NB (March 3 1905) #995					

Date of Application for Enrollment.
April 22/99

109

Choctaw By Blood Enrollment Cards 1898-1914

RESIDENCE: Red River   COUNTY.   **Choctaw Nation**   **Choctaw Roll**   CARD NO.
POST OFFICE: Kullituklo, I.T.   *(Not Including Freedmen)*   FIELD NO.   **710**

Dawes' Roll No.	NAME	Relationship to Person First Named	AGE	SEX	BLOOD	TRIBAL ENROLLMENT Year	County	No.
1726	1 Shoney, Wilson 30	First Named	27	M	Full	1896	Red River	11456
1727	2 " Phelena 35	Wife	38	F	"	1896	" "	13604
DEAD.	3 ~~Walker, Daniel~~ DEAD.	~~S.Son~~	~~16~~	~~M~~	~~"~~	~~1896~~	~~" "~~	~~13605~~
1728	4 " Lorinzy 10	S.Dau	7	F	"	1896	" "	13606
	5							
	6							
	7	ENROLLMENT						
	8	~~OF NOS. 1, 2 and 4~~ HEREON APPROVED BY THE SECRETARY OF INTERIOR DEC 12 1902						
	9							
	10							
	11	No. 3 HEREON DISMISSED UNDER						
	12	ORDER OF THE COMMISSION TO THE FIVE ~~CIVILIZED TRIBES OF MARCH 31, 1905.~~						
	13							
	14							
	15							
	16							
	17							

TRIBAL ENROLLMENT OF PARENTS

	Name of Father	Year	County	Name of Mother	Year	County
1	Alfred Shoney	Dead	Red River	Elsie Shoney	Dead	Red River
2	Foster	"	Blue		"	Blue
3	~~Isom Walker~~	~~1896~~	~~Red River~~	~~No 2~~		
4	" "	"	" "	No 2		
5						
6						
7	No1 on 1896 roll as Wilson Shong.					
8	No2 " 1896 " " Phelena Walker					
9	No3 Died Jany. 6, 1902; proof of death filed March 13,1902.					
10						
11						
12						
13						
14						
15						
16					April 22/99	
17						

110

Choctaw By Blood Enrollment Cards 1898-1914

RESIDENCE: Red River   COUNTY.   **Choctaw Nation**   **Choctaw Roll**   CARD No.
POST OFFICE: Kullituklo, I.T.   *(Not Including Freedmen)*   FIELD No.   711

Dawes' Roll No.		NAME		Relationship to Person	AGE	SEX	BLOOD	TRIBAL ENROLLMENT Year	County	No.
1729	1	Jones, Betsy	36	First Named	33	F	Full	1896	Red River	7021
1730	2	" Mulsie	10	Dau	7	"	"	1896	" "	7022
1731	3	" Frances	5	"	1	"	1/2			
	4									
	5	ENROLLMENT								
	6	OF NOS. 1 2 and 3 HEREON APPROVED BY THE SECRETARY								
	7	OF INTERIOR DEC 12 1902								
	8									
	9									
	10									
	11									
	12									
	13									
	14									
	15									
	16									
	17									

TRIBAL ENROLLMENT OF PARENTS

	Name of Father	Year	County	Name of Mother	Year	County
1	Robuck Foster	Dead	Blue	Siney Foster	Dead	Blue
2	Charley Jones	"	Red River	No 1		
3	Henry DeLoach	"	Non Citz	No 1		
4						
5						
6	No1 on 1896 roll as Betsy Jones					
7	No2 " 1896 " " Molsey "					
8	No3 Affidavit of birth to be supplied. Recd May 4/99					
9						
10						
11						
12						
13				Date of Application for Enrollment.		
14						
15				April 22/99		
16						
17						

111

Choctaw By Blood Enrollment Cards 1898-1914

RESIDENCE: Cedar COUNTY. **Choctaw Nation** Choctaw Roll CARD NO.
POST OFFICE: Alikchi, I.T. (Not Including Freedmen) FIELD NO. 712

Dawes' Roll No.	NAME	Relationship to Person First Named	AGE	SEX	BLOOD	TRIBAL ENROLLMENT		
						Year	County	No.
1732	1 Durant, Amy 33	First Named	30	F	Full	1896	Cedar	3354
1733	2 " Eastman 7	Son	4	M	"	1896	"	3355
	3							
	4 ENROLLMENT							
	5 OF NOS. 1 and 2 HEREON APPROVED BY THE SECRETARY							
	6 OF INTERIOR DEC 12 1902							
	7							
	8							
	9							
	10							
	11 No1 on 1896 roll as Emey Durant							
	12							
	13							
	14							
	15							
	16							
	17							

TRIBAL ENROLLMENT OF PARENTS

Name of Father	Year	County	Name of Mother	Year	County
1 Isaac Jacob	Dead	Cedar	Netsie Jacob	1896	Cedar
2 Grayson Durant	1896	"	No 1		
3					
4					
5					
6					
7					
8					
9					
10					
11					
12					
13					
14				Date of Application for Enrollment.		
15						
16				April 22/99		
17						

Choctaw By Blood Enrollment Cards 1898-1914

RESIDENCE: Nashoba   COUNTY.   **Choctaw Nation**   **Choctaw Roll** (Not Including Freedmen)   CARD No.
POST OFFICE: Alikchi, I.T.   FIELD No. 713

Dawes' Roll No.	NAME	Relationship to Person First Named	AGE	SEX	BLOOD	TRIBAL ENROLLMENT		
						Year	County	No.
1734	1 Stephen, Nancy 30		27	F	Full	1893	Nashoba	P.R. 682
1735	2 Brewer, Darch	Son	22 [sic]	M	"	1896	"	1249
1736	3 Wade, Robinson 10	"	7	"	"	1896	"	13282
1737	4 " Mary 5	Dau	1	F	"			
5								
6								
7	ENROLLMENT OF NOS. 1 2 3 and 4 HEREON							
8	APPROVED BY THE SECRETARY							
9	OF INTERIOR DEC 12 1902							
10								
11								
12								
13								
14								
15								
16								
17								

DIED PRIOR TO SEPTEMBER 25, 1902

TRIBAL ENROLLMENT OF PARENTS

	Name of Father	Year	County	Name of Mother	Year	County
1	Larson Battiest	Dead	Nashoba	Leong Stephen	Dead	Nashoba
2	Ellis Brewer	1896	"	No 1		
3	Kosom Wade	1896	"	No 1		
4	" "	1896	"	No 1		
5						
6	No1 on 1893 Pay roll as Narcy Stephens					
7	No.1 on 1896 Choctaw Census roll page 199; No. 8003 as Nancy Larcen					
8	No2 died January 1, 1900; proof of death filed Dec. 12, 1902.					
9	No2 died Jany - 1900: Enrollment cancelled by Department (remainder illegible)					
10						
11						
12						
13						
14						
15						
16			Date of Application for Enrollment.	April 22/99		
17						

Choctaw By Blood Enrollment Cards 1898-1914

RESIDENCE: Eagle   COUNTY.   **Choctaw Nation**   **Choctaw Roll**   CARD No.
POST OFFICE: Lukfata, I.T.   *(Not Including Freedmen)*   FIELD No.   **714**

Dawes' Roll No.		NAME		Relationship to Person	AGE	SEX	BLOOD	TRIBAL ENROLLMENT		
								Year	County	No.
1738	1	Wilson, Sam		First Named	61	M	Full	1896	Eagle	13551
1739	2	" Sombil		S.Son	19	"	"	1896	"	13516
1740	3	" Isaac	17	Son	14	"	"	1896	"	13531
1741	4	" Molsy	23	Wife	20	F	"	1896	Bok Tuklo	2569
	5									
	6									
	7									
	8									
	9									
	10									
	11									
	12									
	13									
	14									
	15									
	16									
	17									

ENROLLMENT
OF NOS. 1, 2 3 and 4 HEREON
APPROVED BY THE SECRETARY
OF INTERIOR DEC 12 1902

TRIBAL ENROLLMENT OF PARENTS

	Name of Father	Year	County	Name of Mother	Year	County
1	Wilson Mehatiah	Dead	Eagle	Hak-lo-he-ma	Dead	Eagle
2	Joe Wilson	"	"	Salena Wilson	"	"
3	No 1			Mautema Wilson	"	"
4	Sam Amos	Dead	Eagle	Louisa Amos	1896	"
5						
6						
7	No2 on 1896 roll as Sarabel Wilson					
8	No4 " 1896 " " Milcy Crosby					
9	No4 is identified from 1893 payroll Eagle Co page 25 #246 as Malsey Amos					
10	No1 died June, 1900; proof of death filed Dec 15, 1902					
11	No2 " July-1899; " " " " " " "					
	No1 died June-1900; No2 died July-1899; Enrollment cancelled [remainder illegible]					
12						
13						
14						
15				Date of Application for Enrollment.		
16				April 22/99		
17						

114

Choctaw By Blood Enrollment Cards 1898-1914

RESIDENCE: Eagle
POST OFFICE: Lukfata, I.T.

COUNTY.

Choctaw Nation

Choctaw Roll
(Not Including Freedmen)

CARD NO.
FIELD NO. **715**

Dawes' Roll No.	NAME		Relationship to Person First Named	AGE	SEX	BLOOD	TRIBAL ENROLLMENT		
							Year	County	No.
1742	1 Wilson, John	44	Named	41	M	Full	1896	Eagle	13506
1743	2 " Lucy	46	Wife	43	F	"	1896	"	13507
1744	3 " Robert	17	Son	14	M	"	1896	"	13553
1745	4 " Sophie	15	Dau	12	F	"	1896	"	13560
1746	5 " Wade	13	Son	10	M	"	1896	"	13525
1747	6 " Lilly	11	Dau	8	F	"	1896	"	13533
1748	7 " Osborne	10	Son	7	M	"	1896	"	13534
8									
9									
10									
11									
12									
13									
14									
15									
16									
17									

ENROLLMENT
OF NOS. 123456and7 HEREON
APPROVED BY THE SECRETARY
OF INTERIOR Dec 12 1902

TRIBAL ENROLLMENT OF PARENTS

Name of Father	Year	County	Name of Mother	Year	County
1 Ah-to-chin-ubbee	Dead	Eagle	Betsey	Dead	Eagle
2 Sampson Wilson	"	"	Is-ta-ma-huna	"	"
3	No. 1		No. 2		
4	No. 1		No. 2		
5	No. 1		No. 2		
6	No. 1		No. 2		
7	No. 1		No. 2		
8					
9					
10	No6 on 1896 roll as Lily Wilson				
11	For child of No.1 see N.B. (March 3,1905) #1006.				
12					
13					
14				Date of Application for Enrollment.		
15						
16				April	22/99	
17						

115

Choctaw By Blood Enrollment Cards 1898-1914

RESIDENCE: Eagle COUNTY. **Choctaw Nation** Choctaw Roll (Not Including Freedmen) CARD NO.
POST OFFICE: Eagletown, I.T. FIELD NO. 716

Dawes' Roll No.	NAME		Relationship to Person	AGE	SEX	BLOOD	TRIBAL ENROLLMENT		
							Year	County	No.
1749	1 McClure, Peter	26	First Named	23	M	Full	1896	Eagle	9309
1750	2 " Lesina	25	Wife	22	F	"	1896	"	5580
1751	3 " Levisa	4	Dau	9mo	"	"			
1752	4 " Leunie	2	Dau	6mo	F	"			
14581	5 " Anna Dora	1	Dau	2mo	F	"			
	6								
	7								
	8								
	9								
	10								
	11	ENROLLMENT OF NOS. HEREON APPROVED BY THE SECRETARY OF INTERIOR							
	12								
	13								
	14								
	15								
	16								
	17								

TRIBAL ENROLLMENT OF PARENTS

	Name of Father	Year	County	Name of Mother	Year	County
1	Martin McClure	Dead	Eagle	Elsie McClure	1896	Eagle
2	Daniel Hudson	1896	"	Sallie Hudson	1896	"
3	No 1			No 2		
4	No.1			No.2		
5	Nº1			Nº2		
6						
7	No2 on 1896 roll as Levina Hudson					
8	No.4 Enrolled May 21, 1901.					
9	Nº5 Born Sept. 3, 1902. Enrolled Nov. 14, 1902.					
10	For child of Nos 1&2 see NB (Apr 26-06) Card #582					
11						
12						
13						
14						
15				#1 to 3		
16				Date of Application for Enrollment	April 22/99	
17						

Choctaw By Blood Enrollment Cards 1898-1914

RESIDENCE: Eagle
POST OFFICE: Eagletown, I.T.

COUNTY.

Choctaw Nation

Choctaw Roll
(Not Including Freedmen)

CARD NO.
FIELD NO. **717**

Dawes' Roll No.	NAME		Relationship to Person	AGE	SEX	BLOOD	TRIBAL ENROLLMENT		
							Year	County	No.
1753	1 Louis, Bond	32	First Named	29	M	Full	1896	Eagle	8015
DEAD	2 " Learna[sic] DEAD		Wife	28	F	"	1896	"	8016
1754	3 " Ellen	9	Dau	6	"	"	1893	"	P.R. 504
1755	4 " Solomon	4	Son	2	M	"			
1757	5 Tikubbi, Levi	16	S.Son	13	"	"			
1756	6 Louis, Silas	1	Son	1	M	"			
	7								
	8								
	9	ENROLLMENT OF NOS. 1,3,4,5 and 6 HEREON APPROVED BY THE SECRETARY OF INTERIOR Dec. 12, 1902							
	10								
	11								
	12								
	13	No.2 hereon dismissed under order of							
	14	the Commission to the Five Civilized Tribes of March 31, 1905.							
	15								
	16								
	17								

TRIBAL ENROLLMENT OF PARENTS

	Name of Father	Year	County	Name of Mother	Year	County
1	Gilbert Louis	Dead	Eagle	Ah-tok-lan-tema	Dead	Eagle
2	Franklin	"	Bok Tuklo	Liza Ann Franklin	1896	Bok Tuklo
3	No.1			No.2		
4	No. 1			No.2		
5	Bob Tikubbi	1896	Bok Tuklo	No.2		
6	No. 1			No. 2		
7						
8						
9	No.2 on 1896 roll as Leima Louis					
10	No.6 Born May 26,1901: enrolled June 13, 1902					
11	No.2 Died April 19,1902: proof of death filed June 13, 1902.					
12						
13						#1 to 5
14						Date of Application for Enrollment.
15						
16						April 22/99
17						

117

Choctaw By Blood Enrollment Cards 1898-1914

RESIDENCE: Nashoba
POST OFFICE: Alikchi, I.T.

COUNTY. **Choctaw Nation**

Choctaw Roll (Not Including Freedmen)

CARD NO.
FIELD NO. **718**

Dawes' Roll No.	NAME	Relationship to Person First Named	AGE	SEX	BLOOD	TRIBAL ENROLLMENT Year	County	No.
1758	1 Columbus, Melwissie 26	First Named	23	F	Full	1896	Nashoba	2525
1759	2 " Silas 6	Son	3	M	"	1896	"	2538
14582	3 Battiest, Larence 1	Son	16mo	M	"			
	4							
	5	ENROLLMENT						
	6	OF NOS. 1 and 2 HEREON APPROVED BY THE SECRETARY						
	7	OF INTERIOR Dec 12, 1902						
	8							
	9							
	10	ENROLLMENT OF NOS. 3 HEREON						
	11	APPROVED BY THE SECRETARY						
	12	OF INTERIOR May 20, 1903						
	13							
	14							
	15							
	16							
	17							

TRIBAL ENROLLMENT OF PARENTS

	Name of Father	Year	County	Name of Mother	Year	County
1	Morris Baker	1896	Nashoba	Yo-to-na	1896	Nashoba
2	Bill Columbus	Dead	"	No. 1		
3	Allington Battiest	1896	Eagle	No. 1		
4						
5						
6						
7		No.2 on 1896 roll as Silas M Columbus				
8		No.1 wife of Allington Battiest Choc card #1306.				
9		No3 Born Aug. 18, 1902: Enrolled Dec. 24, 1902.				
10		For child of No.1 see NB (Apr. 26-06) Card #607.				
		" " " " " " (Mar 3-05) " #948				
11						
12						
13						
14						
15				#1&2		
16				Date of Application for Enrollment	April 22/99	
17	P.O. Bethel, I.T. 4/5/05					

118

Choctaw By Blood Enrollment Cards 1898-1914

RESIDENCE: Red River   COUNTY.   **Choctaw Nation**   **Choctaw Roll** *(Not Including Freedmen)*   CARD NO.

POST OFFICE: Harris, I.T.   FIELD NO. **719**

Dawes' Roll No.		NAME		Relationship to Person First Named	AGE	SEX	BLOOD	Year	TRIBAL ENROLLMENT County	No.
1760	1	Watkins, J. J.	62	First Named	59	M	Full	1896	Red River	13564
1761	2	" Melinda	51	Wife	48	F	"	1896	" "	13565
1761	3	" Emma	19	Ward	16	"	"	1896	" "	13566
1763	4	" Anna	18	Ward	15	"	"	1896	" "	13567
I.W. 629	5	Wilmoth, John W.	32	Hus. of No 4	32	M	I.W.			
	6									
	7									
	8	ENROLLMENT OF NOS. 1 2 3 and 4 HEREON								
	9	APPROVED BY THE SECRETARY OF INTERIOR Dec 12 1902								
	10									
	11									
	12	ENROLLMENT OF NOS. 5 HEREON								
	13	APPROVED BY THE SECRETARY OF INTERIOR Mar 26, 1904								
	14									
	15									
	16									
	17									

TRIBAL ENROLLMENT OF PARENTS

	Name of Father	Year	County	Name of Mother	Year	County
1	Isaac Watkins	Dead	Red River	Winnie Watkins	Dead	Red River
2	Pisa-bunna	"	" "	Pisa-hunna	"	" "
3	Lorin Watkins	"	" "	Jincey Watkins	"	" "
4	Ben Watkins	1896	" "	Lottie Watkins	"	" "
5	William Wilmoth		Intermarried	Martha Wilmoth	"	noncitizen
6						
7						
8	No.2 on 1896 Roll as Malinda Watkins					
9						
10	No.5 transferred from Choctaw card D662 January 25, 1904					
11	See decision of January 7, 1904. For child of Nos 4&5 see NB (March 3, 1905) #1005					
12						
13						
14						#1 to 4
15						Date of Application for Enrollment.
16						April 22/99
17						

119

Choctaw By Blood Enrollment Cards 1898-1914

RESIDENCE: Eagle   COUNTY.   **Choctaw Nation**   Choctaw Roll   CARD NO.
POST OFFICE: Eagletown, I.T.   (Not Including Freedmen)   FIELD NO. **720**

Dawes' Roll No.	NAME		Relationship to Person	AGE	SEX	BLOOD	TRIBAL ENROLLMENT		
							Year	County	No.
1764	1 Joseph, John	41	First Named	38	M	Full	1896	Eagle	6949
1765	2 " , Ellissie	30	Wife	27	F	"	1896	"	6955
1766	3 " , Gibson	17	Son	14	M	"	1896	"	4172
1767	4 " , Meta	15	Dau	12	F	"	1896	"	4177
15658	5 " , Wicy	8	"	4	"	"			
1768	6 " , Mary		"	1	"	"			
1769	7 " , Sillian	1	Dau	10mo	F	"			
	8								
	9								
	10								
	11								
	12								
	13								
	14								
	15								
	16								
	17								

DIED PRIOR TO SEPTEMBER 25, 1902

ENROLLMENT OF NOS. 1,2,3,4,6 and 7 HEREON APPROVED BY THE SECRETARY OF INTERIOR Dec 12, 1902

ENROLLMENT OF NOS. ~5~ HEREON APPROVED BY THE SECRETARY OF INTERIOR Dec 2, 1904

TRIBAL ENROLLMENT OF PARENTS

	Name of Father	Year	County	Name of Mother	Year	County
1	George Joseph	1896	Eagle	Netsey Joseph	Dead	Eagle
2	Tim Jefferson	Dead	"	Sallie Jefferson	1896	"
3	No 1			Louisa Fobb	1896	"
4	No 1			" "	1896	"
5	No 1			No 2		
6	No 1			No 2		
7	No 1			No 2		
8						
9	No2 on 1896 roll as Elsey Joseph					
10	No3 " 1896 " " Gibson Fobb					
11	No4 " 1896 " " Mela "					
	No7 Born Nov 1, 1902; Enrolled Sept. 5, 1902.					
12	No4 is now the wife of Tom H. Willis Choc #1154 11/28/02					
13	[Entry illegible]					
14	[entry illegible]					#1 to 6 inc
15	No.6 died Nov.25-1900;Enrollment cancelled by Department July 8-1904.					
16						
17						

Date of Application for Enrollment.

April 22/99

Choctaw By Blood Enrollment Cards 1898-1914

RESIDENCE: Bok Tuklo
POST OFFICE: Lukfata, I.T.

COUNTY.
Choctaw Nation

Choctaw Roll
(Not Including Freedmen)

CARD NO.
FIELD NO. **721**

Dawes' Roll No.	NAME	Relationship to Person First Named	AGE	SEX	BLOOD	TRIBAL ENROLLMENT Year	County	No. P.R.
1770	1 Ebamhona ~~DIED PRIOR TO SEPTEMBER 25, 1902~~		53	F	Full	1893	Bok Tuklo	110
1771	2 William, Alfred ~~DIED PRIOR TO SEPTEMBER 25, 1902~~	G.Son	14	M	"	1896	" "	13430
1772	3 Cobb, Sam 9	"	6	"	"	1896	" "	2565
	4							
	5							
	6							
	7							
	8							
	9							
	10							
	11							
	12							
	13							
	14							
	15							
	16							
	17							

ENROLLMENT
OF NOS. 1 – 2 and 3 HEREON
APPROVED BY THE SECRETARY
OF INTERIOR Dec 12 1902

TRIBAL ENROLLMENT OF PARENTS

	Name of Father	Year	County	Name of Mother	Year	County
1	Ko-ta-bee	Dead	Bok Tuklo		Dead	Bok Tuklo
2	Wallace Anderson	"	" "	Betsy Anderson	"	" "
3	Calvin Cobb	"	" "		"	" "
4						
5						
6		No1 also on 1896 roll, as Eboni Davis				
7		Page 82 No. 3403, Bok Tuklo Co.				
8						
9		No.1 died Dec. 1, 1900: proof of death filed Dec. 3, 1902				
10		No.2 " Oct. 10, 1901: " " " " " " "				
11	No.1 died Dec.1-1900:No.2 died Oct.10-1901: Enrollment cancelled by Department July 8,1904					
12						
13						
14						
15				Date of Application for Enrollment.		
16				April 22/99		
17						

121

Choctaw By Blood Enrollment Cards 1898-1914

RESIDENCE: Eagle COUNTY.
POST OFFICE: Eagletown, I.T.

Choctaw Nation

Choctaw Roll
(Not Including Freedmen)

CARD No.
FIELD NO. **722**

Dawes' Roll No.	NAME	Relationship to Person	AGE	SEX	BLOOD	TRIBAL ENROLLMENT		
						Year	County	No.
1773	₁ King, Wilson DIED PRIOR TO SEPTEMBER 25, 1902	First Named	28	M	Full	1896	Eagle	7559
1774	₂ " Margaret ⁵²	Wife	49	F	"	1896	"	7560
	₃							
	₄	ENROLLMENT						
	₅	OF NOS. 1 and 2 HEREON APPROVED BY THE SECRETARY						
	₆	OF INTERIOR Dec 12 1902						
	₇							
	₈							
	₉							
	10							
	11							
	12							
	13							
	14							
	15							
	16							
	17							

TRIBAL ENROLLMENT OF PARENTS

	Name of Father	Year	County	Name of Mother	Year	County
₁	Cha-la-ta	Dead	Eagle	Biccy Conchatta	Dead	Eagle
₂	Shon-ta	"	"	Un-te-a-huna	"	Red River
₃						
₄						
₅						
₆						
₇	No.2 on 1896 roll as Margarett King					
₈	No.1 died Nov. 28-1901: Enrollment cancelled by Department July 8-1904					
₉						
10						
11						
12						
13						
14						
15					Date of Application for Enrollment.	
16					April 22/99	
17						

122

Choctaw By Blood Enrollment Cards 1898-1914

Dawes' Roll No.		NAME		Relationship to Person	AGE	SEX	BLOOD	TRIBAL ENROLLMENT		
								Year	County	No.
1775	1	Charley, Netsie	33	First Named	30	F	Full	1896	Bok Tuklo	2555
1776	2	" Eliston	4	Son	6mo	M	"			
	3									
	4	ENROLLMENT								
	5	OF NOS. 1 and 2 HEREON APPROVED BY THE SECRETARY								
	6	OF INTERIOR Dec 12 1902								
	7									
	8									
	9	For child of No 1 see N.B (Apr 26 06) Card #834								
	10									
	11									
	12									
	13									
	14									
	15									
	16									
	17									

TRIBAL ENROLLMENT OF PARENTS

	Name of Father	Year	County	Name of Mother	Year	County
1	An-chach-taby	Dead	Bok Tuklo	Min-te-hona	Dead	Bok Tuklo
2	Willie Charley	1896	" "	No 1		
3						
4						
5						
6						
7						
8						
9						
10						
11						
12						
13						
14						
15						
16				Date of Application for Enrollment.		
17				April 22/99		

123

Choctaw By Blood Enrollment Cards 1898-1914

RESIDENCE: Nashoba COUNTY.
POST OFFICE: Smithville, I.T.

Choctaw Nation

Choctaw Roll
(Not Including Freedmen)

CARD NO.
FIELD NO. 724

Dawes' Roll No.	NAME	Relationship to Person First Named	AGE	SEX	BLOOD	TRIBAL ENROLLMENT Year	County	No.
1777	1 Carterby, Susan 24	Named	21	F	Full	1896	Nashoba	12163
1778	2 " Salinsie 4	Dau	2mo	"	"			
1779	3 Taylor, Simpson G 8	Son	5	M	"	1896	Nashoba	12166
4								
5								
6	ENROLLMENT OF NOS. 1 2 and 3 HEREON							
7	APPROVED BY THE SECRETARY OF INTERIOR DEC 12 1902							
8								
9								
10								
11								
12	No1 on 1896 roll as Susan J. Taylor							
13								
14								
15								
16								
17								

TRIBAL ENROLLMENT OF PARENTS

	Name of Father	Year	County	Name of Mother	Year	County
1	James Taylor	Dead	Nashoba	Sophima Taylor	1896	Nashoba
2	Almon Carterby	1896	"	No 1		
3	Peter Going	1896	"	No 1		
4						
5						
6						
7						
8						
9						
10						
11						
12						
13						
14						
15						
16						
17						

Date of Application for Enrollment.
April 22/99

124

Choctaw By Blood Enrollment Cards 1898-1914

RESIDENCE: Red River   COUNTY. **Choctaw Nation**   **Choctaw Roll**   CARD No.
POST OFFICE: Garvin, I.T.   *(Not Including Freedmen)*   FIELD No.   **725**

Dawes' Roll No.	NAME			Relationship to Person	AGE	SEX	BLOOD	TRIBAL ENROLLMENT		
								Year	County	No.
1780	1 Hotinlubbee, Sena		28	First Named	25	F	Full	1896	Red River	5657
1781	2 "	Alfred	11	Son	8	M	"	1896	" "	5658
1782	3 "	Loring	7	"	4	"	"	1896	" "	5659
DEAD	4 "	Davis DEAD		"	3	"	"			
DEAD	5 "	Susan DEAD		Dau	3mo	F	"			
1783	6 Hotinlubbee, Lena		2	"	1½	F	"			
	7									
	8									
	9									
	10									
	11									
	12	No. 4 and 5 hereon dismissed under								
	13	order of the Commission to the Five								
	14	Civilized Tribes of March 31, 1905.								
	15									
	16									
	17									

[stamp:] ENROLLMENT OF NOS. 1 2 3 and 6 HEREON APPROVED BY THE SECRETARY OF INTERIOR Dec 12 1902

TRIBAL ENROLLMENT OF PARENTS

	Name of Father	Year	County	Name of Mother	Year	County
1	Ho-ten-a-bi	Dead	Bok Tuklo	Kon-e-o-tema	Dead	Red River
2	Frank McAfee	1896	" "	No. 1		
3	" "	1896	" "	No.1		
4	" "	1896	" "	No.1		
5	" "	1896	" "	No.1 No		
6	Wilson Fisher		Choc Card 500	No.1		
7						
8	No.1 on 1896 roll as Simmy Hotilubbi					
9	No.2 " 1896 " " Alfred Hotillubbi					
10	No.3 " 1896 " " Loring "					
11	No.6 born Dec 2 1900; Enrolled July 8, 1902					
12	as to correct surname of these persons see copy of letter of Simon Taylor filed July 8, 1902.					
13	No.4 died June, 1900. proof of death filed Dec 3, 1902					
14	No.5 " Nov. 1900; " " " " " "					
15	No.1 is now the wife of Frank McAfee Choc #1084				#1 to 5 inc
16	For child of No1 see NB (March 3 1905) #880				Date of Application for Enrollment.
17	P.O. Idabel, I.T. 4/11/05		*			April 22/99

125

Choctaw By Blood Enrollment Cards 1898-1914

RESIDENCE: Nashoba COUNTY.
POST OFFICE: Alikchi, I.T.

Choctaw Nation

Choctaw Roll
(Not Including Freedmen)

CARD NO.
FIELD NO. 726

Dawes' Roll No.	NAME	Relationship to Person First Named	AGE	SEX	BLOOD	TRIBAL ENROLLMENT		
						Year	County	No.
1785	1 Watson, Artie Ann 33	First Named	30	F	Full	1896	Nashoba	13331
1785	2 " Nicey 5	Dau	1	"	"			
	3							
	4							
	5	ENROLLMENT						
	6	OF NOS. 1 and 2 HEREON APPROVED BY THE SECRETARY						
	7	OF INTERIOR DEC 12 1902						
	8							
	9							
	10							
	11							
	12							
	13							
	14							
	15							
	16							
	17							

TRIBAL ENROLLMENT OF PARENTS

Name of Father	Year	County	Name of Mother	Year	County
1 Jonas Watson	Dead	Nashoba	Autema Watson	Dead	Nashoba
2 James Jones	1896	"	No 1		
3					
4					
5					
6					
7	No1 on 1896 roll as Artean Watson				
8	For child of No.1 see NB (March 3, 1905) #939				
9					
10					
11					
12					
13					
14				Date of Application for Enrollment.	
15					
16				April	22/99
17					

126

Choctaw By Blood Enrollment Cards 1898-1914

RESIDENCE: Nashoba COUNTY.
POST OFFICE: Alikchi, I.T.

Choctaw Nation

Choctaw Roll
(Not Including Freedmen)

CARD NO.
FIELD NO. 727

Dawes' Roll No.	NAME	Relationship to Person First Named	AGE	SEX	BLOOD	TRIBAL ENROLLMENT		
						Year	County	No.
1786	1 Lowman, Moses ⁸¹		78	M	Full	1896	Nashoba	7977
	2							
	3	ENROLLMENT						
	4	OF NOS. 1 HEREON APPROVED BY THE SECRETARY						
	5	OF INTERIOR DEC 12 1902						
	6							
	7							
	8							
	9	Ellen Harlett						
	10	No.1 is now Husband of ˄ No1 on Choc #2034						
	11							
	12							
	13							
	14							
	15							
	16							
	17							

TRIBAL ENROLLMENT OF PARENTS

	Name of Father	Year	County	Name of Mother	Year	County
1	Hum-ma	Dead	Eagle	Pie-yah	Dead	Eagle
2						
3						
4						
5						
6						
7						
8						
9						
10						
11						
12						
13						
14						
15						
16						
17						

DATE OF APPLICATION FOR ENROLLMENT. April 22/99

127

Choctaw By Blood Enrollment Cards 1898-1914

RESIDENCE: Red River COUNTY.
POST OFFICE: Shawneetown, I.T.

Choctaw Nation

Choctaw Roll
(Not Including Freedmen)

CARD NO.
FIELD NO. **728**

Dawes' Roll No.	NAME	Relationship to Person	AGE	SEX	BLOOD	TRIBAL ENROLLMENT		
						Year	County	No.
1787	1 Tontubbee, Patsy 37	First Named	34	F	Full	1896	Red River	12313
1788	2 " Enos 17	Dau	14	F	"	1896	" "	12314
1789	3 " Sophy 7	Dau	4	F	"	1896	" "	12315
	4							
	5 ~~ENROLLMENT~~							
	6 ~~OF NOS. 1 2 and 3 HEREON~~							
	7 ~~APPROVED BY THE SECRETARY~~							
	~~OF INTERIOR Dec 12 1902~~							
	8							
	9							
	10							
	11							
	12							
	13							
	14							
	15							
	16							
	17							

TRIBAL ENROLLMENT OF PARENTS

	Name of Father	Year	County	Name of Mother	Year	County
1	Taylor Durant	1896	Atoka	Sealy Durant	Dead	Bok Tuklo
2	Gibson Tontubbee	Dead	Red River	No. 1		
3	" "	"	" "	No. 1		
4						
5						
6	Surnames on 1896 as Tanitobe					
7	No.2 is the wife of Monford Harley on Choc #1111 (11/28/02)					
8	For child of No.2 see NB. (March 3 1905) #1136					
9	~~No2 is female sex changed under Departmental Authority~~					
	~~of June 1, 1905 (LTD6242-1905) D.C. 27931-1905~~					
10						
11						
12						
13						
14				Date of Application		
15				for Enrollment.		
16				April 22/99		
17						

Choctaw By Blood Enrollment Cards 1898-1914

RESIDENCE: Nashoba
POST OFFICE: Smithville, I.T.
COUNTY. **Choctaw Nation**
Choctaw Roll (Not Including Freedmen)
CARD NO.
FIELD NO. **729**

Dawes' Roll No.	NAME	Relationship to Person First Named	AGE	SEX	BLOOD	TRIBAL ENROLLMENT Year	County	No.
DEAD Dead	1 Taylor, Sophina J. DEAD		43	F	Full	1896	Nashoba	12161
14588	2 Watkins, Sinsie J. 18	Dau	15	"	"	1896	"	12164
1790	3 Taylor, Nancy J 15	"	12	"	"	1896	"	12165
14589	4 Watkins, Allen 1	Gr.Son	15mo	M	"			
	5							
	6							
	7							
	8							
	9							
	10							
	11							
	12							
	13							
	14							
	15							
	16							
	17							

ENROLLMENT
OF NOS. 3 HEREON
APPROVED BY THE SECRETARY
OF INTERIOR Dec 12 1902

ENROLLMENT
OF NOS. 2 and 4 HEREON
APPROVED BY THE SECRETARY
OF INTERIOR May 20 1903

No. 1 hereon dismissed under order of the Commission to the Five Civilized Tribes of March 31, 1905.

TRIBAL ENROLLMENT OF PARENTS

	Name of Father	Year	County	Name of Mother	Year	County
1	George Watson	Dead	Nashoba	Nancy Watson	Dead	Nashoba
2	James Taylor	"	"	No. 1		
3	" "	"	"	No. 1		
4	Stephen Watkins	1896	"	No. 2		
5						
6						
7						
8						
9						
10						
11						
12						
13						
14						
15						
16						
17						

No.1 died Oct. 21, 1899: proof of death filed July 26, 1902
No2 is now the wife [sic] Stephen Watkins on Choctaw card #565. Evidence of marriage requested Sept. 12, 1902 – Filed Oct. 13, 1902
No.4 Born June 10, 1901, enrolled Sept. 12, 1902.
For child of No2 see NB (March 3, 1905) #945

#1 to 3

Date of Application for Enrollment.

April 22/99

Choctaw By Blood Enrollment Cards 1898-1914

RESIDENCE: Bok Tuklo   COUNTY.   **Choctaw Nation**   **Choctaw Roll**   CARD NO.
POST OFFICE: Lukfata, I.T.   *(Not Including Freedmen)*   FIELD NO. **730**

Dawes' Roll No.	NAME		Relationship to Person	AGE	SEX	BLOOD	TRIBAL ENROLLMENT		
							Year	County	No.
1791	1 Colbert, Sampson	81	First Named	78	M	Full	1896	Bok Tuklo	2547
1792	2 " Sean	42	Wife	39	F	"	1896	" "	2548
1793	3 " Reason	8	Son	5	M	"	1896	" "	2550
	4								
	5								
	6	ENROLLMENT							
	7	OF NOS. 1 2 and 3 HEREON APPROVED BY THE SECRETARY							
	8	OF INTERIOR Dec 2 1902							
	9								
	10								
	11								
	12								
	13	No. 2 on 1896 roll as Sian Colbert							
	14								
	15								
	16								
	17								

TRIBAL ENROLLMENT OF PARENTS

	Name of Father	Year	County	Name of Mother	Year	County
1	An-ti-nubbee	Dead	in Mississippi	Wa-le-hu-na	Dead	in Mississippi
2	Neal-ubbee	"	" "	Loh-mon-hey	"	Bok Tuklo
3	No. 1			No. 2		
4						
5						
6						
7						
8						
9						
10						
11						
12						
13						
14						
15						
16				Date of Application for Enrollment		April 22/99
17						

Choctaw By Blood Enrollment Cards 1898-1914

RESIDENCE: Bok Tuklo   COUNTY.   **Choctaw Nation**   **Choctaw Roll**   CARD No.

POST OFFICE: Lukfata, I.T.   *(Not Including Freedmen)*   FIELD No.   731

Dawes' Roll No.	NAME	Relationship to Person First Named	AGE	SEX	BLOOD	TRIBAL ENROLLMENT		
						Year	County	No.
1794	1 Colbert, Sylwid 22		19	M	Full	1896	Bok Tuklo	2549
DEAD.	2 " Sarah	Wife	20	F	"	1896	" "	10392
	3							
	4							
	5	ENROLLMENT OF NOS. 1 HEREON						
	6	APPROVED BY THE SECRETARY						
	7	OF INTERIOR DEC 12 1902						
	8							
	9							
	10	No. 2 HEREON DISMISSED UNDER						
	11	ORDER OF THE COMMISSION TO THE FIVE						
		CIVILIZED TRIBES OF MARCH 31, 1905.						
	13							
	14							
	15							
	16							
	17							

TRIBAL ENROLLMENT OF PARENTS

Name of Father	Year	County	Name of Mother	Year	County
1 Sampson Colbert	1896	Bok Tuklo	Sealy Colbert	Dead	Bok Tuklo
2 Simon Peter	1896	" "	Sosin Peter	"	" "
3					
4					
5					
6					
7					
8		No2 on 1896 roll as Sarah Peter			
9		Nº2 Died Dec. 20, 1900. Proof of death filed Oct. 13, 1902.			
10		No.2 "Died prior to September 25, 1902, not entitled to land or money." See Indian Office Letter March 18, 1908 (I.T. 8664-1908).			
11					
12					
13					
14					
15					
16			Date of Application for Enrollment April 22/99		
17					

131

Choctaw By Blood Enrollment Cards 1898-1914

RESIDENCE: Eagle   COUNTY.

POST OFFICE: Eagletown, I.T.

Choctaw Nation

Choctaw Roll
(Not Including Freedmen)

CARD NO.

FIELD NO. 732

Dawes' Roll No.		NAME		Relationship to Person	AGE	SEX	BLOOD	TRIBAL ENROLLMENT		
								Year	County	No.
1795	1	Hudson, Daniei H.	*DIED PRIOR TO SEPTEMBER 25, 1902*	First Named	46	M	Full	1896	Eagle	5572
1796	2	" Sallie	*DIED PRIOR TO SEPTEMBER 25, 1902*	Wife	45	F	"	1896	"	5588
1797	3	" Leuvina	19	Dau	16	"	"	1896	"	5583
1798	4	Hudson, Leeana	17	"	14	"	"	1896	"	5578
1799	5	" Enoch	15	Son	12	M	"	1896	"	5576
1800	6	" Willis	11	"	8	"	"	1896	"	5589
1801	7	" Isham	9	"	6	"	"	1896	"	5591
1802	8	" Aleck	*DIED PRIOR TO SEPTEMBER 25, 1902*	"	4	"	"	1896	"	5577
	9									
	10									
	11									
	12									
	13									
	14									
	15									
	16									
	17									

ENROLLMENT
OF NOS. 1234567and8 HEREON
APPROVED BY THE SECRETARY
OF INTERIOR Dec 12 1902

TRIBAL ENROLLMENT OF PARENTS

	Name of Father	Year	County	Name of Mother	Year	County
1	James Hudson	Dead	Eagle	Ah-ho-bot-ema	Dead	Eagle
2	Isom Going	1896	"	Eliza Going	"	"
3	No.1			No.2		
4	No.1			No.2		
5	No.1			No.2		
6	No.1			No.2		
7	No.1			No.2		
8	No.1			No.2		

9   No1 died June8-1901:No2 died Nov-1900:No8 died Feb-1901:Enrollment cancelled by department July 8-1904

10   No.3 is now wife of Calvin Howell Choc 470:Evidence filed 12/10/02

11   No.4 on 1896 roll as Lena Hudson   For child of No.4 see NB (March 3, 1905) #1098
    No.3 " 1896 " " Levina "

12   Nos. 5,6 and 7 are now wards of Peter J. Hudson on Choctaw card #1923

13   Letters of guardianship filed December 15, 1902

14   No.1 died June 8, 1901; proof of death filed Dec 18, 1902
    No.2 " November 1900. " " " " " "

15   No8 " February-1901 · " " " " " " "

16   Date of Application for Enrollment.

17   P.O. Lukfata 4/15/05   April 22/99

132

Choctaw By Blood Enrollment Cards 1898-1914

RESIDENCE: Cedar COUNTY.
POST OFFICE: Doaksville, I.T.

Choctaw Nation

Choctaw Roll CARD NO.
(Not Including Freedmen) FIELD NO. **733**

Dawes' Roll No.	NAME		Relationship to Person First Named	AGE	SEX	BLOOD	TRIBAL ENROLLMENT		
							Year	County	No.
1803	1 Frazier, Robert S	60	First Named	57	M	Full	1896	Cedar	4112
1804	2 " Narcissa	37	Wife	34	F	1/4	1896	"	4113
1805	3 " Noah	23	Son	20	M	Full	1896	"	4114
1806	4 " Julius	15	"	12	"	5/8	1896	"	4115
1807	5 " Emiline	13	Dau	10	F	5/8	1896	"	4116
1808	6 " Maggie W	10	"	7	"	5/8	1896	"	4117
1809	7 " Wilson T	8	Son	5	M	5/8	1896	"	4118
1810	8 " Mary E	6	Dau	3	F	5/8	1896	"	4123
1811	9 " Moseller E	2	Dau	7mo	F				
	10								
	11	ENROLLMENT OF NOS. 123456789 HEREON							
	12	APPROVED BY THE SECRETARY							
	13	OF INTERIOR Dec 12 1902							
	14								
	15								
	16								
	17								

TRIBAL ENROLLMENT OF PARENTS

	Name of Father	Year	County	Name of Mother	Year	County
1	Hah-hana	Dead	Cedar	Mulsey	Dead	Cedar
2	King Ashford	"	Nashoba	Elizabeth Fowler	1896	Kiamitia
3	No.1			Temas Frazier	Dead	Jacks Fork
4	No.1			No.2		
5	No.1			No.2		
6	No.1			No.2		
7	No.1			No.2		
8	No.1			No.2		
9	No.1			No.2		
10						
11	No.1 on 1896 roll as Robert Frazier					
12	No 5 " 1896 " " Emma "					
13	No.7 " 1896 " " Wilson "					
	No9 Enrolled June 10th 1901					
14	No.6 on 1896 roll as Maggie M Frazier				#1 to 8 inc	
15					Date of Application for Enrollment.	
16					April 24/99	
17						

Choctaw By Blood Enrollment Cards 1898-1914

RESIDENCE: Cedar   COUNTY.   **Choctaw Nation**   Choctaw Roll   CARD NO.
POST OFFICE: Doaksville, I.T.   *(Not Including Freedmen)*   FIELD NO. **734**

Dawes' Roll No.	NAME	Relationship to Person First Named	AGE	SEX	BLOOD	TRIBAL ENROLLMENT Year	County	No.
1812	1 Frazier, Samuel 34	First Named	31	M	Full	1896	Cedar	4073
1813	2 " Josephine 24	Wife	21	F	"	1896	"	4074
1814	3 " Jesse 13	Son	10	M	"	1896	"	4075
1815	4 " Willie 10	"	7	"	"	1896	"	4076
1816	5 " Lewie 4	"	2mo	"	"			
1817	6 " Bengiman 1	Son	5mo	M	"			
	7							
	8	ENROLLMENT						
	9	OF NOS. 1,2,3,4,5 and 6 HEREON APPROVED BY THE SECRETARY						
	10	OF INTERIOR Dec. 12, 1902						
	11							
	12							
	13	For child of Nos 1&2 see NB. (Apr26-06) Card #368						
	14	" " " " " " (Mar 3-05) " " 99						
	15							
	16							
	17							

TRIBAL ENROLLMENT OF PARENTS

	Name of Father	Year	County	Name of Mother	Year	County
1	Robert Frazier	1896	Cedar	Temas Frazier	Dead	Jacks Fork
2	Farlis Payne	Dead	"	Litey Payne	"	Cedar
3	No1			Phoebe Frazier	"	"
4	No1			Minnie Frazier	"	Towson
5	No1			No2		
6	No1			No2		
7						
8						
9	No1 on 1896 roll as Sam Frazier					
10	No3 " 1896 " " Jessie "					
11	No6 Enrolled July 5, 1901.					
12						
13						
14						
15					#1 to 5 inc	
16				Date of Application for Enrollment	April 24/99	
17	P.O. Spencerville, I.T. 3/21/05					

134

Choctaw By Blood Enrollment Cards 1898-1914

RESIDENCE: Cedar COUNTY.
POST OFFICE: Doaksville, I.T.

Choctaw Nation

Choctaw Roll (Not Including Freedmen)

CARD NO.
FIELD NO. 735

Dawes' Roll No.	NAME	Relationship to Person Named	AGE	SEX	BLOOD	TRIBAL ENROLLMENT Year	County	No.
1818	1 Payne, Mattie 20	First	17	F	Full	1896	Cedar	10324
1819	2 " Ella 18	Sister	15	"	"	1896	"	10325
1820	3 Frazier, Emaline DIED PRIOR TO SEPTEMBER 25, 1902	Dau	1mo	"	"			
14883	4 " Misson 1	Son	8mo	M	"			
	5							
	6	ENROLLMENT OF NOS. 1, 2 and 3 HEREON APPROVED BY THE SECRETARY OF INTERIOR Dec. 12, 1902						
	7							
	8							
	9							
	10							
	11							
	12	ENROLLMENT OF NOS. 4 HEREON APPROVED BY THE SECRETARY OF INTERIOR May 21, 1903						
	13							
	14							
	15							
	16							
	17							

TRIBAL ENROLLMENT OF PARENTS

	Name of Father	Year	County	Name of Mother	Year	County
1	Forest Payne	Dead	Cedar	Litey Payne	Dead	Cedar
2	" "	"	"	" "	"	"
3	Sam Frazier	1896	"	No1		
4	" "	1896	"	No1		
5						
6						
7						
8						
9						
10						
11	No3 Affidavit of birth to be supplied. Recd May 9/99					
12	No3 died Nov. 30-1901: Enrollment cancelled by Department July 8- 1904 No3 died Nov. 30, 1901. Proof of death filed Dec 9, 1902.					
13	No1 has a child named Missie Frazier: Evidence of birth					
14	to be supplied 12/05/02.					
15	No4 Born April 14, 1902. Application made Dec. 5, 1902. Proof of birth filed March 5, 1903.					
16	For child of No2 see NB (March 3, 1905) #1392					
17				Date of Application for Enrollment April 24/99 1 to 3		

135

Choctaw By Blood Enrollment Cards 1898-1914

RESIDENCE: Cedar		COUNTY.	**Choctaw Nation**				Choctaw Roll (Not Including Freedmen)	CARD NO.	
POST OFFICE: Doaksville, I.T.								FIELD NO. 736	

Dawes' Roll No.	NAME		Relationship to Person	AGE	SEX	BLOOD	TRIBAL ENROLLMENT		
							Year	County	No.
1821	1 Frazier, Reason	37	First Named	34	M	Full	1896	Cedar	4094
1822	2 " Susan	27	Wife	24	F	"	1896	"	4095
1823	3 " Tobias	10	Son	7	M	"	1896	"	4096
1824	4 ~~Robert~~ DIED PRIOR TO SEPTEMBER 25, 1902		"	3	"	"	1896	"	4122
1826	5 " Doror	1	Dau	4mo	F	"			
1825	6 " Rhody	3	Dau	2wk	F	"			
15824	7 " Eli		Son	1	M	"			

8	ENROLLMENT			
9	OF NOS. 1 2 3 4 5 and 6 HEREON APPROVED BY THE SECRETARY		No.4 on 1896 roll as Robt S. Frazier	
10	OF INTERIOR Dec 12 1902			
11	ENROLLMENT		No.7 born Aug.26, 1902: application received and	
12	OF NOS. ~ 7 ~ HEREON APPROVED BY THE SECRETARY		No.7 placed hereon March 28, 1905, under Act of Congress of Mar. 3, 1905	
13	OF INTERIOR Jun 12 1905			
14				
15	For child of Nos 1&2 see NB (Apr 26 06) Card #370			
16				
17				

TRIBAL ENROLLMENT OF PARENTS

	Name of Father	Year	County	Name of Mother	Year	County
1	Robert Frazier	1896	Cedar	Temas Frazier	Dead	Jacks Fork
2	Forest Payne	Dead	"	Liley Payne	"	Cedar
3	No.1			No.2		
4	~~No.1~~			~~No.2~~		
5	No.1			No.2		
6	No.1			No.2		
7	No.1			No.2		
8						
9						
10				New born child, Susan, on Card D-528		
11				No 5 Born Jany.11,1902: enrolled May 19, 1902.		
12				~~No.4 died Aug 1899~~ Enrollment cancelled by Department July 8, 1904 ~~No.6 born November 11, 1899: transferred to this~~		
13				card July 11, 1902.		
14				No.4 died Aug 1899: proof of death filed Dec 5, 1902		
15						#1 to 4 inc
16						Date of Application for Enrollment April 24/99
17	P.O Spencerville I.T	3/27/05				

Choctaw By Blood Enrollment Cards 1898-1914

RESIDENCE: Cedar COUNTY.
POST OFFICE: Doaksville, I.T.

Choctaw Nation

Choctaw Roll
(Not Including Freedmen)

CARD NO.
FIELD NO. 737

Dawes' Roll No.	NAME	Relationship to Person First Named	AGE	SEX	BLOOD	TRIBAL ENROLLMENT Year	County	No.
1827	1 McCoy, Viney DIED PRIOR TO SEPTEMBER 25, 1902		39	F	Full	1893	Cedar	P.R. 336
	2							
	3 ENROLLMENT							
	4 OF NOS. 1 HEREON APPROVED BY THE SECRETARY							
	5 OF INTERIOR DEC 12 1902							
	6							
	7							
	8							
	9							
	10							
	11							
	12					On 1896 roll Page 345, No. 13132		
	13					Boiney Willis, Cedar Co.		
	14							
	15							
	16							
	17							

TRIBAL ENROLLMENT OF PARENTS

Name of Father	Year	County	Name of Mother	Year	County
1 Willis Newton	Dead	Cedar	Harriet Newton	Dead	Cedar
2					
3					
4					
5 No4 died May 6, 1900; Enrollment cancelled by Department May 2, 1906.					
6					
7					
8					
9					
10					
11					
12					
13					
14					
15					
16			Date of Application for Enrollment	April 24/99	
17					

137

Choctaw By Blood Enrollment Cards 1898-1914

RESIDENCE: Cedar COUNTY.
POST OFFICE: Doaksville, I.T.

Choctaw Nation

Choctaw Roll
(Not Including Freedmen)

CARD NO.
FIELD NO. 738

Dawes' Roll No.	NAME	Relationship to Person	AGE	SEX	BLOOD	TRIBAL ENROLLMENT		
						Year	County	No.
1828	DIED PRIOR TO SEPTEMBER 25, 1902 1 Thomas, Robert	First Named	46	M	Full	1896	Towson	12126
1829	2 " James 16	Son	13	"	"	1896	"	12127
	3							
	4							
	5 ENROLLMENT OF NOS. 1 and 2 HEREON							
	6 APPROVED BY THE SECRETARY OF INTERIOR DEC 12 1902							
	7							
	8							
	9							
	10							
	11	No1 is also known as Cole Thomas.						
	12	No2 on 1896 roll as Jim Thomas.						
	13							
	14							
	15							
	16							
	17							

TRIBAL ENROLLMENT OF PARENTS

	Name of Father	Year	County	Name of Mother	Year	County
1	Thomas	Dead	Cedar	Betsey Thomas	Dead	Cedar
2	No1			Mandy Thomas	"	"
3						
4						
5						
6						
7						
8						
9						
10						
11						
12						
13						
14				Date of Application for Enrollment.		
15						
16				April 24/99		
17						

138

Choctaw By Blood Enrollment Cards 1898-1914

RESIDENCE: Red River COUNTY.
POST OFFICE: Rocky Comfort, Ark.

Choctaw Nation

Choctaw Roll (Not Including Freedmen)

CARD NO.
FIELD NO. 739

Dawes' Roll No.	NAME	Relationship to Person Named	AGE	SEX	BLOOD	TRIBAL ENROLLMENT Year	County	No.
DEAD	1 Bailey, Elizabeth A DEAD	First Named	68	F	IW	1896	Red River	14315
	2							
	3							
	4 No. 1 HEREON DISMISSED UNDER							
	5 ORDER OF THE COMMISSION TO THE FIVE CIVILIZED TRIBES OF JULY 18, 1905.							
	6							
	7							
	8							
	9							
	10							
	11							
	12							
	13							
	14							
	15							
	16							
	17							

TRIBAL ENROLLMENT OF PARENTS

Name of Father	Year	County	Name of Mother	Year	County
1 Caleb Earls	Dead	Non Citz	Melvina Earls	Dead	Non Citz
2					
3					
4					
5					
6 Admitted by the Dawes Commission Case No 860.					
7 No appeal taken.					
8					
9					
10 Also see Dawes Commission Case No 636.					
11 No.1 Died October 11, 1899. See letter of John G. Harris filed April 10, 1901.					
12					
13					
14					
15					
16			Date of Application for Enrollment.		April 24/99
17					

Choctaw By Blood Enrollment Cards 1898-1914

RESIDENCE:
POST OFFICE: Denison, Texas

COUNTY.

Choctaw Nation

Choctaw Roll
(Not Including Freedmen)

CARD NO.
FIELD NO. 740

Dawes' Roll No.	NAME		Relationship to Person	AGE	SEX	BLOOD	TRIBAL ENROLLMENT		
							Year	County	No.
14921	1 Randell, Elizabeth L	19	First Named	16	F	1/8	1896	Kiamitia	10865
14922	2 " Robert J.	17	brother	14	M	1/8	1896	"	10866
	3								
	4								
	5								
	6	ENROLLMENT							
	7	OF NOS. 1 and 2 HEREON APPROVED BY THE SECRETARY							
	8	OF INTERIOR OCT 15 1903							
	9								
	10								
	11				No 1 on 1896 roll as Lizzie Randelle					
	12				No 2 " 1896 " " Robert "					
	13								
	14								
	15								
	16								
	17								

TRIBAL ENROLLMENT OF PARENTS

	Name of Father	Year	County	Name of Mother	Year	County
1	George G. Randell	Dead	Non Citz	Mary E. Randell	Dead	Kiamitia
2	" " "	"	" " "	" " "	"	"
3						
4						
5						
6						
7	J M Randell Denison, Texas is legal guardian of					
8	No 1 and No 2					
9	No 1 and 2 admitted as citizens by blood by Dawes Commission					
10	Choctaw Case #666. No appeal.					
11						
12						
13						
14						
15						
16				Date of Application for Enrollment April 24/99		
17						

Choctaw By Blood Enrollment Cards 1898-1914

RESIDENCE: Red River									
POST OFFICE: Janis, I.T.	COUNTY.	**Choctaw Nation**				**Choctaw Roll** (Not Including Freedmen)	CARD NO. FIELD NO. 741		

Dawes' Roll No.		NAME		Relationship to Person	AGE	SEX	BLOOD	TRIBAL ENROLLMENT		
								Year	County	No.
1830	1	Harris, John G.	51	First Named	49	M	1/8	1896	Red River	5720
I.W. 504	2	" Mary F	48	Wife	41	F	I.W.	1896	" "	14629
1831	3	" Nila	19	Dau	16	"	1/16	1896	Red River	5722
1832	4	" Ernest	17	Son	14	M	1/16	1896	" "	5723
1833	5	" Carl	8	"	6	"	1/16	1896	" "	5724
	6									
	7	ENROLLMENT OF NOS. 1 3 4 and 5 HEREON								
	8	APPROVED BY THE SECRETARY OF INTERIOR DEC 12 1902								
	9									
	10									
	11	ENROLLMENT OF NOS. ~~ 2 ~~ HEREON								
	12	APPROVED BY THE SECRETARY OF INTERIOR DEC 24 1903								
	13									
	14									
	15									
	16									
	17									

TRIBAL ENROLLMENT OF PARENTS

	Name of Father	Year	County	Name of Mother	Year	County
1	Lorenza Harris	Dead	Non Citz	Betsy Harris	Dead	Red River
2	Henderson Ward	"	" "	Elizabeth "	1896	Non Citz
3	No1			No2		
4	No1			No2		
5	No1			No2		
6						
7	No2 was admitted by Dawes Commission, Case No 1352. No appeal taken.					
8						
9	No3 on 1896 roll as Nelly Harris					
10	No5 " 1896 " " Cail "					
11	No1 " 1896 " " Jno. G. "					
	For child of No.3 see N.B. (Apr 26,1906) Card No. 78.					
12						
13						
14						
15						
16				Date of Application for Enrollment April 24/99		
17						

141

Choctaw By Blood Enrollment Cards 1898-1914

RESIDENCE: Red River   COUNTY.   **Choctaw Nation**   Choctaw Roll   CARD No.

POST OFFICE: Janis, I.T.   *(Not Including Freedmen)*   FIELD No. 742

Dawes' Roll No.	NAME	Relationship to Person First Named	AGE	SEX	BLOOD	TRIBAL ENROLLMENT Year	County	No.
1834	1 Harris, George T 13	First Named	10	M	1/16	1896	Red River	5675
1835	2 " Virginia 11	Sister	8	F	1/16	1896	" "	5676
1836	3 " Thomas P 9	brother	6	M	1/16	1896	" "	5677
1837	4 " Emma M 6	Sister	3	F	1/16	1896	" "	5678
1838	5 " Arthur F. 4	brother	1	M	1/16			
	6							
	7							
	8							
	9							
	10							
	11							
	12							
	13							
	14							
	15							
	16							
	17							

ENROLLMENT
OF NOS. 1 2 3 4 and 5 HEREON
APPROVED BY THE SECRETARY
OF INTERIOR DEC 12 1902

TRIBAL ENROLLMENT OF PARENTS

	Name of Father	Year	County	Name of Mother	Year	County
1	James L. Harris	Dead	Red River	Laura J Harris	Dead	Non Citz
2	" " "	"	" " "	" " "	"	" " "
3	" " "	"	" " "	" " "	"	" " "
4	" " "	"	" " "	" " "	"	" " "
5	" " "	"	" " "	" " "	"	" " "
6						
7	No 1 on 1896 roll as George Harris					
8	No 2 " 1896 " " Janie "					
9	No 3 " 1896 " " Thomas "					
	No 4 " 1896 " " Emma "					
10						
11						
12						
13						
14					Date of Application for Enrollment.	
15						
16					April 24/99	
17						

142

Choctaw By Blood Enrollment Cards 1898-1914

RESIDENCE: Red River COUNTY.
POST OFFICE: Garvin, I.T.

Choctaw Nation

Choctaw Roll
(Not Including Freedmen)

CARD No.
FIELD No. 743

Dawes' Roll No.		NAME	Relationship to Person	AGE	SEX	BLOOD	TRIBAL ENROLLMENT		
							Year	County	No.
1839	1	William, Sampson	First Named	48	M	Full	1896	Red River	13572
1840	2	" Moses	Son	15	"	"	1896	" "	13575
	3								
	4	ENROLLMENT							
	5	OF NOS. 1 and 2 HEREON APPROVED BY THE SECRETARY							
	6	OF INTERIOR DEC 12 1902							
	7								
	8								
	9								
	10								
	11								
	12								
	13								
	14								
	15								
	16								
	17								

TRIBAL ENROLLMENT OF PARENTS

	Name of Father	Year	County	Name of Mother	Year	County
1	Wm Ochatubbee	Dead	Red River	Betsy Ochatubbee	Dead	Red River
2	No1			Betsy William	"	" "
3						
4						
5						
6						
7	No2 is now husband of Sophia Battiest on Choctaw card #501 11/25/02					
8	For child of No.2 see NB (March 3, 1905) 1021					
9						
10						
11						
12						
13						
14						
15					Date of Application for Enrollment.	
16					April 24/99	
17						

143

Choctaw By Blood Enrollment Cards 1898-1914

Choctaw Nation

Choctaw Roll (Not Including Freedmen)

CARD NO.

FIELD NO. 744

Dawes' Roll No.	NAME	Relationship to Person First Named	AGE	SEX	BLOOD	TRIBAL ENROLLMENT Year	County	No.
1841	1 Scott, Edmond DIED PRIOR TO SEPTEMBER 25, 1902		78	M	Full	1896	Towson	11359
1842	2 William, Thomas ¹⁹	G. Son	16	"	"	1896	"	13163
	3							
	4							
	5							
	6							
	7							
	8							
	9							
	10							
	11							
	12							
	13							
	14							
	15							
	16							
	17							

ENROLLMENT
OF NOS. 1 and 2 HEREON
APPROVED BY THE SECRETARY
OF INTERIOR DEC 12 1902

No 1 on 1896 roll as Edmund Scott

No 1 died July 26, 1902: proof of death filed Dec 3, 1902

TRIBAL ENROLLMENT OF PARENTS

	Name of Father	Year	County	Name of Mother	Year	County
1	Ish-tonuk-fillubbee	Dead	Red River		Dead	Red River
2	Elias William	"	" "	Lilie John	"	Towson
3						
4						
5						
6						
7						
8						
9						
10						
11						
12						
13						
14						
15						
16						
17						

Date of Application for Enrollment   April 24/99

144

Choctaw By Blood Enrollment Cards 1898-1914

RESIDENCE: Nashoba   COUNTY.   **Choctaw Nation**   **Choctaw Roll**   CARD NO.
POST OFFICE: Alikchi, I.T.   *(Not Including Freedmen)*   FIELD NO. 745

Dawes' Roll No.	NAME	Relationship to Person	AGE	SEX	BLOOD	TRIBAL ENROLLMENT Year	County	No.
1843	1 Bacon, Brazil ⁴¹	First Named	38	M	Full	1896	Nashoba	1157
1844	2 " Ske ⁸	Son	5	"	"	1896	"	1159
	3							
	4	ENROLLMENT						
	5	OF NOS. 1 and 2 HEREON APPROVED BY THE SECRETARY						
	6	OF INTERIOR DEC 12 1902						
	7							
	8							
	9							
	10							
	11							
	12	No1 was formerly husband of Adeline Cephus on Choctaw card #806. They						
	13	were divorced Dec. 6, 1901. See Choctaw card #860: June 3, 1902.						
	14							
	15							
	16							
	17							

	TRIBAL ENROLLMENT OF PARENTS					
	Name of Father	Year	County	Name of Mother	Year	County
1	Ned Bacon	Dead	Cedar	Itcy Dacon	Dead	Cedar
2	No 1			Maswis[sic] Bacon	"	Nashoba
3						
4						
5						
6						
7						
8						
9						
10						
11						
12						
13						
14						
15				Date of Application for Enrollment.		
16				April 24/99		
17						

145

Choctaw By Blood Enrollment Cards 1898-1914

RESIDENCE: Towson COUNTY.
POST OFFICE: Garvin, I.T.

Choctaw Nation

Choctaw Roll CARD NO.
(Not Including Freedmen) FIELD NO. 746

Dawes' Roll No.	NAME		Relationship to Person	AGE	SEX	BLOOD	TRIBAL ENROLLMENT		
							Year	County	No.
1845	1 Austin, Iyers	30	First Named	27	M	Full	1896	Red River	327
1846	2 " Lila	24	Wife	21	F	"	1896	" "	328
	3								
	4	ENROLLMENT							
	5	OF NOS. 1 and 2 HEREON APPROVED BY THE SECRETARY							
	6	OF INTERIOR DEC 12 1902							
	7								
	8								
	9								
	10								
	11	No2 on 1896 roll as Lilie Austin.							
	12								
	13								
	14								
	15								
	16								
	17								

TRIBAL ENROLLMENT OF PARENTS

	Name of Father	Year	County	Name of Mother	Year	County
1	Mollis Austin	Dead	Red River	Phoebe Austin	Dead	Red River
2	John Harris	"	Towson	Anna Harris	"	" "
3						
4						
5						
6						
7						
8						
9						
10						
11						
12						
13						
14						
15						
16				Date of Application for Enrollment	April 24/99	
17						

146

Choctaw By Blood Enrollment Cards 1898-1914

RESIDENCE: Nashoba	COUNTY:							

| | | | | | | | CARD NO. | |
| **Choctaw Nation** | | | | | **Choctaw Roll** (Not Including Freedmen) | | FIELD NO. 747 | |

POST OFFICE: Alikchi, I.T.

Dawes' Roll No.	NAME		Relationship to Person First Named	AGE	SEX	BLOOD	TRIBAL ENROLLMENT		
							Year	County	No.
~~1847~~	~~Lowman, Abel~~ DIED PRIOR TO SEPTEMBER 25, 1902	~~1~~	~~Named~~	~~35~~	~~M~~	~~Full~~	~~1896~~	~~Nashoba~~	~~7966~~
1848	" Itie	2 ¹⁰	Dau	7	F	"	1896	"	7968
	3								
	4								
	5 ENROLLMENT								
	6 OF NOS. 1 and 2 HEREON APPROVED BY THE SECRETARY								
	7 OF INTERIOR DEC 12 1902								
	8								
	9								
	10								
	11								
	12								
	13								
	14								
	15								
	16								
	17								

TRIBAL ENROLLMENT OF PARENTS

	Name of Father	Year	County	Name of Mother	Year	County
1	~~Moses Louman~~	~~1896~~	~~Nashoba~~	~~Hoh-yo-ho-ta~~	~~Dead~~	~~Eagle~~
2	No1			Eusie Lowman	"	Nashoba
3						
4						
5	No2 on 1896 roll as Arttie Lowman					
6	Nº1 Died Aug. 18, 1902. proof of death received and returned for correction Jany. 20, 1903					
7	No.1 died Aug 18-1902: Enrollment cancelled by [remainder illegible]					
8						
9						
10						
11						
12						
13						
14						
15						
16				Date of Application for Enrollment April 24/99		
17				No.2 May 22/99		

147

Choctaw By Blood Enrollment Cards 1898-1914

RESIDENCE: Nashoba		COUNTY.							
POST OFFICE: Alikchi, I.T.									

Choctaw Nation

Choctaw Roll (*Not Including Freedmen*)

CARD NO.

FIELD NO. 748

Dawes' Roll No.	NAME		Relationship to Person First Named	AGE	SEX	BLOOD	TRIBAL ENROLLMENT		
							Year	County	No.
1849	1	Baker, Wesley 39	First Named	36	M	Full	1896	Nashoba	1205
1850	2	" Judy 41	Wife	38	F	"	1896	"	1206
1851	3	" Solomon 18	Son	15	M	"	1896	"	1207
1852	4	" Graham 14	"	11	"	"	1896	"	1208
1853	5	" Nettie 12	Dau	9	F	"	1896	"	1209
1854	6	" Simpson 6	Son	3	M	"	1896	"	1210
1855	7	" Grace 4	Dau	1	F	"			
	8								
	9	ENROLLMENT OF NOS. 123456and7 HEREON APPROVED BY THE SECRETARY OF INTERIOR DEC 12 1902							
	10								
	11								
	12								
	13								
	14	No4 on 1896 roll as Grayham Baker							
	15	For child of No 1&2 see NB (March 3 1905) 893							
	16								
	17								

TRIBAL ENROLLMENT OF PARENTS

	Name of Father	Year	County	Name of Mother	Year	County
1	Samuel Baker	Dead	Nashoba	Malinda Baker	Dead	Nashoba
2	To-nich-cha	1896	"	A-pe-sa-ho-na	"	"
3	No1			No2		
4	No1			No2		
5	No1			No2		
6	No1			No2		
7	No1			No2		
8						
9						
10						
11						
12						
13						
14						
15				Date of Application for Enrollment.		
16				April 24/99		
17						

148

Choctaw By Blood Enrollment Cards 1898-1914

RESIDENCE: Towson COUNTY.
POST OFFICE: Garvin, I.T.

Choctaw Nation

Choctaw Roll
(Not Including Freedmen)

CARD No.

FIELD NO. 749

Dawes' Roll No.	NAME		Relationship to Person First Named	AGE	SEX	BLOOD	TRIBAL ENROLLMENT		
							Year	County	No.
1856	1 Taylor, Ellis	47	First Named	44	M	Full	1896	Towson	12103
1858	2 " Lila	41	Wife	38	F	"	1896	"	12104
1859	3 " Agnes	7	Dau	4	"	"	1896	"	12105
	4								
	5								
	6	ENROLLMENT OF NOS. 1 2 and 3 HEREON APPROVED BY THE SECRETARY OF INTERIOR DEC 12 1902							
	7								
	8								
	9								
	10								
	11								
	12								
	13								
	14								
	15								
	16								
	17								

TRIBAL ENROLLMENT OF PARENTS

	Name of Father	Year	County	Name of Mother	Year	County
1	Ma-ha-la	Dead	Red River	Fannie	Dead	Red River
2	Chic-ca	"	Towson	Amy	1896	Towson
3	No 1			No 2		
4						
5						
6						
7	No2 on 1896 roll as Lylie Taylor					
8	No1 is now guardian of Susan and George Austin, Choctaw card #944:					
9	letters of guardianship filed December 3, 1902.					
10						
11						
12						
13						
14						
15						
16				Date of Application for Enrollment		April 24/99
17						

149

Choctaw By Blood Enrollment Cards 1898-1914

RESIDENCE: Red River COUNTY. **Choctaw Nation** Choctaw Roll CARD NO.
POST OFFICE: Garvin, I.T. *(Not Including Freedmen)* FIELD NO. 750

Dawes' Roll No.	NAME	Relationship to Person	AGE	SEX	BLOOD	TRIBAL ENROLLMENT		
						Year	County	No.
1859	1 Forbis, Albert 61	First Named	58	M	Full	1896	Red River	4216
I.W. 505	2 " Jane 61	Wife	58	F	I.W.	1896	" "	14531
	3							
	4							
	5							
	6							
	7							
	8							
	9							
	10							
	11							
	12							
	13							
	14							
	15							
	16							
	17							

ENROLLMENT OF NOS. 1 HEREON APPROVED BY THE SECRETARY OF INTERIOR DEC 12 1902

ENROLLMENT OF NOS. 2 HEREON APPROVED BY THE SECRETARY OF INTERIOR DEC 24 1903

TRIBAL ENROLLMENT OF PARENTS

	Name of Father	Year	County	Name of Mother	Year	County
1	Neh-ka	Dead	Cedar	Pisa-ho-tema	Dead	Cedar
2	Fipps	"	Non Citz	Jane Fipps	"	Non Citz
3						
4						
5						
6						
7						
8						
9						
10						
11						
12						
13						
14					Date of Application for Enrollment.	
15						
16					April 24/99	
17						

Choctaw By Blood Enrollment Cards 1898-1914

RESIDENCE: Red River COUNTY.
POST OFFICE: Kullituklo, I.T.

Choctaw Nation

Choctaw Roll *(Not Including Freedmen)*

CARD No.

FIELD No. **751**

Dawes' Roll No.	Goodwater - 1902 NAME	Relationship to Person Named	AGE	SEX	BLOOD	TRIBAL ENROLLMENT Year	County	No.
1860	1 Baker, Noel ³¹	First Named	28	M	Full	1893	Nashoba	P.R. 103
Dead	2 " Kitty DEAD	Wife	33	F	"	1896	Bok Tuklo	5566
1861	3 Hickman, Simeon ¹¹	Ward	8	M	"	1896	" "	5570
	4							
	5							
	6							
	7							
	8							
	9							
	10							
	11							
	12							
	13							
	14							
	15							
	16							
	17							

ENROLLMENT
OF NOS. 1 and 3 HEREON
APPROVED BY THE SECRETARY
OF INTERIOR Dec 12 1902

No. 2 hereon dismissed under order of the Commission to the Five Civilized Tribes of March 31, 1905.

TRIBAL ENROLLMENT OF PARENTS

	Name of Father	Year	County	Name of Mother	Year	County
1	Samuel Baker	Dead	Nashoba	Malinda Baker	Dead	Nashoba
2	Shabakullo Anderson	"	Eagle	Nancy Jones	"	Red River
3	Waitey Frye	"	Kiamitia	Frances Cann	"	" "
4						
5						
6						
7	No.2 on 1896 roll as Kitty Hickman					
8	No.2 died November 10, 1899: Evidence of death filed May 15, 1901					
9	Nº1 is now the husband of Elizabeth Williston on Choctaw card 522 May 28, 1902 No.3 on 1896 Roll as Simeon Hickman.					
10						
11						
12						
13						
14						
15						
16					Date of Application for Enrollment April 24/99	
17						

151

Choctaw By Blood Enrollment Cards 1898-1914

RESIDENCE: Nashoba   COUNTY.   **Choctaw Nation**   Choctaw Roll   CARD No.
POST OFFICE: Alikchi, I.T.   *(Not Including Freedmen)*   FIELD No.   752

Dawes' Roll No.	NAME		Relationship to Person	AGE	SEX	BLOOD	TRIBAL ENROLLMENT		
							Year	County	No.
1862	1 Cephus, Timothy	37	First Named	34	M	Full	1896	Nashoba	2501
1863	2 DIED PRIOR TO SEPTEMBER 25, 1902 Wysie		Wife	50	F	"	1896	"	5524
1864	3 " Henry	9	Son	6	M	"	1896	"	2503
1865	4 DIED PRIOR TO SEPTEMBER 25, 1902 Lura		Dau	3	F	"	1896	"	2504
	5								
	6	ENROLLMENT							
	7	OF NOS. 1 2 3 and 4 HEREON APPROVED BY THE SECRETARY							
	8	OF INTERIOR DEC 12 1902							
	9								
	10								
	11	1/29/1917 – See enrollment jacket #752 for affidavit as to mother of No.3 hereon,							
	12	said affidavit having been filed in re per capita of No.3							
	13								
	14								
	15								
	16								
	17								

TRIBAL ENROLLMENT OF PARENTS

	Name of Father	Year	County	Name of Mother	Year	County
1	John Cephus	Dead	Nashoba	Chepee Cephus	Dead	Nashoba
2	Tick-bona-by	"	"	E-la-pa-hu-na	"	"
3	No 1			Belinda Cephus	"	"
4	No 1			"	"	"
5						
6				No2 on 1896 roll as Wysie Hicks		
7				No4 " 1896 " " Rora Cephus		
8						
9				No.2 died May 9, 1900: proof of death filed Dec 3, 1902		
10				No4 " Sept 15, 1900: " " " " Dec 3, 1902		
11	No2 died May 9, 1900: No4 died Sept 15 1900 Enrollment cancelled by Department July 8 1904					
12						
13						
14						
15						
16						Date of Application for Enrollment April 24/99
17	P.O. Rufe, I.T. 7/30/07					

152

Choctaw By Blood Enrollment Cards 1898-1914

RESIDENCE: Eagle   COUNTY.
POST OFFICE: Eagletown, I.T.   **Choctaw Nation**   Choctaw Roll *(Not Including Freedmen)*   CARD NO.
FIELD NO.   753

Dawes' Roll No.	NAME	Relationship to Person Named	AGE	SEX	BLOOD	TRIBAL ENROLLMENT Year	County	No.
1866	1 Bunce, Jerry 52	First Named	49	M	Full	1896	Eagle	1283
1867	2 " Aly 14	Dau	11	F	"	1896	"	1267
1868	3 " ~~Minerva~~ DIED PRIOR TO SEPTEMBER 25, 1902	"	8	"	"	1896	"	1298
1869	4 " Bond 7	Son	4	M	"	1896	"	1262
1870	5 " Vicey 6	Dau	3	F	"	1896	"	1328
1871	6 ~~Leo~~ DIED PRIOR TO SEPTEMBER 25, 1902	Son	5mo	M	"			
	7							
	8							
	9	ENROLLMENT OF NOS. 1 2 3 4 5 and 6 HEREON APPROVED BY THE SECRETARY						
	10	OF INTERIOR DEC 12 1902						
	11	No3 died Jan. 21, 1900 No6 died Aug. 16, 1899: Enrollment cancelled by Department July 8, 1904						
	12	No1 on 1896 roll as Jerry Bounce						
	13	No2 " 1896 " " Eli "						
	14	No3 " 1896 " " Minerva "						
	15	No4 " 1896 " " Bon "						
	16	No5 " 1896 " " Vicey "						
	17							

TRIBAL ENROLLMENT OF PARENTS

	Name of Father	Year	County	Name of Mother	Year	County
1	Yah-ho-ka-tubbee	Dead	Eagle	Okla-hay-she	Dead	Eagle
2	No 1			Salina Bunce	"	"
3	No 1			" "	"	"
4	No 1			" "	"	"
5	No 1			" "	"	"
6	No 1			" "	"	"
7						
8	No1 is now the husband of Suson[sic] Tonihka on Choctaw card #884. See statement of					
9	No1 and Susan Tonihka filed in Choctaw case #884 July 29, 1902					
10	No3 died Jan. 21, 1900: proof of death filed Dec. 10, 1902					
11	No6 died Aug 16, 1899: proof of death filed Dec. 10, 1902.					
12						
13						
14						
15					Date of Application for Enrollment	
16					April 24/99	
17						

153

Choctaw By Blood Enrollment Cards 1898-1914

RESIDENCE: Eagle COUNTY.
POST OFFICE: Eagletown, I.T.

Choctaw Nation

Choctaw Roll *(Not Including Freedmen)*

CARD NO. FIELD NO. **754**

Dawes' Roll No.	NAME		Relationship to Person First Named	AGE	SEX	BLOOD	TRIBAL ENROLLMENT		
							Year	County	No.
1872	1 Elliott, Anderson	29	First Named	26	M	Full	1896	Eagle	3759
1873	2 " Eliza	26	Wife	23	F	"	1896	"	3760
~~1874~~	Died prior to September 25, 1902 3 " Lilly	6	Dau	2	"	"			
1875	4 " Coleman	1	Son	6mo	M	"			
	5								
	6								
	7								
	8	ENROLLMENT							
	9	OF NOS. 1 2 3 and 4 HEREON APPROVED BY THE SECRETARY							
	10	OF INTERIOR Dec 12 1902							
	11								
	12								
	13								
	14								
	15								
	16								
	17								

TRIBAL ENROLLMENT OF PARENTS

	Name of Father	Year	County	Name of Mother	Year	County
1	Harris Elliott	Dead	Eagle	Siney Elliott	Dead	Eagle
2	Jerry Bunce	1896	"	Salina Bunce	"	"
3	~~No.1~~			~~No.2~~		
4	No.1			No.2		
5						
6			No.4 Enrolled Aug 27, 1901			
7						
8			No.3 Died February 1902 Enrollment cancelled by Department May 2 1906			
9			For child of No.2 see NB (March 3, 1905) #875			
10						
11						
12						
13						
14				#1 to 3 inc		
15				Date of Application for Enrollment,		
16				April 24/99		
17	No.2 P.O. Lukfata I.T. 4/12/05					

Choctaw By Blood Enrollment Cards 1898-1914

RESIDENCE: Eagle COUNTY. **Choctaw Nation** Choctaw Roll CARD NO.
POST OFFICE: Eagletown, I.T. *(Not Including Freedmen)* FIELD NO. **755**

Dawes' Roll No.	NAME		Relationship to Person First Named	AGE	SEX	BLOOD	TRIBAL ENROLLMENT		
							Year	County	No.
1876	1 Elliott, Abbott	31		28	M	Full	1893	Eagle	P.R. 227
1877	2 " Mollie	25	Wife	22	F	"	1896	"	6944
1878	3 " Aleta	4	Dau	5mo	"	"			
	4								
	5								
	6	ENROLLMENT							
	7	OF NOS. 1 2 and 3 HEREON APPROVED BY THE SECRETARY OF INTERIOR Dec 12 1902							
	8								
	9								
	10								
	11								
	12								
	13								
	14								
	15								
	16								
	17								

TRIBAL ENROLLMENT OF PARENTS

	Name of Father	Year	County	Name of Mother	Year	County
1	Harris Elliott	Dead	Eagle	Siney Elliott	Dead	Eagle
2	Jonas Jones	"	"	Allitie Jones	"	"
3	No.1			No.2		
4						
5						
6			No.2 on 1896 roll as Mollie Jones			
7			No.1 on 1896 Choctaw Census roll: page 136: No. 5571 as			
8			Abbot Harris			
9			For child of No.1 see NB (March 3, 1905) #967			
10						
11						
12						
13						
14						
15						
16				Date of Application for Enrollment April 24/99		
17						

Choctaw By Blood Enrollment Cards 1898-1914

RESIDENCE:	Eagle	COUNTY.	**Choctaw Nation**			Choctaw Roll	CARD NO.	
POST OFFICE:	Eagletown					(Not Including Freedmen)	FIELD NO.	**756**

Dawes' Roll No.	NAME		Relationship to Person First Named	AGE	SEX	BLOOD	TRIBAL ENROLLMENT		
							Year	County	No.
1879	1 Bobb, Joseph	58	First Named	55	M	Full	1896	Eagle	1287
1880	2 " Atkins	20	Son	17	"	"	1896	"	1261
	3								
	4								
	5	ENROLLMENT							
	6	OF NOS. 1 and 2 HEREON							
	7	APPROVED BY THE SECRETARY							
	8	OF INTERIOR Dec. 12, 1902							
	9	2/25/1915 – Question as to date of death of Nos 1 and 2; under investigation.							
	10								
	11								
	12								
	13								
	14								
	15								
	16								
	17								

TRIBAL ENROLLMENT OF PARENTS

	Name of Father	Year	County	Name of Mother	Year	County
1	Lick Bobb	Dead	Eagle	Na-ne-ma-hohke	Dead	Eagle
2	No 1			Betty Bobb		"
3						
4						
5						
6						
7						
8						
9						
10						
11						
12						
13						
14						
15					Date of Application for Enrollment.	
16					April 24/99	
17						

156

Choctaw By Blood Enrollment Cards 1898-1914

RESIDENCE: Eagle COUNTY. **Choctaw Nation** Choctaw Roll CARD NO.
POST OFFICE: Eagletown, I.T. *(Not Including Freedmen)* FIELD NO. **757**

Dawes' Roll No.	NAME	Relationship to Person	AGE	SEX	BLOOD	TRIBAL ENROLLMENT		
						Year	County	No.
1881	1 Sheaheke, Washington	57 First Named	53	M	Full	1896	Eagle	11432
	2							
	3							
	4	ENROLLMENT						
	5	OF NOS. 1 HEREON APPROVED BY THE SECRETARY						
	6	OF INTERIOR Dec 12, 1902						
	7							
	8							
	9							
	10							
	11							
	12							
	13							
	14							
	15							
	16							
	17							

TRIBAL ENROLLMENT OF PARENTS

	Name of Father	Year	County	Name of Mother	Year	County
1	Sheaheke	Dead	Eagle	Me-a-she-ma	Dead	Eagle
2						
3						
4						
5						
6						
7						
8						
9						
10						
11						
12						
13						
14						
15				Date of Application for Enrollment.		
16				April 24/99		
17						

157

Choctaw By Blood Enrollment Cards 1898-1914

RESIDENCE: Eagle   COUNTY.   **Choctaw Nation**   Choctaw Roll   CARD No.
POST OFFICE: Eagletown, I.T.   *(Not Including Freedmen)*   FIELD No. 758

Dawes' Roll No.	NAME	Relationship to Person First Named	AGE	SEX	BLOOD	TRIBAL ENROLLMENT Year	County	No.
1882	₁ Eba-ho-tubbe, Ellis ³⁶	First Named	33	M	Full	1896	Eagle	3745
1883	₂ DIED PRIOR TO SEPTEMBER 25, 1902 " Sia	Wife	40	F	"	1896	"	3757
1884	₃ " Charles ¹⁴	Son	11	M	"	1896	"	3747
1885	₄ " Sukey	Dau	5	F	"	1896	"	3758
	5							
	6							
	7							
	8							
	9							
	10							
	11							
	12							
	13							
	14	No2 on 1896 roll as Sai Ebahotubbe						
	15	No4 " 1896 " " Sokie "						
	16	No.2 died May – 1901 Enrollment cancelled by Department July 8 1904						
	17							

```
ENROLLMENT
OF NOS. 1,2,3 and 4 HEREON
APPROVED BY THE SECRETARY
OF INTERIOR DEC 12 1902
```

TRIBAL ENROLLMENT OF PARENTS

	Name of Father	Year	County	Name of Mother	Year	County
1	John Ebahotubbee	Dead	Eagle	Susan Ebahotubbee	Dead	Eagle
2	Tick-be-na-by	"	Nashoba	E-lap-a-hona	"	Nashoba
3	No1			No2		
4	No1			No2		
5						
6						
7						
8						
9						
10						
11						
12						
13						
14						
15				Date of Application for Enrollment.		
16				April 24/99		
17						

158

Choctaw By Blood Enrollment Cards 1898-1914

RESIDENCE: Eagle
POST OFFICE: Eagletown, I.T.

COUNTY.

Choctaw Nation

Choctaw Roll
(Not Including Freedmen)

CARD NO.
FIELD NO. **759**

Dawes' Roll No.		NAME		Relationship to Person	AGE	SEX	BLOOD	TRIBAL ENROLLMENT		
								Year	County	No.
1886	1	Harrison, Ziad	37	First Named	34	M	Full	1896	Eagle	5628
1887	2	" Insey	27	Wife	24	F	"	1896	"	5622
1888	3	" Eliza	9	Dau	6	"	"	1896	"	5624
1889	4	" Silas	8	Son	5	M	"	1896	"	5652
	5									
	6									
	7									
	8									
	9									
	10									
	11									
	12									
	13									
	14									
	15									
	16									
	17									

ENROLLMENT
OF NOS. 1 2 3 and 4 HEREON
APPROVED BY THE SECRETARY
OF INTERIOR Dec 12 1902

TRIBAL ENROLLMENT OF PARENTS

	Name of Father	Year	County	Name of Mother	Year	County
1	Stephen Harrison	Dead	Eagle	Che-ma-la-hohke	Dead	Eagle
2	Thomas Billy	"	"	Sallie Billy	1896	"
3	No1			No2		
4	No1			No2		
5						
6			No3 also on 1896 roll as Eliza Billy, Page 32,			
7			No 2 192 Eagle Co.			
8			No.1 is husband of Malena Thomas on Choctaw card No. 849;			
9			Certificate of marriage filed Dec. 16/1902.			
10			No2 is said to be dead			
11			#4 = "Died prior to September 25, 1902; not entitled to land or money"			
12			See Indian Office letter May 13, 1910, D.C. #657 – 1910			
13			No2 = "Died prior to September 25, 1902; not entitled to land or money"			
14			(See Indian Office letter of June 20, 1910, D.C. #837 – 1910)			
15						
16						
17			No3 in Wheelock Academy			

Date of Application for Enrollment.

April 24/99

11-28 '02

159

Choctaw By Blood Enrollment Cards 1898-1914

RESIDENCE: Eagle   COUNTY.   **Choctaw Nation**   **Choctaw Roll** CARD NO.
POST OFFICE: Eagletown, I.T.   *(Not Including Freedmen)*   FIELD NO. **760**

Dawes' Roll No.	NAME	Relationship to Person	AGE	SEX	BLOOD	TRIBAL ENROLLMENT		
						Year	County	No.
1890	1 Jefferson, Sampson 31	First Named	28	M	Full	1896	Eagle	6956
1891	2 " Hoteza 33	Wife	30	F	"	1896	"	6957
1892	3 " Wilton 10	Son	7	M	"	1896	"	6960
1893	4 " Sophie 7	Dau	4	F	"	1896	"	6961
1894	5 Wilson, Sarah 12	S.Dau	9	"	"	1896	"	13670
	6							
	7	ENROLLMENT						
	8	OF NOS. 1,2,3,4 and 5 HEREON APPROVED BY THE SECRETARY						
	9	OF INTERIOR Dec. 12, 1902						
	10							
	11							
	12							
	13	No 3 on 1896 roll as Witten Jefferson						
	14							
	15							
	16							
	17							

TRIBAL ENROLLMENT OF PARENTS

	Name of Father	Year	County	Name of Mother	Year	County
1	Timothy Jefferson	Dead	Eagle	Sallie Jefferson	1896	Eagle
2	Simon Johnson	"	"	Suillie[sic] Johnson	1896	Red River
3	No 1			No 2		
4	No 1			No 2		
5	Dean Wilson	Dead	Red River	No 2		
6						
7						
8						
9						
10						
11						
12						
13						
14						Date of Application for Enrollment.
15						April 24/99
16						
17	P.O. Hochatown I.T. 5/21/07					

160

Choctaw By Blood Enrollment Cards 1898-1914

RESIDENCE: Bok Tuklo
POST OFFICE: Lukfata, I.T.
COUNTY.

Choctaw Nation

Choctaw Roll
(Not Including Freedmen)

CARD NO.
FIELD NO. **761**

Dawes' Roll No.	NAME		Relationship to Person	AGE	SEX	BLOOD	TRIBAL ENROLLMENT		
							Year	County	No.
IW630	1 Johnson, William	44	First Named	41	M	IW	1896	Bok Tuklo	14693
1895	2 " Sophy	31	Wife	28	F	Full	1896	" "	6906
1896	3 " Dan	14	Son	11	M	1/2	1896	" "	6907
1897	4 " Richard	12	"	9	"	1/2	1896	" "	6908
1898	5 " Henry	11	"	8	"	1/2	1896	" "	6909
1899	6 " James	5	"	1	"	1/2			
1900	7 ~~Mattie~~ DIED PRIOR TO SEPTEMBER 25, 1902		~~Dau~~	~~3mo~~	~~F~~	~~1/2~~			
1901	8 " Laura May	1	Dau	2m	F	1/2			

9
10 ENROLLMENT OF NOS. 2,3,4,5,6,7,and 8 HEREON
11 APPROVED BY THE SECRETARY OF INTERIOR Dec 12, 1902

12
13 ENROLLMENT OF NOS. HEREON
14 APPROVED BY THE SECRETARY OF INTERIOR Mar 26, 1904
15

16

17

TRIBAL ENROLLMENT OF PARENTS

	Name of Father	Year	County	Name of Mother	Year	County
1	Daniel Johnson	1896	Non Citz		Dead	Non Citz
2	William Anderson	Dead	Bok Tuklo	Me-har-dy	"	Bok Tuklo
3	No 1			No 2		
4	No 1			No 2		
5	No 1			No 2		
6	No 1			No 2		
7	No 1			No 2		
8	No 1			No 2		

9
10   No3 on 1896 roll as Ben Johnson
11   For child of Nos 1&2 see N.B.(March 3,1905) #1040
12   License exhibited, was duly issued by Ben Watkins Clerk 2nd Judicial District, Choctaw Nation to William Johnson to marry Sophia
13   Anderson on the 14th day of April 1887 with certificate of marriage on
14   back. Instrument in many pieces so it cannot be filed
15 No7 died July 23 1900, proof of death filed Dec.6,1902.
    ~~No7 Enrolled June 23d 1900~~
16   No8 Born May 6.1901:Enrolled July 22nd 1902
17 No7 died July23,21900:Enrollment cancelled by Department July 8, 1904

#1 to 6 inc
Date of Application for Enrollment.
April 24/99

Choctaw By Blood Enrollment Cards 1898-1914

RESIDENCE: Red River   COUNTY.   **Choctaw Nation**   Choctaw Roll   CARD NO.

POST OFFICE: Harris, I.T.   *(Not Including Freedmen)*   FIELD NO. **762**

Dawes' Roll No.		NAME		Relationship to Person First Named	AGE	SEX	BLOOD	TRIBAL ENROLLMENT		
								Year	County	No.
I.W. 506	1	White, John R	44	First Named	40	M	I.W.	1896	Red River	15180
1902	2	" Lena	26	Wife	23	F	3/8	1896	" "	13690
1903	3	" Julius	10	Son	7	M	3/16	1896	" "	13691
1904	4	" May	7	Dau	4	F	3/16	1896	" "	13692
1905	5	" Ola	5	"	2	"	3/16			
1906	6	" Tuck S.	3	Son	6wk	M	3/16			
	7									
	8									
	9									
	10									
	11									
	12									
	13									
	14									
	15									
	16									
	17									

ENROLLMENT
OF NOS. 2,3,4,5 and 6 HEREON
APPROVED BY THE SECRETARY
OF INTERIOR Dec. 12, 1902

ENROLLMENT
OF NOS. ~1~ HEREON
APPROVED BY THE SECRETARY
OF INTERIOR Dec. 24, 1903

No 1 on 1896 roll as Johnny White

Name appears in marriage license as John White

TRIBAL ENROLLMENT OF PARENTS

	Name of Father	Year	County	Name of Mother	Year	County
1	William S White	Dead	Non Citz	Frances M. White	1896	Non Citz
2	Tucker Simpson	"	" "	Jincy Simpson	Dead	Red River
3	No 1			No 2		
4	No 1			No 2		
5	No 1			No 2		
6	No 1			No 2		
7						
8						
9						
10			No5 Affidavit of birth to be supplied Recd May 6/99			
11						
12			Tuck S White born Dec 3/99. On Card No D – 555			
13			No6 born December 3, 1899: transferred to this card May 24, 1902			
14			For child of Nov 1&2 see N.B. (March 3, 1905) #898			
15						
16	P.O. Idabel IT 4/11/05				Date of Application for Enrollment	April 24/99
17	P.O. Norwood I.T. 11/26/02					

162

Choctaw By Blood Enrollment Cards 1898-1914

RESIDENCE: Red River		COUNTY.	**Choctaw Nation**			**Choctaw Roll** (Not Including Freedmen)	CARD No.	
POST OFFICE: Harris, I.T.							FIELD No.	**763**

Dawes' Roll No.	NAME	Relationship to Person First Named	AGE	SEX	BLOOD	TRIBAL ENROLLMENT		
						Year	County	No.
Dead	1 ~~Harris, H. C.~~		~~62~~	~~M~~	~~1/8~~	~~1896~~	~~Red River~~	~~5701~~
I.W. 631	2 " Maggie E. 63	Wife	58	F	IW	1896	" "	14628
1907	3 Brady, Clarence 18	Ward	15	M	1/4	1893	" "	P.R. 71
1908	4 " Arthur 15	"	12	"	1/4	1893	" "	70
	5							
	6	ENROLLMENT						
	7	~~OF NOS. 3 and 4 HEREON~~ APPROVED BY THE SECRETARY						
	8	OF INTERIOR Dec 12, 1902						
	9	ENROLLMENT						
	10	OF NOS. 2 HEREON APPROVED BY THE SECRETARY						
	11	OF INTERIOR Mar 26, 1904						
	12							
	13							
	14	~~No. 1 Hereon dismissed under order~~						
	15	of the Commission to the Five Civilized						
	16	Tribes of March 31, 1905.						
	17							

TRIBAL ENROLLMENT OF PARENTS						
Name of Father	Year	County	Name of Mother	Year	County	
1 ~~William R. Harris~~	~~Dead~~	~~Non Citz~~	~~Eliza Harris~~	~~Dead~~	~~Eagle~~	
2 William Lee	"	" "	Nancy Lee	"	Non Citz	
3 Brady	"	" "	Josephine Brady	"	Sans Bois	
4 "	"	" "	"	"	" "	
5						
6						
7						
8	Evidence of marriage filed with Dawes Commission in 1897					
9	Married in 1862 in Senter County, Ark. under laws of that					
10	State. No1 is now Associate Justice of Supreme Court ~~Choctaw Nation.~~					
11	#2 Admitted by Dawes Com in '96 Case # 1413, as Margaret E Harris					
12	No3 on 1893 Pay roll as Clarence Brady					
13	No3 also on 1896 roll, Red River Co, Page 117, No 4804 as Clarence Grady No4 " " 1896 " " " " 117, " 4805 " Arthur "					
14	No.1 Died October 26, 1899 Evidence of death filed March 22, 1901				April 24/99	
15						
16					Nos 3 + 4 Apr 28/99	
17	Nos 3&4 P.O. McAlester, I.T.				~~Date of Application~~ for Enrollment.	

163

Choctaw By Blood Enrollment Cards 1898-1914

RESIDENCE: Red River   COUNTY.   **Choctaw Nation**   **Choctaw Roll**   CARD NO.
POST OFFICE: Harris, I.T.   *(Not Including Freedmen)*   FIELD NO. **764**

Dawes' Roll No.	NAME	Relationship to Person	AGE	SEX	BLOOD	TRIBAL ENROLLMENT		
						Year	County	No.
1909	1 Victor, Charlie ³³	First Named	30	M	1/2	1896	Atoka	12637
	2							
	3	ENROLLMENT						
	4	OF NOS. 1 HEREON APPROVED BY THE SECRETARY						
	5	OF INTERIOR Dec. 12, 1902						
	6							
	7							
	8							
	9							
	10	No1 is in Penitentiary at Huntsville, Texas						
	11							
	12							
	13							
	14							
	15							
	16							
	17							

TRIBAL ENROLLMENT OF PARENTS

Name of Father	Year	County	Name of Mother	Year	County
1 Robert Victor	Dead	Red River	Siney Victor	Dead	Red River
2					
3					
4					
5					
6					
7					
8					
9					
10					
11					
12					
13					
14					
15					
16			Date of Application for Enrollment April 24/99		
17 P.O. Davis, I.T. 1/9/03					

164

Choctaw By Blood Enrollment Cards 1898-1914

RESIDENCE: Red River   COUNTY.   **Choctaw Nation**   **Choctaw Roll**   CARD NO.
POST OFFICE: Harris, I.T.   *(Not Including Freedmen)*   FIELD NO. 765

Dawes' Roll No.	NAME	Relationship to Person	AGE	SEX	BLOOD	TRIBAL ENROLLMENT		
						Year	County	No.
1910	1 Hampton, Carrie	First Named	58	F	1/8	1896	Red River	5699
	2							
	3	ENROLLMENT						
	4	OF NOS. 1 HEREON APPROVED BY THE SECRETARY						
	5	OF INTERIOR DEC 12 1902						
	6							
	7							
	8							
	9							
	10	On 1896 roll as Carrie F Hampton						
	11							
	12							
	13							
	14							
	15							
	16							
	17							

TRIBAL ENROLLMENT OF PARENTS

	Name of Father	Year	County	Name of Mother	Year	County
1	W. R. Harris	Dead	Non Citz	Eliza Harris	Dead	Eagle
2						
3						
4						
5						
6						
7						
8						
9						
10						
11						
12						
13						
14						
15						
16				Date of Application for Enrollment		April 24/99
17						

165

Choctaw By Blood Enrollment Cards 1898-1914

RESIDENCE: Red River	COUNTY.								
POST OFFICE: Harris, I.T.		**Choctaw Nation**				Choctaw Roll *(Not Including Freedmen)*	CARD No. FIELD No. 766		

Dawes' Roll No.	NAME	Relationship to Person	AGE	SEX	BLOOD	TRIBAL ENROLLMENT		
						Year	County	No.
1911	1 Houston, Emma	First Named	21	F	Full	1896	Red River	5704
	2							
	3							
	4	ENROLLMENT OF NOS. 1 HEREON						
	5	APPROVED BY THE SECRETARY						
	6	OF INTERIOR DEC 12 1902						
	7							
	8							
	9							
	10							
	11	Name of parents to be supplied by H.C. Harris						
	12							
	13							
	14							
	15							
	16							
	17							

TRIBAL ENROLLMENT OF PARENTS

	Name of Father	Year	County	Name of Mother	Year	County
1	John Houston	Dead	Sugar Loaf	Martha Houston	Dead	Sugar Loaf
2						
3						
4						
5						
6						
7						
8						
9						
10						
11						
12						
13						
14				Date of Application for Enrollment.		
15				April 24/99		
16						
17						

166

Choctaw By Blood Enrollment Cards 1898-1914

RESIDENCE: Eagle COUNTY. **Choctaw Nation** **Choctaw Roll** CARD No.
POST OFFICE: Eagletown, I.T. *(Not Including Freedmen)* FIELD No. 767

Dawes' Roll No.	NAME	Relationship to Person	AGE	SEX	BLOOD	TRIBAL ENROLLMENT		
						Year	County	No.
1912	1 Frazier, Dwight 22	First Named	19	M	Full	1893	Eagle	P.R. 558
	2							
	3	ENROLLMENT OF NOS. 1 HEREON						
	4	APPROVED BY THE SECRETARY						
	5	OF INTERIOR DEC 12 1902						
	6							
	7							
	8							
	9							
	10							
	11	Also on 1896 roll as Dwight Fobb,						
	12	Page 102, No 4196, Eagle Co.						
	13							
	14							
	15							
	16							
	17							

TRIBAL ENROLLMENT OF PARENTS

	Name of Father	Year	County	Name of Mother	Year	County
1	Loman Frazier	Dead	Nashoba	Putchie Frazier	Dead	Nashoba
2						
3						
4						
5						
6						
7						
8						
9						
10						
11						
12						
13						
14						
15						
16				Date of Application for Enrollment	April 24/99	
17						

167

Choctaw By Blood Enrollment Cards 1898-1914

RESIDENCE: Towson   COUNTY. **Choctaw Nation**   **Choctaw Roll**   CARD No.
POST OFFICE: Alikchi, I.T.   *(Not Including Freedmen)*   FIELD No. 768

Dawes' Roll No.	NAME		Relationship to Person	AGE	SEX	BLOOD	TRIBAL ENROLLMENT		
							Year	County	No.
1913	1 Payne, Nebus	32	First Named	29	M	Full	1896	Towson	10346
	2								
	3	ENROLLMENT							
	4	OF NOS. 1 HEREON APPROVED BY THE SECRETARY							
	5	OF INTERIOR DEC 12 1902							
	6								
	7								
	8								
	9								
	10								
	11								
	12								
	13								
	14								
	15								
	16								
	17								

TRIBAL ENROLLMENT OF PARENTS

	Name of Father	Year	County	Name of Mother	Year	County
1	Morris Payne	Dead	Towson	Boh-li-ho-na	Dead	Nashoba
2						
3						
4						
5						
6						
7						
8						
9						
10						
11						
12						
13						
14						
15						
16						Date of Application for Enrollment April 24/99
17						

Choctaw By Blood Enrollment Cards 1898-1914

RESIDENCE: Nachoba[sic]
POST OFFICE: Smithville, I.T.

COUNTY. **Choctaw Nation**

Choctaw Roll *(Not Including Freedmen)*

CARD NO.
FIELD NO. **769**

Dawes' Roll No.	NAME		Relationship to Person Named	AGE	SEX	BLOOD	TRIBAL ENROLLMENT		
							Year	County	No.
1914	₁ Wilson, Raymond	33	First Named	30	M	Full	1896	Nashoba	13240
IW1287	₂ " Matilda	30	Wife	26	F	I.W.	1896	"	15173
1915	₃ " Evadne	6	Dau	2	"	1/2			
1916	₄ " Dukes	4	Son	6mo	M	1/2			
1917	₅ " Ethelind	1	Dau	5mo	F	1/2			
	6								
	7	ENROLLMENT							
	8	OF NOS. 1, 3, 4, and 5 HEREON APPROVED BY THE SECRETARY							
	9	OF INTERIOR Dec. 12, 1902							
	10								
	11	ENROLLMENT							
	12	OF NOS. 2 HEREON APPROVED BY THE SECRETARY							
	13	OF INTERIOR Mar 14, 1905							
	14								
	15								
	16								
	17								

TRIBAL ENROLLMENT OF PARENTS

	Name of Father	Year	County	Name of Mother	Year	County
₁	Aleck Wilson	1896	Nashoba	Liza Wilson	1896	Nashoba
₂	Willie Smith	1896	Non Citz	Martha Smith	1896	Non Citz
₃	No 1			No 2		
₄	No 1			No 2		
₅	No 1			No 2		
₆						
₇	For child of Nos 1&2 see N.B. (Apr 26-06) Card #701					
₈						
₉	Affidavits as to birth of Nos 3 and 4 to be supplied. Recd May 1/99					
₁₀	No.5 Enrolled Aug 3, 1901					
₁₁	Evidence of marriage between Nos 1 and 2 filed Mar 18 ,04 Intermarried status taken of No 2					
₁₂						
₁₃						
₁₄						
₁₅						
₁₆			Date of Application for Enrollment	April 24/99		
₁₇	P.O. seems now to be Octavia, I.T.					

Choctaw By Blood Enrollment Cards 1898-1914

RESIDENCE: Nashoba   COUNTY.   **Choctaw Nation**   Choctaw Roll   CARD NO.
POST OFFICE: Smithville, I.T.   *(Not Including Freedmen)*   FIELD NO.   770

Dawes' Roll No.	NAME		Relationship to Person	AGE	SEX	BLOOD	TRIBAL ENROLLMENT		
							Year	County	No.
1918	1 Wilson, Alexander	73	First Named	70	M	Full	1896	Nashoba	13226
1919	2 " Liza	74	Wife	71	F	"	1896	"	13227
1920	~~3 DIED PRIOR TO SEPTEMBER 25, 1902 Silaney~~		Dau	16	"	"	1896	"	13230
	4								
	5	ENROLLMENT							
	6	OF NOS. 1, 2, and 3 HEREON APPROVED BY THE SECRETARY							
	7	OF INTERIOR DEC 12 1902							
	8								
	9								
	10								
	11								
	12								
	13								
	14								
	15								
	16								
	17								

TRIBAL ENROLLMENT OF PARENTS

	Name of Father	Year	County	Name of Mother	Year	County
1	Pe-sa-chubby	Dead	Eagle	Li-se-ma	Dead	Eagle
2		Died	in Mississippi		"	"
3	~~No 1~~			~~No 2~~		
4						
5						
6		Names of parents of No2 could not be ascertained				
7		No.3 Died June 12" 1902: Proof of Death filed December 20" 1902				
8		No.3 died June 12 1902: Enrollment cancelled by Department July 8, 1904				
9						
10						
11						
12						
13						
14						
15						
16					Date of Application for Enrollment	April 24/99
17						

Choctaw By Blood Enrollment Cards 1898-1914

RESIDENCE: Eagle   COUNTY.   **Choctaw Nation**   **Choctaw Roll**   CARD NO.
POST OFFICE: Eagletown, I.T.   *(Not Including Freedmen)*   FIELD NO.   771

Dawes' Roll No.	NAME	Relationship to Person Named	AGE	SEX	BLOOD	TRIBAL ENROLLMENT Year	County	No.
1921	1 Loma, Thomas 35	First Named	32	M	Full	1896	Eagle	801
1922	2 " Annie 33	Wife	30	F	"	1893	Bok Tuklo	3
1923	3 Nakintaya, Reuben 11	S.Son	8	M	"	1896	Eagle	9728
1924	4 " Pisona 7	S.Dau	4	F	"	1896	"	9727
14590	5 Loma, James 1	Son	2mo	M	"			
	6							
	7	ENROLLMENT OF NOS. 1 2 3 and 4 HEREON						
	8	APPROVED BY THE SECRETARY						
	9	OF INTERIOR DEC 12 1902						
	10							
	11	ENROLLMENT						
	12	OF NOS. 5 HEREON APPROVED BY THE SECRETARY						
	13	OF INTERIOR MAY 20 1903						
	14							
	15							
	16							
	17							

TRIBAL ENROLLMENT OF PARENTS

	Name of Father	Year	County	Name of Mother	Year	County
1	Loma		Eagle	O na to ma	Dead	Eagle
2		Dead	Bok Tuklo	Sho-na	"	Bok Tuklo
3	Davis Nakintaya	"	Eagle	No2		
4	" "	"	"	No2		
5	Nº1			Nº2		
6						
7			No2 on 1893 Pay Roll as Annie			
8			Davis. Was then wife of Davis			
9			Nakintaya			
10			No.4 on 1896 Roll as Pisaona Nakintaya.			
			Nº5 Born Aug. 24, 1902, enrolled Oct. 20, 1902.			
11						
12						
13						
14						
15					#1 to 4	
16				Date of Application for Enrollment April 24/99		
17						

Choctaw By Blood Enrollment Cards 1898-1914

RESIDENCE: Eagle   COUNTY.   **Choctaw Nation**   **Choctaw Roll** *(Not Including Freedmen)*   CARD NO.
POST OFFICE: Lukfata, I.T.   FIELD NO. 772

Dawes' Roll No.	NAME	Relationship to Person	AGE	SEX	BLOOD	TRIBAL ENROLLMENT Year	County	No.
1925	1 Lo-ma 73	First Named	70	M	Full	1896	Eagle	8018
	2							
	3	ENROLLMENT						
	4	OF NOS. 1 HEREON APPROVED BY THE SECRETARY						
	5	OF INTERIOR DEC 12 1902						
	6							
	7							
	8							
	9							
	10							
	11							
	12							
	13							
	14							
	15							
	16							
	17							

TRIBAL ENROLLMENT OF PARENTS

Name of Father	Year	County	Name of Mother	Year	County
1 Lu-se-te-by	Dead	Eagle	Sho-na	Dead	Eagle
2					
3					
4					
5					
6					
7					
8					
9					
10					
11					
12					
13					
14					
15			DATE OF APPLICATION FOR ENROLLMENT.	April 24/99	
16					
17					

172

Choctaw By Blood Enrollment Cards 1898-1914

RESIDENCE: Red River COUNTY.
POST OFFICE: Janis, I.T.

Choctaw Nation

Choctaw Roll
(Not Including Freedmen)

CARD NO.
FIELD NO. 773

Dawes' Roll No.		NAME	Relationship to Person Named	AGE	SEX	BLOOD	TRIBAL ENROLLMENT		
							Year	County	No.
1926	1	Lawechobe, Hopewell T	First Named	33	M	Full	1896	Red River	8040
dead	2	" Sophy DEAD.	Wife	28	F	"	1896	" "	8041
1927	3	" Abner	Son	7	M	"	1896	" "	8041
1928	4	" Gertrude	Dau	4	F	"	1896	" "	8043
Dead	5	" Ida DEAD.	"	1	"	"			
	6								
	7	ENROLLMENT							
	8	OF NOS. 13 and 4 HEREON APPROVED BY THE SECRETARY							
	9	OF INTERIOR DEC 12 1902							
	10								
	11	No. 2 and 5 HEREON DISMISSED UNDER ORDER OF THE COMMISSION TO THE FIVE							
	12	CIVILIZED TRIBES OF MARCH 31, 1905.							
	13								
	14								
	15								
	16								
	17								

TRIBAL ENROLLMENT OF PARENTS

	Name of Father	Year	County	Name of Mother	Year	County
1	Thos Lawechobe	Dead	Red River	Yoh-kee	Dead	Red River
2	Thos Jefferson	"	" " "	Mary Jefferson	"	" " "
3	No 1			No 2		
4	No 1			No 2		
5	No 1			No 2		
6						
7	No 1 on 1896 roll as H.T. Lawechobe					
8	No.1 is no the Husband of Tennessee Jefferson on Choctaw Card No. 774					
9	No2 died June 21, 1899; proof of death filed Dec 3, 1902					
10	No5 " July 8, 1899; " " " " Dec 3, 1902					
	For child of No.1 see NB (March 3, 1905) #1401.					
11						
12						
13						
14						
15						
16			Date of Application for Enrollment.	April 24/99		
17						

173

Choctaw By Blood Enrollment Cards 1898-1914

RESIDENCE: Red River   COUNTY.   **Choctaw Nation**   Choctaw Roll   CARD No.
POST OFFICE: Janis, I.T.   *(Not Including Freedmen)*   FIELD No. **774**

Dawes' Roll No.	NAME	Relationship to Person	AGE	SEX	BLOOD	TRIBAL ENROLLMENT		
						Year	County	No.
1929	1 Jefferson, Mary [DIED PRIOR TO SEPTEMBER 25, 1902]	First Named	60	F	Full	1896	Red River	7030
1930	2 " Tennessee 27	Dau	24	"	"	1896	" "	7031
	3							
	4							
	5	ENROLLMENT OF NOS. 1 and 2 HEREON						
	6	APPROVED BY THE SECRETARY OF INTERIOR Dec 12 1902						
	7							
	8							
	9							
	10							
	11							
	12							
	13							
	14							
	15							
	16							
	17							

TRIBAL ENROLLMENT OF PARENTS

	Name of Father	Year	County	Name of Mother	Year	County
1	La-po-ta-bee	Dead	Eagle	E-oh-to-na	Dead	Eagle
2	Thos Jefferson	"	Red River	No 1		
3						
4						
5	No1 died May 5, 1902; proof of death filed Dec. 3, 1902					
6	No2 is now the wife of Hopewell T. Lawechobe on Choctaw Card No. 773					
7	Evidence of marriage exhibited dated Aug 13, 1900.					
8	No1 died May 5, 1902: Enrollment cancelled by Department July 8, 1904.					
	For child of No2 see N.B. (March 3, 1905) #1401					
9						
10						
11						
12						
13						
14				Date of Application for Enrollment.		
15						
16				April 24/99		
17	No2 P.O. Goodwater I.T. 4/10/05					

174

Choctaw By Blood Enrollment Cards 1898-1914

RESIDENCE: Eagle   COUNTY.   **Choctaw Nation**   **Choctaw Roll**   CARD No.
POST OFFICE: Eagletown, I.T.   (Not Including Freedmen)   FIELD No. **775**

Dawes' Roll No.	NAME		Relationship to Person Named	AGE	SEX	BLOOD	TRIBAL ENROLLMENT		
							Year	County	No.
1931	1 Johnson, Lonis	37	First Named	34	M	Full	1896	Eagle	6970
1932	2 " Lila	26	Wife	23	F	"	1896	"	6971
1933	3 " Irene	8	Dau	5	"	"	1896	"	6972
1934	4 " Bobb	5	Son	1	M	"			
~~1935~~	~~5 Brown, J. L.~~	2	~~Dau No2~~	~~4mo~~	~~F~~	~~1/2~~	~~Illegitimate~~		
14591	6 Johnson, Sylvester	3	Son	3	M	Full			
	7								
	8	ENROLLMENT							
	9	OF NOS. 1 2 3 4 and 5 HEREON APPROVED BY THE SECRETARY							
	10	OF INTERIOR Dec 12, 1902							
	11								
	12	ENROLLMENT							
	13	OF NOS. 6 HEREON APPROVED BY THE SECRETARY							
	14	OF INTERIOR May 20 1903							
	15								
	16								
	17								

TRIBAL ENROLLMENT OF PARENTS

	Name of Father	Year	County	Name of Mother	Year	County
1	Samuel Johnson	Dead	Eagle	Suwillie Johnson	1896	Red River
2	Joseph Bobb	1896	"	Beckie Bobb	Dead	Eagle
3	No 1			No 2		
4	No 1			No 2		
5	~~Johnny Brown~~			~~No 2~~		
6	No 1			No 2		
7						
8						
9	No2 on 1896 roll as Lylie Johnson					
10	No3 " 1896 " Greeney "					
11	No6 Born June 14, 1899, enrolled Nov. 11, 1902					
12	~~No5 is duplicate of Johnnie Lee Brown, Choctaw Freedman Card No185 Approved roll of Choctaw Freedmen No92 Enrollment of No5 cancelled by Secretary of Interior Aug 23-1904. See Departmental~~					
13	letter of that date (I.T.D. 6672-1904) D.C. № 30905-1904 No.5. Enrolled May 2, 1900.					
14	For child of Nos. 1&2 see N.B. (March 3, 1905) #1417					#1 to 4
15						Date of Application for Enrollment.
16						April 24/99
17	P.O. Hochatown, Okla 2/11/09					

175

Choctaw By Blood Enrollment Cards 1898-1914

RESIDENCE: Eagle COUNTY.
POST OFFICE: Eagletown, I.T.

Choctaw Nation

Choctaw Roll *(Not Including Freedmen)*

CARD NO.
FIELD NO. **776**

Dawes' Roll No.		NAME		Relationship to Person First Named	AGE	SEX	BLOOD	TRIBAL ENROLLMENT		
								Year	County	No.
1936	1	Wall, James	DIED PRIOR TO SEPTEMBER 25, 1902		66	M	Full	1896	Eagle	13452
1937	2	" Lina	48	wife	45	F	"	1896	"	13457
1938	3	" Joe	23	son	20	M	"	1896	"	13454
1939	4	" Morris	DIED PRIOR TO SEPTEMBER 25, 1902	"	5	"	"	1896	"	13460
	5									
	6									
	7	ENROLLMENT								
	8	OF NOS. 1,2,3 and 4 HEREON APPROVED BY THE SECRETARY OF INTERIODec 12 1902R								
	9									
	10									
	11							No		
	12									
	13									
	14									
	15									
	16									
	17									

TRIBAL ENROLLMENT OF PARENTS

	Name of Father	Year	County	Name of Mother	Year	County
1	Nuk-a-sti-ya	Dead	in Mississippi	Ta-hoh-ke	Dead	Eagle
2	Jackson Chubby	"	Eagle	E-chap-e-hona	"	"
3	No 1			No 2		
4	No 1			No 2		
5						
6	No2 on 1896 roll as Linny Wall					
7	No3 is now the husband of Nicey Sampson on Choctaw card #1057 Sept24/1902					
8	No1 died March 1, 1901, proof of death filed Dec. 15, 1902					
	No4 " June 21, 1899, " " " " Dec. 15, 1902					
9	No1 died March1,1901. No4 died June 21,1899; Enrollment cancelled by Department July8,1904					
10						
11						
12						
13						
14						
15						
16				Date of Application for Enrollment	April 24/99	
17						

RESIDENCE: Eagle   COUNTY.   **Choctaw Nation**   Choctaw Roll   CARD NO.
POST OFFICE: Eagletown, I.T.   *(Not Including Freedmen)*   FIELD NO.   **777**

Dawes' Roll No.		NAME		Relationship to Person	AGE	SEX	BLOOD	TRIBAL ENROLLMENT		
								Year	County	No.
1940	1	Bohanan, Benjamin	34	First Named	31	M	Full	1896	Eagle	1263
1941	2	" Timesy	29	Wife	26	F	"	1896	"	1337
1942	3	" Maley	14	Dau	11	"	"	1896	"	1300
1943	4	" Sillis	10	"	7	"	"	1896	"	1314
1944	5	" Lucy	7	"	4	"	"	1896	"	1291
1945	6	" Elizabeth	6	"	2	"	"			
1946	7	" Williston	1	Son	5mo	M	"			
15825	8	" Sissie	7	Dau	4	F	"			
	9									
	10	ENROLLMENT OF NOS. 1, 2, 3, 4, 5 6 and 7 HEREON APPROVED BY THE SECRETARY OF INTERIOR Dec. 12, 1902								
	11									
	12									
	13									
	14	ENROLLMENT OF NOS. ~~~ 8 ~~~ HEREON APPROVED BY THE SECRETARY OF INTERIOR Jun 12 1905								
	15									
	16									
	17									

TRIBAL ENROLLMENT OF PARENTS

	Name of Father	Year	County	Name of Mother	Year	County
1	Julius Bohanan	Dead	Nashoba	Sophie Bohanan	Dead	Eagle
2	James Wall	1896	Eagle	Lina Wall	1896	"
3	No 1			No 2		
4	No 1			No 2		
5	No 1			No 2		
6	No 1			No 2		
7	No 1			No 2		
8	No 1			No 2		
9	No2 on 1896 roll as Tennessee Bohanan					
10	No3 " 1896 " " Meley "					
11	No4 " 1896 " " Silis "					
	No7 Born Feb. 18th 1902: Enrolled July 16th 1902.					
12	No8 born June 6, 1898: Application received and No8 placed on					
13	this card April 17, 1905 under Act of Congress approved Mar 3, 1905					
14	For child of No2 see N.B. (March 3, 1905) #931			Date of Application for Enrollment.		#1 to 6
15				April 24/99		
16						
17						

Choctaw By Blood Enrollment Cards 1898-1914

POST OFFICE: Doaksville, I.T.   *(Not Including Freedmen)*   FIELD No. **778**

Dawes' Roll No.	NAME	Relationship to Person First Named	AGE	SEX	BLOOD	TRIBAL ENROLLMENT Year	County	No.
1947	1 Tims, Emiline ⁶⁰	Named	57	F	1/4	1896	Towson	12116
1948	2 " Johnny ²⁹	Son	26	M	5/8	1896	Cedar	12081
VOID	3 " Rosanna	Dau	18	F	5/8	1896	Towson	12119
1949	4 " Calvin ¹⁷	Son	14	M	5/8	1896	"	12120
	5							
	6							
	7							
	8	ENROLLMENT						
	9	OF NOS. 12 and 4 HEREON APPROVED BY THE SECRETARY						
	10	OF INTERIOR Dec 12, 1902						
	11							
	12							
	13							
	14							
	15							
	16							
	17							

TRIBAL ENROLLMENT OF PARENTS

	Name of Father	Year	County	Name of Mother	Year	County
1	John Steadman	Dead	Non Citz	O-we-na	Dead	Towson
2	Benson Tims	"	Towson	No 1		
3	" "	"	"	No 1		
4	" "	"	"	No 1		
5						
6	No3 on 1896 roll as Rosa Tims					
7	No3 transferred to Choctaw Card #1281 with her husband, James Wilson					
8	No1 on 1896 Roll as Emeline Tims Oct 26, 1900					
9						
10						
11						
12						
13						
14						
15						
16				Date of Application for Enrollment April 24/99		
17						

178

Choctaw By Blood Enrollment Cards 1898-1914

RESIDENCE: Cedar COUNTY.
POST OFFICE: Doaksville, I.T.

Choctaw Nation

Choctaw Roll (Not Including Freedmen)

CARD NO.
FIELD NO. 779

Dawes' Roll No.		NAME		Relationship to Person First Named	AGE	SEX	BLOOD	TRIBAL ENROLLMENT		
								Year	County	No.
1950	1	DIED PRIOR TO SEPTEMBER 25, 1902 Wesley, Campbell			36	M	Full	1896	Cedar	13146
1951	2	" Eliza	33	Wife	30		"	1896	"	13147
1952	3	" Eben	12	Son	9		"	1896	"	13148
	4									
	5	ENROLLMENT								
	6	OF NOS. 1 2 and 3 HEREON								
	7	APPROVED BY THE SECRETARY OF INTERIOR DEC 12 1902								
	8									
	9									
	10									
	11									
	12									
	13									
	14									
	15									
	16									
	17									

TRIBAL ENROLLMENT OF PARENTS

	Name of Father	Year	County	Name of Mother	Year	County
1	Moses Wesley	Dead	Cedar	Kan-ohl-hu-na	Dead	Cedar
2	Wallen Lewis	"	"	Silmee Lewis	"	"
3	No 1			No 2		
4						
5						
6						
7			No3 on 1896 roll as Elum Wesley			
8			No1 died Aug 11, 1902: proof of death file Dec 30, 1902			
9			No1 died Aug 11, 1902: Enrollment cancelled -------- July 8, 1904			
10						
11						
12						
13						
14						
15						
16				Date of Application for Enrollment April 24/99		
17						

Choctaw By Blood Enrollment Cards 1898-1914

RESIDENCE: Nashoba COUNTY. **Choctaw Nation** Choctaw Roll *(Not Including Freedmen)* CARD NO.
POST OFFICE: Alikchi, I.T. FIELD NO. 780

Dawes' Roll No.	NAME	Relationship to Person	AGE	SEX	BLOOD	TRIBAL ENROLLMENT		
						Year	County	No.
1953	1 Noah, Brazil ³³	First Named	30	M	Full	1896	Nashoba	9699
	2							
	3	ENROLLMENT						
	4	OF NOS. 1 HEREON APPROVED BY THE SECRETARY						
	5	OF INTERIOR DEC 12 1902						
	6							
	7							
	8							
	9							
	10							
	11							
	12							
	13							
	14							
	15							
	16							
	17							

TRIBAL ENROLLMENT OF PARENTS

	Name of Father	Year	County	Name of Mother	Year	County
1	Hah-ne-by	Dead	Wade	Hannah	Dead	Nashoba
2						
3						
4						
5						
6						
7						
8						
9						
10						
11						
12						
13						
14						
15						
16			Date of Application for Enrollment April 24/99			
17						

RESIDENCE: Nashoba   COUNTY.
POST OFFICE: Smithville, I.T.

Choctaw Nation

Choctaw Roll *(Not Including Freedmen)*

CARD NO. FIELD NO. **781**

Dawes' Roll No.	NAME	Relationship to Person First Named	AGE	SEX	BLOOD	TRIBAL ENROLLMENT Year	County	No.
1954	1 Loman, Greek L. 51		48	M	Full	1896	Nashoba	7961
1955	2 " Emiline 52	Wife	49	F	"	1896	"	7962
1956	3 " Malsie 11	Dau	8	"	"	1896	"	7963
1957	4 " Roxie 7	"	4	"	"	1896	"	7964
5								
6	ENROLLMENT OF NOS. 1,2,3 and 4 HEREON APPROVED BY THE SECRETARY OF INTERIOR Dec. 12, 1902							
7								
8								
9								
10								
11								
12								
13								
14								
15								
16								
17								

TRIBAL ENROLLMENT OF PARENTS

	Name of Father	Year	County	Name of Mother	Year	County
1	Ok-chubbee	Dead	Nashoba	Sophie	Dead	Nashoba
2	Eli Hickubbee	"	"	Anna Hickubbee	"	"
3	No 1			No 2		
4	No 1			No 2		
5						
6						
7	No1 on 1896 roll as Greek L. Lowman					
8	No3 " 1896 " " Malsie "					
9	No4 " 1896 " " Roxie					
10	No2 " 1896 " " Emiline Loman					
11						
12						
13						
14						
15						
16				Date of Application for Enrollment	April 24/99	
17						

Choctaw By Blood Enrollment Cards 1898-1914

RESIDENCE: Nashoba   COUNTY.   **Choctaw Nation**   Choctaw Roll   CARD NO.
POST OFFICE: Smithville, I.T.   *(Not Including Freedmen)*   FIELD NO. **782**

Dawes' Roll No.	NAME		Relationship to Person First Named	AGE	SEX	BLOOD	TRIBAL ENROLLMENT		
							Year	County	No.
1958	1 Cusher, Ellis	57	First Named	54	M	Full	1896	Nashoba	2479
14592	2 " Elias	16	Son	13	"	1/2	1896	"	2480
14593	3 " Simeon	14	"	11	"	1/2	1896	"	2481
14594	4 " Peter	12	"	9	"	1/2	1896	"	2482
14595	5 " Mary	8	Dau	5	F	1/2	1896	"	2484
14596	6 " Harrison	10	Son	7	M	1/2	1896	"	2483
~~Dead~~	7 ~~" Lola~~		~~Dau~~	~~2~~	~~F~~	~~1/2~~			
IW1554	8 Cusher, Martha		Wife	52	F	I.W.			
	9								
	10 ENROLLMENT OF NOS. 1 HEREON APPROVED BY THE SECRETARY								
	11 OF INTERIOR Dec 12, 1902								
	12 ENROLLMENT								
	13 OF NOS. 2,3,4,5 and 6 HEREON APPROVED BY THE SECRETARY								
	14 OF INTERIOR May 20, 1903								
	15 No 7								
	16 Dismissed Jan 23, 1906		No 1 Married by A.R. Durant, Minister His affidavit to be supplied.						
	17								

TRIBAL ENROLLMENT OF PARENTS

	Name of Father	Year	County	Name of Mother	Year	County
1	Kash-sha	Died	in Mississippi	Yus-ba-no-lie	Died	in Mississippi
2	No 1			Martha Cushee[sic]	1896	Non Citz
3	No 1			" "	1896	" "
4	No 1			" "	1896	" "
5	No 1			" "	1896	" "
6	No 1			" "	1896	" "
7	~~No 1~~			~~" "~~	~~1896~~	~~" "~~
8	William Labor		Mexican	Crecy Labor		Mexican
9						

10	No 8 placed hereon under order of Commissioner to the Five Civilized Tribes of April 23, 1906 holding ~~application was made for her enrollment within time provided by act of July 1 1902 (32 Stat 641)~~
11	Wife of No 1 and mother of children hereon on 1896 Choctaw Roll No 14405
12	Nos 1,2,3,4&6 on Nashoba County 1893 pay roll as "Kasho"
13	~~No 8 Granted Jun 13, 1906~~
	~~No 7 proof of death requested 7/3/05~~
14	No 7 Proof of death filed showing death Dec 21,1902 While
15	notation "Dead" was placed on card by Mr. Reuter prior to Feb, 1900.
16	
17	

#1 to 7 inc
~~Date of Application for Enrollment.~~
April 24/99

P.O. Belch I.T. Nov 22/05

Choctaw By Blood Enrollment Cards 1898-1914

RESIDENCE: Nashoba   COUNTY.   **Choctaw Nation**   **Choctaw Roll**   CARD NO.
POST OFFICE: Smithville, I.T.   *(Not Including Freedmen)*   FIELD NO.   **783**

Dawes' Roll No.		NAME		Relationship to Person	AGE	SEX	BLOOD	TRIBAL ENROLLMENT		
								Year	County	No.
1959	1	Taylor, Charles J.	48	First Named	45	M	Full	1896	Nashoba	12137
1960	2	" Sarfin	42	Wife	39	F	"	1896	"	12138
1961	3	" Simpson	15	Son	12	M	"	1896	"	12139
	4									
	5									
	6									
	7									
	8									
	9									
	10									
	11									
	12									
	13									
	14									
	15									
	16									
	17									

ENROLLMENT
OF NOS. 1 2 and 3 HEREON
APPROVED BY THE SECRETARY
OF INTERIOR Dec 12, 1902

No 1 on 1896 roll as Chas. J. Taylor

TRIBAL ENROLLMENT OF PARENTS

	Name of Father	Year	County	Name of Mother	Year	County
1	James Taylor	Ded[sic]	Nashoba	Nancy	1896	Nashoba
2	Ka-na-li-chubbee	"	"	No-wat-i-Ma	Ded	"
3	No 1			No 2		
4						
5						
6						
7						
8						
9						
10						
11						
12						
13						
14						
15						
16						
17						

Date of Application for Enrollment. April 24/99

Choctaw By Blood Enrollment Cards 1898-1914

RESIDENCE: Nashoba COUNTY. **Choctaw Nation** **Choctaw Roll** CARD NO.
POST OFFICE: Smithville, I.T. (Not Including Freedmen) FIELD NO. 784

Dawes' Roll No.	NAME	Relationship to Person First Named	AGE	SEX	BLOOD	TRIBAL ENROLLMENT		
						Year	County	No.
1962	1 Benn, Simon 23		20	M	Full	1896	Nashoba	1112
1963	2 " Lula 20		17	F	"	1896	"	13231
	3							
	4	ENROLLMENT						
	5	OF NOS. 1 and 2 HEREON APPROVED BY THE SECRETARY OF INTERIOR DEC 12 1902						
	6							
	7							
	8							
	9							
	10							
	11	No2 on 1896 roll as Lula Wilson also on 1896						
	12	roll Page 402, No1517, as Laura Wilson						
	13	Nashoba.						
	14							
	15							
	16							
	17							

TRIBAL ENROLLMENT OF PARENTS

	Name of Father	Year	County	Name of Mother	Year	County
1	Davis Benn	Dead	Nashoba	Martha Benn	1896	Nashoba
2	Cal Wilson	1896	"	Sarah Wilson	Dead	Eagle
3						
4						
5						
6						
7						
8						
9						
10						
11						
12						
13						
14						
15						
16						
17						

Date of Application for Enrollment April 24/99

RESIDENCE: Nashoba   COUNTY.

POST OFFICE: Smithville, I.T.

Choctaw Nation

Choctaw Roll
(Not Including Freedmen)

CARD NO.

FIELD NO. **785**

Dawes' Roll No.	NAME		Relationship to Person	AGE	SEX	BLOOD	TRIBAL ENROLLMENT		
							Year	County	No.
1964	1 Watson, Rampsey	44	First Named	41	M	Full	1896	Nashoba	13267
1965	2 " , Amy	42	Wife	39	F	"	1896	"	13268
1966	3 " , Larsen	17	Son	14	M	"	1896	"	13269
1967	4 Lewis, Littie	14	Dau	11	F	"	1896	"	13270
1968	5 Watson, Sally Ann	11	"	8	"	"	1896	"	13271
1969	6 " , Lena	7	"	4	"	"	1896	"	13272
1970	7 " , Clistie	5	"	1	"	"			
1971	8 " , Sophie	2	"	8mo	F	"			
1972	9 Lewis, Wilson	1	Son of No4	6mo	M	"			
	10								
	11	ENROLLMENT OF NOS: 1,2,3,4,5,6,7,8 and 9 HEREON APPROVED BY THE SECRETARY OF INTERIOR Dec 12, 1902							
	12								
	13								
	14								
	15								
	16								
	17								

TRIBAL ENROLLMENT OF PARENTS

	Name of Father	Year	County	Name of Mother	Year	County
1	George Watson	Dead	Nashoba	Nancy Watson	Dead	Nashoba
2	James Wall	1896	Eagle	Pisa-hi-ma	"	Eagle
3	No 1			No 2		
4	No 1			No 2		
5	No 1			No 2		
6	No 1			No 2		
7	No 1			No 2		
8	No 1			No 2		
9	Simon Lewis		Choctaw Card #827	No 4		

10 No5 on 1896 roll as Silly Ann Watson

11 No4 " 1896 " " Littie Jane "

No8 Enrolled June 8th 1901

12 No4 now the wife of Simmon Lewis on Choctaw Card #827 Evidence of marriage filed June

13 No9 Born Decr. 21st 1901; Enrolled June 26th, 1902.   26th, 1902.

14 For child of No4 See N.B.(March 3, 1905) #867.

#1 to 8

Date of Application for Enrollment.

April 24/99

Choctaw By Blood Enrollment Cards 1898-1914

RESIDENCE: Nashoba   COUNTY.   **Choctaw Nation**   Choctaw Roll   CARD NO.
POST OFFICE: Smithville, I.T.   *(Not Including Freedmen)*   FIELD NO. **786**

Dawes' Roll No.	NAME	Relationship to Person First Named	AGE	SEX	BLOOD	TRIBAL ENROLLMENT Year	County	No.
~~1973~~	1 ~~Carney, Locus~~	~~Named~~	~~24~~	~~M~~	~~Full~~	~~1896~~	~~Nashoba~~	~~2493~~
1974	2 " Bettie 47	Wife	44	F	"	1896	"	9700
1975	3 Homer, Sosephine 10	S.Dau	7	"	"	1896	"	5544
1976	4 " Elliot 9	S.Son	6	M	"	1896	"	5545
	5							
	6							
	7							
	8							
	9							
	10							
	11							
	12							
	13							
	14							
	15							
	16							
	17							

~~DIED PRIOR TO SEPTEMBER 25, 1902~~

ENROLLMENT OF NOS. 1, 2, 3 and 4 HEREON APPROVED BY THE SECRETARY OF INTERIOR Dec 12, 1902

TRIBAL ENROLLMENT OF PARENTS

	Name of Father	Year	County	Name of Mother	Year	County
1	~~Charles Payne~~	~~Dead~~	~~Nashoba~~	~~Jinnie Payne~~	~~Dead~~	~~Nashoba~~
2	John Homa	"	Eagle	Yo-to-na	1896	"
3	Pierce Homer	1896	Nashoba	No 2		
4	" "	1896	"	No 2		
5						
6						
7	No2 on 1896 roll as Bettie Noshobi					
8	No4 " 1896 " " Ellot Homer					
9	No1 died - 1899; Enrollment cancelled by Department July 8, 1904					
10						
11						
12						
13						
14						
15						
16				Date of Application for Enrollment.	April 24/99	
17						

186

Choctaw By Blood Enrollment Cards 1898-1914

RESIDENCE: Nashoba COUNTY.
POST OFFICE: Alikchi, I.T.

Choctaw Nation

Choctaw Roll *(Not Including Freedmen)*

CARD NO.
FIELD NO. **787**

Dawes' Roll No.	NAME	Relationship to Person	AGE	SEX	BLOOD	TRIBAL ENROLLMENT Year	County	No.
1977	1 Johnson, Elean ⁴⁶	First Named	43	F	Full	1896	Nashoba	6848
1978	2 Columbus, Nicholas ¹⁵	son	12	M	"	1896	"	6850
	3							
	4	ENROLLMENT						
	5	OF NOS. 1 and 2 HEREON APPROVED BY THE SECRETARY						
	6	OF INTERIOR Dec. 12, 1902						
	7							
	8							
	9							
	10							
	11	No2 on 1896 roll as Nicholas C. Johnson.						
	12							
	13							
	14							
	15							
	16							
	17							

TRIBAL ENROLLMENT OF PARENTS

Name of Father	Year	County	Name of Mother	Year	County
1 Wash Johnson	Dead	Nashoba	Susan Cobb	Dead	Nashoba
2 Bill Columbus	"	"	No 1		

Date of Application for Enrollment April 24/99

187

Choctaw By Blood Enrollment Cards 1898-1914

RESIDENCE: Nashoba   COUNTY.   **Choctaw Nation**   Choctaw Roll   CARD No.
POST OFFICE: Smithville, I.T.   (Not Including Freedmen)   FIELD No. **788**

Dawes' Roll No.		NAME		Relationship to Person First Named	AGE	SEX	BLOOD	TRIBAL ENROLLMENT Year	County	No.
1979	1	Peter, Davis	55	First Named	52	M	Full	1896	Nashoba	10355
1980	2	" , Becky	25	Wife	22	F	"	1896	"	10356
1981	3	" , Samuel	18	Son	15	M	"	1896	"	10357
1982	4	" , Lula	12	Dau	9	F	"	1896	"	10358
1983	5	" , Lillie	12	"	9	"	"	1896	"	10359
1984	6	" , Ener	7	"	4	"	"	1896	"	10360
14597	7	" , Abbie	3	Dau	1mo	"	"			
	8	ENROLLMENT								
	9	OF NOS. 1,2,3,4,5 and 6 HEREON APPROVED BY THE SECRETARY								
	10	OF INTERIOR Dec 12, 1902								
	11	ENROLLMENT								
	12	OF NOS. ~~7~~ HEREON APPROVED BY THE SECRETARY				No				
	13	OF INTERIOR May 20, 1903								
	14									
	15									
	16									
	17									

TRIBAL ENROLLMENT OF PARENTS

	Name of Father	Year	County	Name of Mother	Year	County
1	Ah-bey	Dead	Atoka	Ba-chey	Dead	Nashoba
2	Lake John	"	Nashoba	Etney John	"	"
3	No 1			Plensie Peter	"	"
4	No 1			" "	"	"
5	No 1			" "	"	"
6	No 1			No 2		
7	No 1			No 2		
8	No2 died in 1900: Enrollment cancelled by Department March 2, 1907.					
9	No4 died June 4, 1902: Enrollment cancelled by Depart Dec. 8, 1906.					
10	No6 died in Sept 1900: Enrollment cancelled by Department March 4, 1907.					
11	March 19,1909 Department request reports to Nos 2, 4 and 6 hereon April 2, 1909, Reports to Department					
12	For child of No5 see N.B. (Apr 26-06) Card #860.					
13	June 14,1909 Department holds these cases are not analogous to Goldsby					
14	case and declines to take action looking to restoration of Nos 2, 4 and 6 to roll.					
15						Date of Application for Enrollment.
16						April 24/99
17	P.O. Seems to be Bethel					

Choctaw By Blood Enrollment Cards 1898-1914

RESIDENCE: Red River	COUNTY.	**Choctaw Nation**				**Choctaw Roll** *(Not Including Freedmen)*	CARD NO.	
POST OFFICE: Kully Tuk-lo I.T.							FIELD NO. 789	

Dawes' Roll No.	NAME	Relationship to Person	AGE	SEX	BLOOD	TRIBAL ENROLLMENT		
						Year	County	No.
1985	₁ Brown, James ⁷³	First Named	70	M	Full	1896	Red River	1341
	2							
	3							
	4	ENROLLMENT OF NOS. 1 HEREON						
	5	APPROVED BY THE SECRETARY OF INTERIOR DEC 12 1902						
	6							
	7							
	8							
	9							
	10							
	11							
	12							
	13							
	14							
	15							
	16							
	17							

TRIBAL ENROLLMENT OF PARENTS

	Name of Father	Year	County	Name of Mother	Year	County
₁	Unknown	Ded	Blue	Unknown	Ded	Blue
2						
3						
4						
5						
6						
7						
8						
9						
10						
11						
12						
13						
14						
15						
16				Date of Application for Enrollment		4-24-99
17						

189

Choctaw By Blood Enrollment Cards 1898-1914

RESIDENCE: Nashoba COUNTY.
POST OFFICE: Smithville, I.T.

Choctaw Nation

Choctaw Roll
(Not Including Freedmen)

CARD NO.
FIELD NO. 790

Dawes' Roll No.	NAME	Relationship to Person First Named	AGE	SEX	BLOOD	TRIBAL ENROLLMENT		
						Year	County	No.
1986	1 Benn, Louis 28	First Named	25	M	1/2	1896	Nashoba	1111
1987	2 Sallie	Wife	20	F	Full	1896	"	3381
1988	3 " Eveline 4	Dau	1	"	3/4			
1989	4 " Jackson 3	Son	4mo	M	3/4			
14598	5 " Lewis 3	Son	3	M	3/4			
	6							
	7							
	8							
	9							
	10							
	11							
	12							
	13							
	14							
	15							
	16							
	17							

ENROLLMENT
OF NOS. 1,2,3 and 4 HEREON
APPROVED BY THE SECRETARY
OF INTERIOR Dec 12, 1902

TRIBAL ENROLLMENT OF PARENTS

	Name of Father	Year	County	Name of Mother	Year	County
1	Davis Benn	De'd	Nashoba	Martha Benn	1896	Nashoba
2	Rice Durant	"	Kiamatia[sic]	Betsy Durant	Ded	Towson
3	No 1			No 2		
4	No 1			No 2		
5	No 1			No 2		
6						
7	No2 on 1896 roll as Sallie Durant					
8	No2 died May 25, 1900: Proof of death filed Dec. 13, 1902.					
9	No5 born Feb. 25, 1900: Enrolled Dec 13, 1902.					
10	No.2 Died May 25, 1900; Enrollment cancelled by Department July 8, 1904.					
11						
12						
13						
14					Date of Application for Enrollment.	4-24-99
15				No4 Enrolled Nov. 24/99		
16						
17	P.O. Hatfield, Ark 2/19/09					

Choctaw By Blood Enrollment Cards 1898-1914

RESIDENCE: **Nashoba** COUNTY.
POST OFFICE: **Smithville, I.T.**

Choctaw Nation

Choctaw Roll
(Not Including Freedmen)

CARD NO.
FIELD NO. **791**

Dawes' Roll No.	NAME	Relationship to Person First Named	AGE	SEX	BLOOD	TRIBAL ENROLLMENT		
						Year	County	No.
~~1990~~	~~1 Columbus, Tecumseh~~ DIED PRIOR TO SEPTEMBER 25, 1903	First Named	~~17~~	~~M~~	~~Full~~	~~1896~~	~~Nashoba~~	~~6849~~
1991	2 " Celin	Wife	17	F	"	1896	"	7533
~~1992~~	~~3 " Mack~~ DIED PRIOR TO SEPTEMBER 25, 1902	~~Son~~	~~New~~	~~M~~	~~"~~	~~New~~	~~"~~	~~New~~
	4							
	5							
	6	ENROLLMENT						
	7	OF NOS. 1 2 and 3 HEREON APPROVED BY THE SECRETARY						
	8	OF INTERIOR DEC 12 1902						
	9							
	10							
	11							
	12							
	13	No 1 enrolled as Tecumseh C. Johnson						
	14	No 2 " " Celine Kochette						
	15	No 3 new born, 1 month old						
	16							
	17							

TRIBAL ENROLLMENT OF PARENTS

	Name of Father	Year	County	Name of Mother	Year	County
1	~~Dill Columbus~~	De'd	~~Nashoba~~	~~Elean Johnson~~	1896	~~Nashoba~~
2	Moses McCoy	1896	"	Louisa McCoy	1896	"
3	~~No 1~~			~~No 2~~		
4						
5						
6						
7	~~No 1 died Jan 1900 Enrollment cancelled by Department July 8, 1904~~					
8	~~No 3 " Jan. 9. 1900 " " " " Dec 24. 1904~~					
9	For child of No.2 see NB (March 3,1905) #1408					
	" " " " " (April 26,1906) #454					
10						
11						
12						
13						
14						
15					Date of Application for Enrollment	
16					4-24-99	
17						

Choctaw By Blood Enrollment Cards 1898-1914

RESIDENCE: Nashoba   COUNTY.   **Choctaw Nation**   Choctaw Roll   CARD NO.
POST OFFICE: Smithville, I.T.   *(Not Including Freedmen)*   FIELD NO.   792

Dawes' Roll No.	NAME		Relationship to Person	AGE	SEX	BLOOD	TRIBAL ENROLLMENT		
							Year	County	No.
1993	1 McCoy, Holman	24	First Named	21	M	Full	1896	Nashoba	7531
1994	2 " " Sillis	26	Wife	23	F	"	1896	"	9281
1995	3 " " Robert A	6	S Son	3	M	"	1896	"	9282
1996	4 DIED PRIOR TO SEPTEMBER 25, 1902 Laney		Dau	2mo	F	"			
1997	5 " " Freeman	2	Son	3mo	M	"			
	6								
	7	ENROLLMENT OF NOS. HEREON							
	8	APPROVED BY THE SECRETARY OF INTERIOR							
	9								
	10								
	11								
	12								
	13								
	14	No3 died in March 1900: Enrollment cancelled by Department March 2, 1907							
	15	No 1 enrolled as Holman Kochette							
	16	No3 on 1896 roll as Robt. Allen McCoy.							
	17	No.5 Enrolled June 26, 1901.							

TRIBAL ENROLLMENT OF PARENTS

	Name of Father	Year	County	Name of Mother	Year	County
1	Moses McCoy	1896	Nashoba	Louisa McCoy	1896	Nashoba
2	Morgan Robert	Ded	"	Nelsy Robert	Ded	"
3	Nelson McCoy	"	"	No 2		
4	No 1			No 2		
5	No.1			No.2		
6						
7	No 4 died Aug 28, 1900: Enrollment cancelled by Department July 8, 1904					
8	For child of No.2 see NB (Apr 26-06) Card #851					
9	" " " No1 " " (Mar 3-05) " #977					
10	7/8/36 Nos 1 and 2 Divorced [illegible]					
11	July 14, 1903					
12						
13						
14						
15				No4 enrolled Nov 24/99		
16				Date of Application for Enrollment 4-24-99		
17				1 to 3		

Choctaw By Blood Enrollment Cards 1898-1914

RESIDENCE: **Nashoba** COUNTY. **Choctaw Nation** **Choctaw Roll** CARD NO.
POST OFFICE: **Smithville, I.T.** *(Not Including Freedmen)* FIELD NO. **793**

Dawes' Roll No.	NAME	Relationship to Person First Named	AGE	SEX	BLOOD	TRIBAL ENROLLMENT Year	County	No.
1998	1 McCoy Moses 56	First Named	53	M	Full	1896	Nashoba	7529
1999	2 " " Louisa 53	Wife	50	F	"	1896	"	7530
2000	3 " " Elias 21	Son	18	M	"	1896	"	7532
2001	4 " " Sallie 18	Dau	15	F	"	1896	"	7534
2002	5 " " Alson 15	Son	13	M	"	1896	"	7535
~~2003~~	~~6 DIED PRIOR TO SEPTEMBER 25, 1902 Silwe~~	~~Dau~~	~~9~~	~~F~~	~~"~~	~~1896~~	~~"~~	~~7536~~
2004	7 " " Sam 8	Son	5	M	"	1896	"	7537
	8							
	9							
	10							
	11							
	12							
	13							
	14							
	15							
	16							
	17							

```
ENROLLMENT
OF NOS. 1 2 3 4 5 6 and 7 HEREON
APPROVED BY THE SECRETARY
OF INTERIOR   DEC 12 1902
```

TRIBAL ENROLLMENT OF PARENTS

	Name of Father	Year	County	Name of Mother	Year	County
1	Ko-chit-ty	De'd	Eagle	Mary Ko-chit-ty	Ded	Eagle
2	Simon Jones	"	"		"	Red River
3	No 1			No 2		
4	No 1			No 2		
5	No 1			No 2		
6	No 1			No 2		
7	No 1			No 2		
8	No.3 is the husband of Lilian McCoy on Choc. Card #2078.					
9			No 1 on roll as Moses Kochette			
10			No 2 " " " Lowisa "			
11			No 3 " " " Elias "			
12			No 4 " " " Sallie "			
			No 5 " " " Alson "			
13			No 6 " " " Silwe "			
14			No 7 " " " Sam "			
15						Date of Application for Enrollment.
16	For child of No.4 see NB(March 3, 1905) #944					4-24-99
17	No.6 died June 1, 1902; Enrollment cancelled by Department Sept 16-1904					

Choctaw By Blood Enrollment Cards 1898-1914

RESIDENCE: Nashoba   COUNTY.   **Choctaw Nation**   Choctaw Roll   CARD NO.
POST OFFICE: Alik-chi I.T.   *(Not Including Freedmen)*   FIELD NO. 794

Dawes' Roll No.	NAME	Relationship to Person First Named	AGE	SEX	BLOOD	TRIBAL ENROLLMENT		
						Year	County	No.
2005	1 Choate, Robert 27	First Named	24	M	Full	1896	Nashoba	2546
2006	2 Elizy DIED PRIOR TO SEPTEMBER 25, 1902	Wife	45	F	"	1893	Cedar	P.R. 458
2007	3 Willis, Martha 15	Dau	13	"	"	1896	Nashoba	13314
	4							
	5							
	6							
	7							
	8							
	9							
	10							
	11							
	12							
	13							
	14							
	15							
	16							
	17							

ENROLLMENT
OF NOS. 1-2 and 3 HEREON
APPROVED BY THE SECRETARY
OF INTERIOR DEC 12 1902

TRIBAL ENROLLMENT OF PARENTS

Name of Father	Year	County	Name of Mother	Year	County
1 Joel Choate	De'd	Towson	Lucy Choate	Ded	Nashoba
2 Barney No-wat-ub-bi	"	Nashoba		"	"
3 Marcus Willis	1896	Cedar	No 2		
4					
5		No.3 on 1896 Choctaw Census roll as Martina Wallis			
6		No2 on p. 43 - #458 as Eliza Wallace			
7		Cedar Co pay roll 1893			
		No2 died March 31, 1900: prof of death filed Dec 3, 1902.			
8	No.2 died March 31, 1900; Enrollment cancelled by Department July 8, 1904				
9		For child of No3 see NB (March 3, 1905) #1086			
10					
11					
12					
13					
14					
15					Date of Application for Enrollment.	
16					4-24-99	
17						

Choctaw By Blood Enrollment Cards 1898-1914

RESIDENCE: Cedar COUNTY.
POST OFFICE: Doaksville, Ind. Terr.

Choctaw Nation

Choctaw Roll
(Not Including Freedmen)

CARD NO.
FIELD NO. **795**

Dawes' Roll No.	NAME	Relationship to Person	AGE	SEX	BLOOD	TRIBAL ENROLLMENT		
						Year	County	No.
2008	1 Jackson, Litie 48	First Named	45	F	Full	1896	Cedar	6746
14599	2 " , Silas 17	Ad. Son	30[sic]	M	"	1896	"	6748
2009	3 " , Anderson 10	Son	8	"	"	1896	"	6747
	4							
	5	ENROLLMENT						
	6	OF NOS. 1 and 3 HEREON						
	7	APPROVED BY THE SECRETARY OF INTERIOR Dec 12, 1902						
	8							
	9	ENROLLMENT						
	10	OF NOS. 2 HEREON						
	11	APPROVED BY THE SECRETARY OF INTERIOR May 20, 1903						
	12							
	13	No 1 Enrolled as Rhoda Jackson						
	14							
	15							
	16							
	17	Mistake as to age of No.2. He is now 17 years old 12/1-02						

TRIBAL ENROLLMENT OF PARENTS

	Name of Father	Year	County	Name of Mother	Year	County
1	Pis-u-ho-nubbi	De'd	Skullyville	Sallie	De'd	Skullyville
2	Bill A-ho katubbi	"	Nashoba	Sik-a-ue	"	Cedar
3	Albert Jackson	"	Cedar	No.1		
4						
5						
6						
7						
8						
9						
10						
11						
12						
13						
14					Date of Application for Enrollment.	
15						
16					4-24-99	
17						

195

Choctaw By Blood Enrollment Cards 1898-1914

RESIDENCE: Cedar COUNTY. **Choctaw Nation** **Choctaw Roll** CARD No.
POST OFFICE: Doaksville, I.T. *(Not Including Freedmen)* FIELD No. 796

Dawes' Roll No.	NAME	Relationship to Person	AGE	SEX	BLOOD	TRIBAL ENROLLMENT Year	TRIBAL ENROLLMENT County	TRIBAL ENROLLMENT No.
2010	1 Bond, Eliza 55	First Named	52	F	Full	1896	Cedar	1048
	2							
	3							
	4							
	5	ENROLLMENT						
	6	OF NOS. 1 HEREON APPROVED BY THE SECRETARY						
	7	OF INTERIOR DEC 12 1902						
	8							
	9							
	10							
	11							
	12							
	13							
	14							
	15							
	16							
	17							

TRIBAL ENROLLMENT OF PARENTS

Name of Father	Year	County	Name of Mother	Year	County
1 John Mul-e-tub-bi	Ded	Skullyville	On-tai-i-ana	Ded	Skullyville
2					
3					
4					
5					
6					
7					
8					
9					
10					
11					
12					
13					
14					
15					
16				Date of Application for Enrollment 4-24-99		
17					

Choctaw By Blood Enrollment Cards 1898-1914

Choctaw Nation

Choctaw Roll (Not Including Freedmen)

CARD NO.

FIELD NO. 797

Dawes' Roll No.	NAME	Relationship to Person First Named	AGE	SEX	BLOOD	TRIBAL ENROLLMENT Year	County	No.
DEAD.	1 Billy Sim DEAD	First Named	21	M	F.	1896	Eagle	1326
	2							
	3							
	4							
	5	No. 1 HEREON DISMISSED UNDER						
	6	ORDER OF THE COMMISSION TO THE FIVE						
	7	CIVILIZED TRIBES OF MARCH 31, 1905.						
	8							
	9							
	10							
	11							
	12	No.1 Died August 10, 1900 Evidence of death filed April 6, 1901.						
	13							
	14							
	15							
	16							
	17							

TRIBAL ENROLLMENT OF PARENTS

	Name of Father	Year	County	Name of Mother	Year	County
1	Billy	Ded	Bok Tuklo	Ha yak atima	Ded	Eagle
2						
3						
4						
5						
6						
7						
8						
9						
10						
11						
12						
13						
14						
15						
16				Date of Application for Enrollment	4-24-99	
17						

197

Choctaw By Blood Enrollment Cards 1898-1914

Choctaw Nation

Choctaw Roll
(Not Including Freedmen)

CARD NO.
FIELD NO. 798

Dawes' Roll No.		NAME		Relationship to Person First Named	AGE	SEX	BLOOD	TRIBAL ENROLLMENT		
								Year	County	No.
2011	1	Christie, Alfred	53	First Named	50	M	Full	1896	Towson	2451
2012	2	" Mary	43	Wife	40	F	"	1896	"	2451
2013	3	" David	21	Son	18	M	"	1896	"	2453
2014	4	" Emma	18	Dau	15	F	"	1896	"	2454
2015	5	" Moses	15	Son	12	M	"	1896	"	2455
2016	6	" Peter	11	"	8	"	"	1896	"	2456
	7									
	8									
	9									
	10									
	11	ENROLLMENT OF NOS. 1 2 3 4 5 and 6 HEREON								
	12	APPROVED BY THE SECRETARY								
	13	OF INTERIOR DEC 12 1902								
	14									
	15									
	16									
	17									

TRIBAL ENROLLMENT OF PARENTS

	Name of Father	Year	County	Name of Mother	Year	County
1	Josie Christie	Dead	Red River	Mary Christie	Dead	Eagle
2	Concho-tombee	"	" "	Winnie	"	Towson
3	No1			No2		
4	No1			No2		
5	No1			No2		
6	No1			No2		
7						
8						
9						
10						
11						
12						
13						
14						
15						
16				Date of Application for Enrollment	April 24/99	
17						

Choctaw By Blood Enrollment Cards 1898-1914

RESIDENCE: Nashoba COUNTY. **Choctaw Nation** **Choctaw Roll** CARD No.
POST OFFICE: Smithville, I.T. *(Not Including Freedmen)* FIELD No. **799**

Dawes' Roll No.	NAME		Relationship to Person Named	AGE	SEX	BLOOD	TRIBAL ENROLLMENT		
							Year	County	No.
2017	1 Bohanan, Jesse	42	First Named	39	M	Full	1896	Nashoba	1135
2018	2 " Sophia	24	Wife	21	F	"	1896	"	1136
2019	3 " Lucy	18	Dau	15	"	"	1896	"	1137
2020	4 " Listie	16	"	13	"	"	1896	"	1138
2021	5 " Richard	14	Son	11	M	"	1896	"	1139
2022	6 " Wilson	9	"	6	"	"	1896	"	1140
2023	7 " Liza	8	Dau	5	F	"	1896	"	1141
2024	8 " Elizabeth	6	"	3	"	"	1896	"	1142
2025	9 ~~" Mitchell~~ DIED PRIOR TO SEPTEMBER 25, 1902		~~Son~~	~~1~~	~~M~~	"			
14600	10 " Nicholas	1	Son	18mo	M	"			
	11								
	12 ENROLLMENT OF NOS. 1 2 3 4 5 6 7 8 and 9 HEREON								
	13 APPROVED BY THE SECRETARY OF INTERIOR Dec 12 1902								
	14								
	15 ENROLLMENT OF NOS 10 HEREON								
	16 APPROVED BY THE SECRETARY OF INTERIOR May 20 1903								
	17								

TRIBAL ENROLLMENT OF PARENTS

	Name of Father	Year	County	Name of Mother	Year	County
1	Julius Bohanan	Dead	Nashoba	Sallie Bohanan	1896	Nashoba
2	Lewis Bean	"	"	Martha Bean	1896	"
3	No 1			Susan Bohanan	Dead	"
4	No 1			" "	"	"
5	No 1			" "	"	"
6	No 1	No		No 2		
7	No 1			No 2		
8	No 1			No 2		
9	No 1			No 2		
10	No 1			No 2		
11	No 10 Born May 8, 1901 enrolled Nov. 4, 1902					
12	No.3 is Mother of No5 on Choctaw Card No2062 (dead)					
13	No9 died Sept 4, 1900: proof of death filed Dec. 11, 1902					
13	No9 died Sept 4, 1900: Enrollment cancelled by Department July 8, 1904					
14	No4 " Feby 27, 1906: Proof on file.					#1 to 9
15	For child of Nos 1&2 see N.B. (Apr26-06) Card No 710				Date of Application for Enrollment.	
15	" " " No4 " " " 200					
16	" " " Nos 1&2 " " (Mar 3-05) " " 889				April 24/99	
17						

199

Choctaw By Blood Enrollment Cards 1898-1914

RESIDENCE: Bok Tuklo   COUNTY.   **Choctaw Nation**   Choctaw Roll   CARD NO.
POST OFFICE: Lukfata, I.T.   *(Not Including Freedmen)*   FIELD NO.   **800**

Dawes' Roll No.	NAME	Relationship to Person First Named	AGE	SEX	BLOOD	TRIBAL ENROLLMENT		
						Year	County	No.
2026	1 Colbert, Davison ³¹	First Named	29	M	Full	1896	Bok Tuklo	2551
2027	2 " Daviney ⁴¹	Wife	38	F	"	1896	" "	2552
	3 " ~~Bicey DEAD~~	~~Dau~~	~~6~~	~~"~~	~~"~~	~~1896~~	~~" "~~	~~2553~~
2028	4 " Dickson ⁷	Son	4	M	"	1896	" "	2554
2029	5 " Emiline ⁴	Dau	9mo	F	"			
2030	6 " Marswes ⁴	Dau	9mo	"	"			
	7							
	8	ENROLLMENT						
	9	OF NOS. 1 2 4 5 and 6 HEREON APPROVED BY THE SECRETARY						
	10	OF INTERIOR DEC 12 1902						
	11							
	12	No. 3 HEREON DISMISSED UNDER						
	13	ORDER OF THE COMMISSION TO THE FIVE CIVILIZED TRIBES OF MARCH 31, 1905						
	14							
	15							
	16							
	17							

TRIBAL ENROLLMENT OF PARENTS

	Name of Father	Year	County	Name of Mother	Year	County
1	Sampson Colbert	1896	Bok Tuklo	Okla-hona	Dead	Bok Tuklo
2	Alex Frazier	Dead	Red River		"	Red River
3	~~No1~~			~~No2~~		
4	No1			No2		
5	No1			No2		
6	No1			No2		
7						
8	~~No3 on 1896 roll as Byissie Colbert~~					
9	No.3 Died January 8, 1900. Evidence of death filed Oct. 26, 1902.					
10	For child of Nos. 1&2 see NB (March 3, 1905) #1409					
11						
12						
13						
14					~~Date of Application~~	
15					for Enrollment.	
16					April 24/99	
17						

Choctaw By Blood Enrollment Cards 1898-1914

RESIDENCE: Nashoba   COUNTY.   **Choctaw Nation**   **Choctaw Roll** *(Not Including Freedmen)*   CARD NO.
POST OFFICE: Alikchi, I.T.   FIELD NO. **801**

Dawes' Roll No.	NAME	Relationship to Person First Named	AGE	SEX	BLOOD	TRIBAL ENROLLMENT		
						Year	County	No.
2031	1 Billy, Daniel 56	First Named	53	M	Full	1896	Nashoba	1192
2032	2 " Eli [DIED PRIOR TO SEPTEMBER 25, 1902]	Son	18	"	"	1896	"	1197
2033	3 " Delilah 16	Dau	13	F	"	1896	"	1194
2034	4 " Calom 13	Son	10	M	"	1896	"	1195
	5							
	6							
	7							
	8							
	9							
	10							
	11							
	12							
	13							
	14							
	15							
	16							
	17							

ENROLLMENT
OF NOS. 1 2 3 and 4 HEREON
APPROVED BY THE SECRETARY
OF INTERIOR Dec 12 1902

TRIBAL ENROLLMENT OF PARENTS

	Name of Father	Year	County	Name of Mother	Year	County
1	Bi-na-ta-ya	Dead	Nashoba	Ha-ish-tona	Dead	Nashoba
2	No 1			Lina Billy	"	"
3	No 1			" "	"	"
4	No 1			" "	"	"
5						
6	No2 also on 1896 Choctaw census roll, page 28; No 1104 as Eli Billie					
7	No3 is wife of Pitchlynn Bathest[sic] Choctaw Card #1293. See statements					
8	of Allington Battiest and Beyington Bond filed Dec. 23, 1902 also copy of letter from Pitchlynn Battiest Jany. 3, 1903.					
9	No2 Died before Sept. 25, 1902 Enrollment cancelled by Department May 2, 1906.					
10	For child of No3 see N.B. (Apr 26-06) Card #611					
11	" " " " " " (Mrch3-05) " #951					
12						
13						
14						
15					Date of Application for Enrollment.	
16					April 24/99	
17	No 3 P.O. Bethel I.T. 4/5/05					

Choctaw By Blood Enrollment Cards 1898-1914

RESIDENCE: Nas-hoba COUNTY.
POST OFFICE: Smithville, I.T.

Choctaw Nation

Choctaw Roll
(Not Including Freedmen)

CARD NO.
FIELD NO. **802**

Dawes' Roll No.	NAME	Relationship to Person	AGE	SEX	BLOOD	TRIBAL ENROLLMENT		
						Year	County	No.
2035	1 Bohanan, Wismon 22	First Named	19	M	Full	1896	Nashoba	1121
	2							
	3							
	4							
	5	ENROLLMENT						
	6	OF NOS. 1 HEREON APPROVED BY THE SECRETARY						
	7	OF INTERIOR DEC 12 1902						
	8							
	9							
	10							
	11							
	12							
	13							
	14							
	15							
	16							
	17							

TRIBAL ENROLLMENT OF PARENTS

Name of Father	Year	County	Name of Mother	Year	County
1 Julius Bohanan	Dead	Nashoba	Sallie Bohanan	1891	Nashoba
2					
3					
4					
5					
6					
7					
8					
9					
10					
11					
12					
13					
14					
15			Date of Application for Enrollment.	April 24/99	
16					
17					

Choctaw By Blood Enrollment Cards 1898-1914

RESIDENCE: Nashoba COUNTY. **Choctaw Nation** Choctaw Roll CARD NO.
FFICE: Alikchi, I.T. (Not Including Freedmen) FIELD NO. 803

	NAME		Relationship to Person	AGE	SEX	BLOOD	TRIBAL ENROLLMENT		
							Year	County	No.
1	Baker, Phelan	38	First Named	35	M	Full	1896	Nashoba	1161
2	" Charkesis	33	Wife	30	F	"	1896	"	1162
3	" Olarney	9	Dau	6	"	"	1896	"	1164
4	" Chimon	8	Son	5	M	"	1896	"	1165
5	" Ida	5	Dau	1	F	"			
6	" Somis	2	Son	1year	M	"			
2042 7	" Joseph	1	Son	2mo	M	"			
8									
9									
10									
11	ENROLLMENT								
12	OF NOS. 123456and7 HEREON APPROVED BY THE SECRETARY								
13	OF INTERIOR DEC 12 1902								
14									
15									
16									
17									

TRIBAL ENROLLMENT OF PARENTS

	Name of Father	Year	County	Name of Mother	Year	County
1	Samuel Baker	Dead	Nashoba	Melinda Baker	Dead	Nashoba
2	Sylvester Williams	"	"	Bicey John	1896	"
3	No 1			No 2		
4	No 1			No 2		
5	No 1			No 2		
6	No 1			No 2		
7	Nº1			Nº2		
8						
9	No3 on 1896 roll as Rainie Baker					
10	No4 " 1896 " " Chalmon "					
11	No6 Enrolled January 3, 1901.					
	Nº7 Born March 8, 1902: enrolled May 14, 1902.					
12						
13						
14				#1 to 5		
15				Date of Application for Enrollment.		
16	Present P.O. address Bethel I.T. Jany 3, 1901.			April 24/99		
17						

Choctaw By Blood Enrollment Cards 1898-1914

RESIDENCE: Nashoba   COUNTY.   **Choctaw Nation**   Choctaw Roll   CARD NO.
POST OFFICE: Alikchi, I.T.   *(Not Including Freedmen)*   FIELD NO.   804

Dawes' Roll No.	NAME	Relationship to Person	AGE	SEX	BLOOD	Year	County	No.
2043	1 Carterby, Eben 32	First Named	29	M	Full	1896	Nashoba	2518
2044	2 " Isabelle 48	Wife	45	F	"	1896	"	2519
2045	3 " Ben 10	Son	7	M	"	1896	"	2520
	4							
	5							
	6	ENROLLMENT						
	7	OF NOS. 1 2 and 3 HEREON						
		APPROVED BY THE SECRETARY						
	8	OF INTERIOR DEC 12 1902						
	9							
	10							
	11							
	12							
	13	No1 on 1896 roll as Aben Carterby						
	14							
	15							
	16							
	17							

TRIBAL ENROLLMENT OF PARENTS

Name of Father	Year	County	Name of Mother	Year	County
1 Phillie Carterby	Dead	Nashoba	Emiline Carterby	1896	Nashoba
2 Chon-tubbee	"	"	Lu-tush	Dead	"
3 No 1			No 2		
4					
5					
6					
7					
8					
9					
10					
11					
12					
13					Date of Application for Enrollment.
14					
15				April 24/99	
16					
17					

RESIDENCE: Red River COUNTY.
POST OFFICE: Cerrogordo[sic], I.T.

Choctaw Nation

Choctaw Roll (Not Including Freedmen)

CARD NO.
FIELD NO. 805

Dawes' Roll No.	NAME		Relationship to Person First Named	AGE	SEX	BLOOD	TRIBAL ENROLLMENT		
							Year	County	No.
2046	1 McKinney, Samuel	53	First Named	50	M	Full	1896	Red River	9340
2047	2 " Eliza		Wife	40	F	"	1896	" "	9341
2048	3 " Robinson	14	Son	11	M	"	1896	" "	9342
2049	4 " Mana	6	Dau	3	F	"	1896	" "	9343
2050	5 " Ida	5	"	1	"	"			
2051	6 " John	3	Son	3mo	M	"			
	7								
	8								
	9								
	10								
	11								
	12								
	13								
	14								
	15								
	16								
	17								

(row 2047: DIED PRIOR TO SEPTEMBER 25, 1902)

ENROLLMENT
OF NOS. 1 2 3 4 5 and 6 HEREON
APPROVED BY THE SECRETARY
OF INTERIOR DEC 12 1902

TRIBAL ENROLLMENT OF PARENTS

	Name of Father	Year	County	Name of Mother	Year	County
1	A-tok-lan-tubbee	Dead	Red River		Dead	Red River
2	Billis Dyer	"	Eagle		"	Eagle
3	No 1			No 2		
4	No 1			No 2		
5	No 1			No 2		
6	No.1			No.2		
7						
8	No4 on 1896 roll as Mamie McKinney					
9	For child of No.1 see NB (March 3, 1905) #1000					
10	No.6 Enrolled May 24, 1900					
	No2 died Feb. 1901; proof of death filed Dec 3, 1902					
11	No1 now married to Lucy Ann Loman on Choctaw card #1104					
12	No2 died Feb. - 1901: Enrollment cancelled by Department July 8, 1904					
13						
14				Date of Application for Enrollment		
15				April 25/99		
16						
17	P.O. Goodwater 11/28 '02					

205

Choctaw By Blood Enrollment Cards 1898-1914

RESIDENCE: **Cedar** COUNTY.

POST OFFICE: **Doaksville, I.T.**

Choctaw Nation

Choctaw Roll
(Not Including Freedmen)

CARD NO.

FIELD NO. **806**

Dawes' Roll No.	NAME		Relationship to Person First Named	AGE	SEX	BLOOD	TRIBAL ENROLLMENT		
							Year	County	No.
2052	1 Choate, Gilbert	48	First Named	45	M	Full	1896	Cedar	2412
2053	2 " , Sophie	25	Wife	22	F	"	1896	"	2413
~~Dead~~	3 ~~" , Louisa~~		~~Dau~~	~~3~~	~~"~~	~~"~~	~~1896~~	~~"~~	~~2415~~
~~Dead~~	4 ~~" , Jim Crow~~		~~Son~~	~~1~~	~~M~~	~~"~~			
14884	5 Taylor, Bynie	2	Dau of No2	2½	F	"			
	6								
	7	ENROLLMENT							
	8	OF NOS. 1 and 2 HEREON APPROVED BY THE SECRETARY							
	9	OF INTERIOR Dec. 12, 1902							
	10	ENROLLMENT							
	11	OF NOS. 5 HEREON APPROVED BY THE SECRETARY							
	12	OF INTERIOR May 21, 1903							
	13								
	14	No.3 and 4 hereon dismissed under							
	15	order of the Commission to the Five							
	16	Civilized Tribes of March 31, 1905.							
	17								

TRIBAL ENROLLMENT OF PARENTS

	Name of Father	Year	County	Name of Mother	Year	County
1	Lyman Choate	Dead	Wade	Loh-no	Dead	Nashoba
2	Martin Peter	"	Towson	Bickie Peter	1896	Cedar
3	~~No 1~~			~~No 2~~		
4	~~No 1~~			~~No 2~~		
5	Selin Taylor	1893	Cedar	No 2		
6						
7	No2 on 1896 roll as Sopha Choate					
8	No3 Died April 3,1898. Evidence of death filed March 30,1901.					
9	~~No4 Died July 29, 1898. Evidence of death filed March 30, 1901/~~ ~~No2 is now - married to Paul Homma on Choctaw Card #1826; Evidence of~~					
10	~~separated from No.P and~~ marriage filed Dec. 6, 1902.					
11	No5 Born July 3,1900. Application received Oct.3,1900 returned for information					
12	~~relative to mother. Affidavits as to birth filed March 13, 1903.~~ ~~The above notation relative to No2 is an error. She was married to Selin~~					
13	Taylor Choctaw Card #1021 Jany or Feby,1900 See testimony of Selin					
14	Taylor and Reason Hopson of May 22, 1903.					
15	For child of No.2 see NB (Mar.3-1905) Card #20					
16						
17						

Date of Application for Enrollment.

April 25/99

Choctaw By Blood Enrollment Cards 1898-1914

RESIDENCE: Nashoba		COUNTY.	**Choctaw Nation**				**Choctaw Roll**	CARD NO.	
POST OFFICE: Smithville, I.T.							*(Not Including Freedmen)*	FIELD NO.	807

Dawes' Roll No.	NAME		Relationship to Person First Named	AGE	SEX	BLOOD	TRIBAL ENROLLMENT		
							Year	County	No.
~~2054~~	~~1 James, Molsey~~	DIED PRIOR TO SEPTEMBER 25, 1902		~~52~~	~~F~~	~~Full~~	~~1896~~	~~Nashoba~~	~~6807~~
2055	2 " Lucy	18	Dau	15	"	"	1896	"	6809
2056	3 " Reuben	17	Son	14	M	"	1896	"	6810
2057	4 " Lina	15	Dau	12	F	"	1896	"	6811
	5								
	6								
	7								
	8								
	9								
	10								
	11	ENROLLMENT							
	12	OF NOS. 1 2 3 and 4 HEREON APPROVED BY THE SECRETARY							
	13	OF INTERIOR DEC 12 1902							
	14								
	15								
	16								
	17								

TRIBAL ENROLLMENT OF PARENTS

	Name of Father	Year	County	Name of Mother	Year	County
1	~~Dead~~				~~Dead~~	
2	Bobb James	"	Nashoba	No 1		
3	" "	"	"	No 1		
4	" "	"	"	No 1		
5						
6			No4 on 1896 roll as Lainey S James			
7			No1 " 1896 " " Malsey "			
8			Names of parents of No1 waived by Commissioner McKinney			
9	~~No 1 died Aug 1901. Enrollment cancelled by Department Sept. 16, 1904~~					
10			For child of No3 see NB (Apr 26-06) Card #343			
11			" " " No2 " " " " #843			
12			" " " No2 " " (Mar 3-05) " #979			
13						
14				Date of Application for Enrollment.		
15						
16				April 25/99		
17	P.O. Bethel IT 4/6/05					

207

Choctaw By Blood Enrollment Cards 1898-1914

RESIDENCE: Towson COUNTY.
POST OFFICE: Doaksville, I.T.

Choctaw Nation

Choctaw Roll
(Not Including Freedmen)

CARD NO.

FIELD NO. 808

Dawes' Roll No.		NAME	Relationship to Person First Named	AGE	SEX	BLOOD	TRIBAL ENROLLMENT		
							Year	County	No.
2058	1	Snead, Thomas K	First Named	14	M	1/2	1896	Towson	11370
2059	2	" Edward P.	brother	12	"	1/2	1896	"	11371
2060	3	" Susan J	sister	8	F	1/2	1896	"	11372
2061	4	" Roberta	"	6	"	1/2	1896	"	11373
2062	5	" John G	brother	3	M	1/2	1896	"	11374
	6								
	7								
	8								
	9								
	10								
	11	ENROLLMENT OF NOS. 1 2 3 4 and 5 HEREON							
	12	APPROVED BY THE SECRETARY							
	13	OF INTERIOR DEC 2 1902							
	14								
	15								
	16								
	17								

TRIBAL ENROLLMENT OF PARENTS

	Name of Father	Year	County	Name of Mother	Year	County
1	Ben Snead	Dead	Non Citz	Manda Snead	Dead	Towson
2	" "	"	" "	" "	"	"
3	" "	"	" "	" "	"	"
4	" "	"	" "	" "	"	"
5	" "	"	" "	" "	"	"
6						
7	No 5 on 1896 roll as Ino. G. Snead					
8	Thomas E. Sanguim is guardian of children on this card. Guardianship					
9	papers issued by Towson Co Court filed Jany. 17, 1903					
10						
11						
12						
13						
14				Date of Application for Enrollment.		
15						
16				April 25/99		
17	P.O. Naples I.T. 7/2/06					

Choctaw By Blood Enrollment Cards 1898-1914

RESIDENCE: Cedar COUNTY.
POST OFFICE: Doaksville, I.T.

Choctaw Nation

Choctaw Roll
(Not Including Freedmen)

CARD No.
FIELD No. 809

Dawes' Roll No.	NAME		Relationship to Person	AGE	SEX	BLOOD	TRIBAL ENROLLMENT		
							Year	County	No.
2063	₁ LaFlore, Edmond	58	First Named	55	M	Full	1896	Cedar	7898
2064	₂ " Osborne	23	Son	20	"	"	1896	"	7901
2065	₃ " Daniel	9	"	6	"	"	1896	"	7900
	4								
	5								
	6								
	7								
	8								
	9								
	10								
	11	ENROLLMENT				No			
	12	OF NOS. 1 – 2 and 3 HEREON APPROVED BY THE SECRETARY							
	13	OF INTERIOR DEC 12 1902							
	14								
	15								
	16								
	17								

TRIBAL ENROLLMENT OF PARENTS

	Name of Father	Year	County	Name of Mother	Year	County
1	Joel LaFlore	Dead	Bok Tuklo	Mary LaFlore	Dead	Cedar
2	No 1			Mulsey LaFlore	"	"
3	No 1			Susan LaFlore	"	"
4						
5						
6	No1 on 1896 roll as Edmund LaFlore					
7	No1 died Feb.9 1901: proof of death filed Dec 1, 1902					
8	No1 died Feb 9, 1901: Enrollment cancelled by Department [remainder illegible]					
9	For child of No.2 see NB (March 3, 1905) #1392					
10						
11						
12						
13						
14						
15					Date of Application for Enrollment.	
16					April 25/99	
17						

P.O. [Illegible] I.T.

Choctaw By Blood Enrollment Cards 1898-1914

RESIDENCE: Red River COUNTY.
POST OFFICE: Cerrogordo[sic], Ark

Choctaw Nation

Choctaw Roll
(Not Including Freedmen)

CARD NO.
FIELD NO. **810**

Dawes' Roll No.	NAME		Relationship to Person	AGE	SEX	BLOOD	TRIBAL ENROLLMENT		
							Year	County	No.
2066	1 MᶜKinney, Jamison	52	First Named	49	M	Full	1896	Red River	9348
Dead	2 DEAD Hannah	45	Wife	42	F	"	1896	" "	9349
2067	3 " David	22	Son	19	M	"	1896	" "	9350
2068	4 " Jackson	9	"	6	"	"	1896	" "	9351
2069	5 " Susan	6	Dau	3	F	"	1896	" "	9352
2070	6 Jefferson, Fannie	19	Ward	16	"	"	1896	" "	7057
2071	7 " Wellington	17	"	14	M	"	1896	" "	7058
2072	8 " Nina	15	"	12	F	"	1896	" "	7059
14601	9 Hall, Joseph	1	Son of No6	6mo	M	"			
	10								
	11	ENROLLMENT					ENROLLMENT		
	12	OF NOS. 134567and8 HEREON APPROVED BY THE SECRETARY					OF NOS. 9 HEREON APPROVED BY THE SECRETARY		
	13	OF INTERIOR Dec. 12, 1902					OF INTERIOR May 20, 1903		

14 No, 2. Hereon dismissed under order of
For child of No6 see N.B. (Apr.26-06) card #578 the Commission to the Five Civilized
16 "   "   "   "   " (March 3,1905) " #1100 Tribes of March 31, 1905.

17

TRIBAL ENROLLMENT OF PARENTS

	Name of Father	Year	County	Name of Mother	Year	County
1	Jack MᶜKinney	Dead	Red River		Dead	Red River
2	George Graham	"	" " "	Jincy Graham	"	" " "
3	No 1			Saline MᶜKinney	"	" " "
4	No 1			No 2		
5	No 1			No 2		
6	Timothy Jefferson	Dead	Red River	Annie Jefferson	Dead	Red River
7	" "	"	" " "	" "	"	" " "
8	" "	"	" " "	" "	"	" " "
9	Joshua Hall			No 6		

10 No3 on 1896 roll as Davis MᶜKinney
11 No6 " 1896 " " Lina Jefferson
12 No8 " 1896 " Mina
No2 Died Oct23,1900. Proof of death filed March 26,1901
13 No3 is now the husband of Minerva Going on Choctaw Card #1120 June 9, 1902
14 No9 born May 25,1902: Enrolled Dec.2,1902   #1 to 8
15 No6 is now wife of Joshua Hall a citizen of the Choctaw Nation
Choctaw Card #585 evidence of marriage filed Dec. 6, 1902

Date of Application for Enrollment.
April 25/99

16

17 P.O. Janis, I.T. 12/2 '02

210

Choctaw By Blood Enrollment Cards 1898-1914

RESIDENCE: Cedar   COUNTY.   **Choctaw Nation**   **Choctaw Roll**   CARD NO.
POST OFFICE: Doaksville, I.T.   *(Not Including Freedmen)*   FIELD NO. 811

Dawes' Roll No.	NAME		Relationship to Person	AGE	SEX	BLOOD	TRIBAL ENROLLMENT		
							Year	County	No.
2073	1 Frazier, Edward	52	First Named	49	M	Full	1896	Cedar	4077
2074	2 " Wisey	41	Wife	38	F	"	1896	"	4078
2075	3 " Susan	18	Dau	15	"	"	1896	"	4080
	4								
	5								
	6	ENROLLMENT							
	7	OF NOS. 1 2 and 3 HEREON APPROVED BY THE SECRETARY							
	8	OF INTERIOR DEC 12 1902							
	9								
	10								
	11								
	12								
	13	No3 on 1896 roll as Susie Frazier							
	14								
	15								
	16								
	17								

TRIBAL ENROLLMENT OF PARENTS

	Name of Father	Year	County	Name of Mother	Year	County
1	Smith Frazier	Dead	Cedar	E-la-ho-tema	Dead	Cedar
2	Augustine Cole	"	"	Minnie Cole	"	"
3	No 1			No 2		
4						
5						
6						
7						
8						
9						
10						
11						
12						
13						
14						
15				Date of Application for Enrollment.		
16				April 25/99		
17						

Choctaw By Blood Enrollment Cards 1898-1914

RESIDENCE: Cedar COUNTY.
POST OFFICE: Doaksville, I.T.

Choctaw Nation

Choctaw Roll
(Not Including Freedmen)

CARD No.
FIELD No. 812

Dawes' Roll No.	NAME	Relationship to Person	AGE	SEX	BLOOD	TRIBAL ENROLLMENT		
						Year	County	No.
2076	1 Cole, Harrison ~~DIED PRIOR TO SEPTEMBER 25, 1902~~	First Named	22	M	Full	1896	Cedar	2405
	2							
	3							
	4							
	5	ENROLLMENT						
	6	OF NOS. 1 HEREON ~~APPROVED BY THE SECRETARY~~						
	7	OF INTERIOR DEC 12 1902						
	8							
	9							
	10							
	11							
	12							
	13	No1 died December 1899: proof of death filed Dec. 10, 1902						
	14	No1 died Jan. 9, 1900[sic]: Enrollment cancelled [remainder illegible]						
	15							
	16							
	17							

TRIBAL ENROLLMENT OF PARENTS

	Name of Father	Year	County	Name of Mother	Year	County
1	Nicholas Cole	Dead	Cedar	Susanna Cole	Dead	Cedar
2						
3						
4						
5						
6						
7						
8						
9						
10						
11						
12						
13						
14				Date of Application for Enrollment.		
15						
16				April	25/99	
17						

Choctaw By Blood Enrollment Cards 1898-1914

RESIDENCE: Nashoba   COUNTY.   **Choctaw Nation**   **Choctaw Roll** (Not Including Freedmen)   CARD No.
POST OFFICE: Smithville, I.T.   FIELD No. **813**

Dawes' Roll No.	NAME	Relationship to Person First Named	AGE	SEX	BLOOD	TRIBAL ENROLLMENT Year	County	No.
2077	1 Bohanan, Sallie ⁶³	First Named	60	F	Full	1896	Nashoba	1116
2078	2 " , Sianer ⁴²	Dau	39	"	"	1896	"	1117
2079	3 " , Amy ²⁹	"	26	"	"	1896	"	1119
*2080	4 " , Laymon ¹⁴	G. Son	11	M	"	1896	"	1122
*2081	5 " , Stewart ¹⁰	G. "	7	"	"	1896	"	1123
	6							
	7							
	8							
	9							
	10							
	11							
	12							
	13							
	14							
	15							
	16							
	17							

ENROLLMENT
OF NOS. 1 2 3 4 and 5 HEREON
APPROVED BY THE SECRETARY
OF INTERIOR Dec. 12, 1902

TRIBAL ENROLLMENT OF PARENTS

Name of Father	Year	County	Name of Mother	Year	County
1 Un-te-a-tubbee	Dead	Nashoba		Dead	Nashoba
2 Julius Bohanan	"	"	No 1		
3 " "	"	"	No 1		
4 Hilburn Kiah			No 2		
5 " "			No 2		
6					
7	As to parents of Nos 4 and 5 see testimony of				
8	Nos. 2 and 3 of July 6, 1903				
9	11-21-23				
10	*Letter "G" Placed on Nos 4 and 5 as to relationship of No 1 to conformity of testimony of 7/6/03				
11					
12					
13					
14				Date of Application for Enrollment.	
15					
16				April 25/99	
17					

213

Choctaw By Blood Enrollment Cards 1898-1914

RESIDENCE: Red River   COUNTY.   **Choctaw Nation**   **Choctaw Roll** CARD NO.
POST OFFICE: Garvin, I.T.   *(Not Including Freedmen)*   FIELD NO.   814

Dawes' Roll No.	NAME	Relationship to Person First Named	AGE	SEX	BLOOD	TRIBAL ENROLLMENT		
						Year	County	No.
2082	1 Taylor, Watson		28	M	Full	1896	Red River	12293
	2							
	3							
	4							
	5							
	6							
	7							
	8							
	9							
	10							
	11							
	12							
	13							
	14							
	15							
	16							
	17							

DIED PRIOR TO SEPTEMBER 25, 1902

ENROLLMENT
OF NOS. 1 HEREON
APPROVED BY THE SECRETARY
OF INTERIOR DEC 12 1902

No1 died August 13, 1899: Enrollment [remainder illegible]

TRIBAL ENROLLMENT OF PARENTS

	Name of Father	Year	County	Name of Mother	Year	County
1	Alec Taylor	1896	Red River	Julia A. Taylor	Dead	Red River
2						
3						
4						
5						
6						
7						
8						
9						
10						
11						
12						
13						
14						
15				Date of Application for Enrollment.		
16				April 25/99		
17						

Choctaw By Blood Enrollment Cards 1898-1914

RESIDENCE: Towson COUNTY.
POST OFFICE: Fowlerville, I.T.

Choctaw Nation

Choctaw Roll (Not Including Freedmen)

CARD NO.
FIELD NO. 815

Dawes' Roll No.	NAME	Relationship to Person First Named	AGE	SEX	BLOOD	TRIBAL ENROLLMENT Year	County	No.
2083	1 Durant, Betsy 10	First Named	7	F	Full	1896	Towson	3369
2084	2 Harkins, Elsy 9	Sister	6	"	1/2	1896	"	5471
	3							
	4							
	5	ENROLLMENT						
	6	OF NOS. 1 and 2 HEREON APPROVED BY THE SECRETARY						
	7	OF INTERIOR DEC 12 1902						
	8							
	9							
	10							
	11	No2 on 1896 roll as Elsie Harkin						
	12							
	13							
	14							
	15							
	16							
	17							

TRIBAL ENROLLMENT OF PARENTS

	Name of Father	Year	County	Name of Mother	Year	County
1	Charlie Durant	Dead	Bok Tuklo	Frances Durant	Dead	Towson
2	Daniel Harkins	"	Non Citz	" "	"	"
3						
4						
5						
6						
7						
8						
9						
10						
11						
12						
13						
14						
15						
16				Date of Application for Enrollment	April 25/99	
17						

215

Choctaw By Blood Enrollment Cards 1898-1914

CE: Cedar COUNTY.

POST OFFICE: Doaksville, I.T.

Choctaw Nation

Choctaw Roll
(Not Including Freedmen)

CARD NO.

FIELD NO. 816

NAME	Relationship to Person First Named	AGE	SEX	BLOOD	TRIBAL ENROLLMENT		
					Year	County	No.
1 Tims, Robert 28	First Named	25	M	3/4	1896	Cedar	12088
2 " Fannie	Wife	18	F	3/4	1896	"	12089
3							
4							
5	ENROLLMENT						
6	OF NOS. 1 and 2 HEREON APPROVED BY THE SECRETARY						
7	OF INTERIOR DEC 12 1902						
8							
9							
10							
11							
12							
13							
14							
15							
16							
17							

TRIBAL ENROLLMENT OF PARENTS

Name of Father	Year	County	Name of Mother	Year	County
1 Vincent Tims	Dead	Towson	Emiline Tims	1896	Towson
2 John Wesley	"	Cedar	Winnie Wesley	1896	Cedar
3					
4					
5					
6					
7					
8					
9					
10					
11					
12					
13					
14					
15					
16			Date of Application for Enrollment	April 25/99	
17					

Choctaw By Blood Enrollment Cards 1898-1914

RESIDENCE: Nashoba   COUNTY.   **Choctaw Nation**   **Choctaw Roll**   CARD NO.

POST OFFICE: Alikchi, I.T.   *(Not Including Freedmen)*   FIELD NO. 817

Dawes' Roll No.		NAME		Relationship to Person	AGE	SEX	BLOOD	TRIBAL ENROLLMENT		
								Year	County	No.
2087	1	Stephens, Bynum	43	First Named	40	M	Full	1896	Nashoba	11419
2088	2	" Elsy	41	Wife	39	F	"	1893	Wade	P.R. 189
2089	3	" Minnie	4	S. Dau	1	"	"			
	4									
	5									
	6	~~ENROLLMENT~~								
	7	~~OF NOS. 1 2 and 3 HEREON~~ ~~APPROVED BY THE SECRETARY~~								
	8	~~OF INTERIOR~~ DEC 12 1902								
	9									
	10									
	11									
	12									
	13									
	14									
	15									
	16									
	17									

TRIBAL ENROLLMENT OF PARENTS

	Name of Father	Year	County	Name of Mother	Year	County
1	Elija Stephens	Dead	Nashoba	Eran Stephens	Dead	Nashoba
2	Elija Tom	"	Wade	Lucy A. Tom	"	"
3	Stage Wilson	"	"	No2		
4						
5						
6						
7	No1 on 1896 roll as Benjamin Stephen					
8	No2 " 1893 " " Sibi Dyer also on 1896					
9	roll, Page 344 No 13117, Wade Co. as Silvie ~~Wilson~~					
10						
11						
12						
13						
14				Date of Application for Enrollment.		
15						
16				April 25/99		
17						

Choctaw By Blood Enrollment Cards 1898-1914

RESIDENCE: Cedar COUNTY.
POST OFFICE: Doaksville, I.T

Choctaw Nation

Choctaw Roll
(Not Including Freedmen)

CARD NO.
FIELD NO. 818

Dawes' Roll No.	NAME	Relationship to Person	AGE	SEX	BLOOD	TRIBAL ENROLLMENT		
						Year	County	No.
2090	1 Wesley, Winnie ³³	First Named	30	F	Full	1893	Cedar	P.R. 469
	2							
	3							
	4							
	5	ENROLLMENT						
	6	OF NOS. 1 HEREON APPROVED BY THE SECRETARY						
	7	OF INTERIOR DEC 12 1902						
	8							
	9							
	10							
	11							
	12	On 1893 Pay roll as Willy Wesley, wife of Johnson Wesley						
	13							
	14							
	15							
	16							
	17							

TRIBAL ENROLLMENT OF PARENTS

	Name of Father	Year	County	Name of Mother	Year	County
1	Isaac Yarlin	Dead	Cedar	Sallie Yarlin	Dead	Eagle
2						
3						
4						
5						
6						
7						
8						
9						
10						
11						
12						
13						
14						
15						
16				Date of Application for Enrollment	April 25/99	
17						

218

Choctaw By Blood Enrollment Cards 1898-1914

RESIDENCE: Cedar   COUNTY.   **Choctaw Nation**   **Choctaw Roll**   CARD NO.
POST OFFICE: Doaksville, I.T.   *(Not Including Freedmen)*   FIELD NO.   **819**

Dawes' Roll No.	NAME	Relationship to Person	AGE	SEX	BLOOD	TRIBAL ENROLLMENT		
						Year	County	No.
2091	1 Reed, Alexander H. ⁵¹	First Named	48	M	Full	1896	Cedar	10781
~~2092~~	~~2 Martha~~ DIED PRIOR TO SEPTEMBER 25, 1902	~~Wife~~	~~46~~	~~F~~	~~"~~	~~1896~~	~~"~~	~~10782~~
2093	3 " Michael ¹²	Son	9	M	"	1896	"	10783
	4							
	5							
	6							
	7	ENROLLMENT						
	8	OF NOS. 1 – 2 and 3 HEREON APPROVED BY THE SECRETARY						
	9	OF INTERIOR Dec. 12, 1902						
	10							
	11							
	12							
	13							
	14							
	15							
	16							
	17							

TRIBAL ENROLLMENT OF PARENTS

	Name of Father	Year	County	Name of Mother	Year	County
1	Sho-ko-po-homa	Dead	Cedar	A-fih-no-tona	Dead	Cedar
2	~~Isaac Lewis~~	"	~~Skullyville~~	~~Oka-tha-le-huna~~	"	~~Towson~~
3	No 1			No 2		
4						
5						
6						
7	No2 died Oct 29 1901; proof of death filed Dec 5, 1902					
8	No1 is now the husband of Bicey Taylor – Choctaw card #1353 12/1/02					
9	No2 died Oct 29, 1901; Enrollment cancelled by Department July 8, 1904					
10						
11						
12						
13						
14						
15				Date of Application for Enrollment.		
16				April 25/99		
17						

219

Choctaw By Blood Enrollment Cards 1898-1914

RESIDENCE: Eagle   COUNTY.   **Choctaw Nation**   Choctaw Roll   CARD No.
POST OFFICE: Eagletown, I.T.   *(Not Including Freedmen)*   FIELD No. 820

Dawes' Roll No.	NAME	Relationship to Person First Named	AGE	SEX	BLOOD	TRIBAL ENROLLMENT Year	County	No.
2094	1 Ashshalintubbi, Kale 32	First Named	29	M	Full	1896	Eagle	305
2095	2 " Elsey 23	Wife	20	F	"	1896	"	276
2096	3 " Iris 9	Dau	6	"	"	1896	"	267
2097	4 " Eben 6	Son	3	M	"	1896	"	268
2098	5 " Isaac 3	"	3mo	"				
	6							
	7							
	8							
	9							
	10							
	11	ENROLLMENT						
	12	OF NOS. 1 2 3 4 and 5 HEREON APPROVED BY THE SECRETARY						
	13	OF INTERIOR DEC 12 1902						
	14							
	15							
	16							
	17							

TRIBAL ENROLLMENT OF PARENTS

	Name of Father	Year	County	Name of Mother	Year	County
1	Ashshalintubbi	Dead	Eagle	Ti-mus	Dead	Eagle
2	Sewee Fobb	"	"	Ish-ti-mi-hoke	"	"
3	No 1			No 2		
4	No 1			No 2		
5	No 1			No 2		
6						
7	No1 on 1896 roll as Kate Ashshalintubbi					
8	No3 " 1896 " " Ainis "					
9	No2 " 1896 " " Elsy "					
	No4 " 1896 " " Aben "					
10	Feby 7, 1920 – No5 born January 5, 1899 – See birth affidavits on file.					
11				W.H.A.		
12						
13						
14				Date of Application for Enrollment.		
15						
16				April 25/99		
17						

220

Choctaw By Blood Enrollment Cards 1898-1914

RESIDENCE: Eagle
POST OFFICE: Eagletown, I.T.

COUNTY. **Choctaw Nation**

Choctaw Roll
(Not Including Freedmen)

CARD No.
FIELD No. **821**

Dawes' Roll No.	NAME	Relationship to Person First Named	AGE	SEX	BLOOD	TRIBAL ENROLLMENT Year	County	No.
2099	1 Fobb, Wallice ~~DIED PRIOR TO SEPTEMBER 25, 1902~~		35	M	Full	1896	Eagle	4188
2100	2 " Sien	Son	12	"	"	1896	"	4179
2101	3 " Carson	"	9	"	"	1896	"	4193
2102	4 " Soloman	"	7	"	"	1896	"	4184
	5							
	6							
	7							
	8							
	9							
	10							
	11	ENROLLMENT						
	12	OF NOS. 1 2 3 and 4 HEREON APPROVED BY THE SECRETARY						
	13	OF INTERIOR DEC 12 1902						
	14							
	15							
	16							
	17							

TRIBAL ENROLLMENT OF PARENTS

	Name of Father	Year	County	Name of Mother	Year	County
1	Sewee Fobb	Dead	Eagle	Ish tim ho ke	Dead	Eagle
2	No 1			Emiline Fobb	"	"
3	No 1			" "	"	"
4	No 1			" "	"	"
5						
6						
7	No3 on 1896 roll as Cars Fobb					
8	No1 " 1896 " " Wallace Fobb					
9						
10						
11						
12						
13						
14						
15						
16				Date of Application for Enrollment	April 25/99	
17						

221

Choctaw By Blood Enrollment Cards 1898-1914

RESIDENCE: Eagle COUNTY.	Choctaw Nation	Choctaw Roll (Not Including Freedmen)	CARD No.
POST OFFICE: Eagletown, I.T.			FIELD No. 822

Dawes' Roll No.	NAME	Relationship to Person First Named	AGE	SEX	BLOOD	TRIBAL ENROLLMENT		
						Year	County	No.
2103	1 Fobb, Louisa 83	First Named	80	F	Full	1896	Eagle	4174
	2							
	3							
	4							
	5							
	6	ENROLLMENT						
	7	OF NOS. 1 HEREON APPROVED BY THE SECRETARY						
	8	OF INTERIOR Dec 12, 1902						
	9							
	10							
	11							
	12							
	13							
	14							
	15							
	16							
	17							

TRIBAL ENROLLMENT OF PARENTS

	Name of Father	Year	County	Name of Mother	Year	County
1	Battiest Bobb	Dead	Eagle		Died	in Mississippi
2						
3						
4						
5						
6						
7						
8						
9						
10						
11						
12						
13						
14						
15						
16					Date of Application for Enrollment	April 25/99
17						

Choctaw By Blood Enrollment Cards 1898-1914

RESIDENCE: Bok Tuklo   COUNTY.   **Choctaw Nation**   **Choctaw Roll**   CARD No.
POST OFFICE: Lukfata, I.T.   *(Not Including Freedmen)*   FIELD No.   823

Dawes' Roll No.	NAME	Relationship to Person First Named	AGE	SEX	BLOOD	TRIBAL ENROLLMENT Year	County	No.
dead 1	Billy, Hudson	Named	47	M	Full	1896	Bok Tuklo	1251
dead 2	" Sillen	Wife	35	F	"	1896	" "	1252
3								
4								
5								
6								
7								
8								
9								
10	No. 1 & 2 HEREON DISMISSED UNDER							
11	ORDER OF THE COMMISSIONER TO THE FIVE CIVILIZED TRIBES OF JULY 18, 1905.							
12								
13								
14								
15								
16								
17								

TRIBAL ENROLLMENT OF PARENTS

	Name of Father	Year	County	Name of Mother	Year	County
1	Sampson Colbert	1896	Bok Tuklo	Okla ho nah	Dead	Bok Tuklo
2	George Graham	Dead	" "	Ma-ta-nah	"	" "
3						
4						
5						
6						
7	No1 died several years prior to Sept 25, 1902. Proof of death filed June 9, 1906.					
8	No2 " " " " " " "		" " " " " "			
9						
10						
11						
12						
13						
14						
15						
16					Date of Application for Enrollment	April 25/99
17						

Choctaw By Blood Enrollment Cards 1898-1914

RESIDENCE: Nashoba COUNTY.
POST OFFICE: Alikchi, I.T.

Choctaw Nation

Choctaw Roll *(Not Including Freedmen)*

CARD NO.
FIELD NO. **824**

Dawes' Roll No.	NAME		Relationship to Person	AGE	SEX	BLOOD	TRIBAL ENROLLMENT		
							Year	County	No.
2104	₁ Emeyabbi, Isham	25	First Named	22	M	Full	1896	Nashoba	3735
2105	₂ " Lucen	24	Wife	21	F	"	1896	"	11416
2106	₃ " Crosby	4	Son	2mo	M	"			
2107	₄ Stephen, Simmie	6	S. Dau	3	F	"	1896	Nashoba	11417
15937	₅ Emeyabbi, Abina		Son	1	M	"			
	₆								
	₇								
	₈								
	₉	ENROLLMENT							
	₁₀	OF NOS. 1 2 3 and 4 HEREON APPROVED BY THE SECRETARY							
	₁₁	OF INTERIOR Dec. 12, 1902							
	₁₂								
	₁₃								
	₁₄	ENROLLMENT							
	₁₅	OF NOS. ~~~ 5 ~~~ HEREON APPROVED BY THE SECRETARY							
	₁₆	OF INTERIOR Nov. 24 1905							
	₁₇								

TRIBAL ENROLLMENT OF PARENTS

	Name of Father	Year	County	Name of Mother	Year	County
₁	Forbis Emeyabbi	1896	Nashoba	Elean Johnson	1896	Nashoba
₂	Bynum Stephens	1896	"	Missouri Stephens	Dead	Skullyville
₃	No 1			No 2		
₄	Granson Stephen	1896	Nashoba	No 2		
₅	No 1			No 2		
₆						
₇	No2 on 1896 roll as Lucen Stephen					
₈	No4 " 1896 " " Sinie "					
₉	No5 was born Sept. 12, 1902; application received and No5 placed on this card April 13, 1905 under Act of Congress approved Mar. 3, 1905					
₁₀						
₁₁						
₁₂						
₁₃						
₁₄						
₁₅				#1 to 3 inc		
₁₆				Date of Application for Enrollment		April 25/99
₁₇	P.O. Noah, I.T. 4/8/05			No.4 "		26/99

Choctaw By Blood Enrollment Cards 1898-1914

RESIDENCE: Red River   COUNTY.   **Choctaw Nation**   **Choctaw Roll**   CARD No.
POST OFFICE: Garvin, I.T.   *(Not Including Freedmen)*   FIELD No.   **825**

Dawes' Roll No.	NAME	Relationship to Person First Named	AGE	SEX	BLOOD	TRIBAL ENROLLMENT Year	County	No.
2108	1 Thompson, Peter ⁴⁵	First Named	42	M	Full	1896	Red River	12317
2109	2 " , Rhoda ⁵⁸	Wife	55	"	"	1896	" "	12318
2110	3 " , Simeon ²²	Ward	19	"	"	1896	" "	12319
	4							
	5							
	6							
	7	ENROLLMENT						
	8	OF NOS. 1 – 2 and 3 HEREON APPROVED BY THE SECRETARY						
	9	OF INTERIOR Dec 12, 1902						
	10							
	11							
	12							
	13	No3 on 1896 roll as Simmon Thompson						
	14							
	15							
	16							
	17							

TRIBAL ENROLLMENT OF PARENTS

	Name of Father	Year	County	Name of Mother	Year	County
1	Yah-hesh-taby	Dead	Towson	Bole-hu-na	Dead	Towson
2	Jackson McClure	"	Red River	Isabelle McClure	"	Red River
3	Umpsion Daniel	"	Towson	Bicey Christie	"	Towson
4						
5						
6						
7						
8						
9						
10						
11						
12						
13						
14						
15				Date of Application		
16				for Enrollment.		
17				April 25/99		

225

RESIDENCE: Eagle COUNTY. **Choctaw Nation** Choctaw Roll CARD NO.
POST OFFICE: Eagletown, I.T. *(Not Including Freedmen)* FIELD NO. 826

Dawes' Roll No.	NAME	Relationship to Person Named	AGE	SEX	BLOOD	TRIBAL ENROLLMENT		
						Year	County	No.
2111	1 Harrison, Johnson ~~DIED PRIOR TO SEPTEMBER 25, 1902~~	First Named	39	M	Full	1896	Eagle	5621
2112	2 Sophie ~~DIED PRIOR TO SEPTEMBER 25, 1902~~	Wife	47	F	"	1896	"	5650
2113	3 " Calvin	Son	8	M	"	1896	"	5605
2114	4 Steven, Tom	Ward	15	"	"	1896	"	11430
	5							
	6							
	7	ENROLLMENT						
	8	OF NOS. 1 2 3 and 4 HEREON APPROVED BY THE SECRETARY						
	9	OF INTERIOR DEC 12 1902						
	10							
	11							
	12							
	13							
	14							
	15							
	16							
	17							

TRIBAL ENROLLMENT OF PARENTS

	Name of Father	Year	County	Name of Mother	Year	County
1	John Harrison	Dead	Eagle	Ye-me-ta-huna	Dead	Eagle
2	Ach ne tubbee	"	"	Mollie	"	"
3	No 1			No 2		
4	John Stephen	Dead	Eagle	Leviney Stephen	Dead	Eagle
5						
6	No1 died Dec 4, 1907; proof of death filed Dec 3, 1902.					
7	No2 " Jan 21,1902; " " " " " " "					
8	Nos 3 and 4 are now living with Sampson Jefferson, Choc. #760.					
9	~~No1 died Dec 4,1901; No2 died Jan 21, 1902; Enrollment cancelled by Department July 8, 1904~~					
10						
11						
12						
13						
14						
15					Date of Application for Enrollment.	
16					April 25/99	
17						

Choctaw By Blood Enrollment Cards 1898-1914

RESIDENCE: Nashoba COUNTY.
POST OFFICE: Smithville, I.T.

Choctaw Nation

Choctaw Roll
(Not Including Freedmen)

CARD NO.
FIELD NO. 827

Dawes' Roll No.	NAME	Relationship to Person First Named	AGE	SEX	BLOOD	TRIBAL ENROLLMENT		
						Year	County	No.
2115	1 Lewis, Simmon	First Named	24	M	Full	1896	Nashoba	7965
	2							
	3							
	4							
	5							
	6	ENROLLMENT						
	7	OF NOS. 1 HEREON APPROVED BY THE SECRETARY						
	8	OF INTERIOR DEC 12 1902						
	9							
	10							
	11							
	12							
	13							
	14							
	15							
	16							
	17							

TRIBAL ENROLLMENT OF PARENTS

	Name of Father	Year	County	Name of Mother	Year	County
1	Louis, Emacombey	Dead	Eagle	Isabelle Benjamin	Dead	Nashoba
2						
3						
4						
5						
6	No1 now the Husband of Lettie Jane Watson Choctaw Card #785. Evidence of marriage filed June 26th 1902					
7	For child of No.1 see NB (March 3, 1905) #867					
8						
9						
10						
11						
12						
13						
14						
15						
16				Date of Application for Enrollment	April 25/99	
17						

RESIDENCE: Nashoba COUNTY.
POST OFFICE: Smithville, I.T.

Choctaw Nation

Choctaw Roll
(Not Including Freedmen)

CARD NO.
FIELD NO. 828

Dawes' Roll No.		NAME	Relationship to Person First Named	AGE	SEX	BLOOD	TRIBAL ENROLLMENT		
							Year	County	No.
Dead	1	Benjamin, Charles ~~DIED PRIOR TO SEPTEMBER 25, 1902~~	First Named	32	M	Full	1896	Nashoba	1128
2116	2	" Nelly	Wife	36	F	"	1896	"	1129
2117	3	" Mina	Dau	12	"	"	1896	"	1133
2118	4	" Narsie	"	9	"	"	1896	"	1134
2119	5	" Rosa	"	3	"	"	1896	"	1130
2120	6	" Joe	Son	3m	M	"			
	7								
	8								
	9	ENROLLMENT							
	10	OF NOS. 2 3 4 5 and 6 HEREON APPROVED BY THE SECRETARY							
	11	OF INTERIOR DEC 12 1902							
	12	No. 1 HEREON DISMISSED UNDER							
	13	ORDER OF THE COMMISSION TO THE FIVE CIVILIZED TRIBES OF MARCH 31, 1905.							
	14								
	15								
	16								
	17								

TRIBAL ENROLLMENT OF PARENTS

	Name of Father	Year	County	Name of Mother	Year	County
1	~~Benj. Cohn~~	~~Dead~~	~~Eagle~~	~~Sukey Benjamin~~	~~1896~~	~~Nashoba~~
2	Jonas Colbert	"	Nashoba	Sallie Colbert	Dead	"
3	No 1			Hinny Stechi	1896	"
4	No 1			Elsey Colbert	Dead	"
5	No 1			No 2		
6	No 1			No 2		
7						
8						
9			No3 on 1896 roll as Minnie Benjamin			
10			No4 " 1896 " " Naisie "			
11			No1 Died June 30" 1899: Proof of Death filed December 20" 1902.			
12						
13						
14					#1 to 5 inc	
15				Date of Application for Enrollment.	April 25/99	
16				No6 enrolled Nov 1/99		
17						

Choctaw By Blood Enrollment Cards 1898-1914

RESIDENCE: Nashoba COUNTY. **Choctaw Nation** Choctaw Roll CARD NO.
POST OFFICE: Smithville, I.T. *(Not Including Freedmen)* FIELD NO. 829

Dawes' Roll No.	NAME	Relationship to Person Named	AGE	SEX	BLOOD	TRIBAL ENROLLMENT Year	County	No.
2121	1 Benjamin, Sooke	First Named	85	F	Full	1896	Nashoba	1131
2122	2 Lewis, Massey ~~DIED PRIOR TO SEPTEMBER 25, 1902~~	Dau	20	"	"	1896	"	1132
	3							
	4							
	5							
	6							
	7							
	8							
	9							
	10							
	11	ENROLLMENT						
	12	OF NOS. 1 and 2 HEREON APPROVED BY THE SECRETARY						
	13	OF INTERIOR DEC 12 1902						
	14							
	15							
	16							
	17							

TRIBAL ENROLLMENT OF PARENTS

	Name of Father	Year	County	Name of Mother	Year	County
1		Died	in Mississippi		Died	in Mississippi
2	~~Louis Emacombey~~	Dead	Eagle	~~Isabelle Benjamin~~	Dead	Nashoba
3						
4						
5						
6			No2 on 1896 roll as Missie Benjamin			
7			No2 Died July 16" 1899: Proof of Death filed December 2, 1902			
8			~~No2 died July 16, 1899: Enrollment cancelled by Department July 8, 1904.~~			
9						
10						
11						
12						
13						
14					Date of Application for Enrollment.	
15						
16					April 25/99	
17						

229

Choctaw By Blood Enrollment Cards 1898-1914

RESIDENCE: Eagle	COUNTY.				
POST OFFICE: Eagletown, I.T.	**Choctaw Nation**		Choctaw Roll *(Not Including Freedmen)*	CARD NO. FIELD NO. 830	

Dawes' Roll No.	NAME	Relationship to Person	AGE	SEX	BLOOD	TRIBAL ENROLLMENT		
						Year	County	No.
2123	1 Thomas, William	First Named	19	M	Full	1896	Eagle	12244
	2							
	3							
	4							
	5	ENROLLMENT						
	6	OF NOS. 1 HEREON APPROVED BY THE SECRETARY						
	7	OF INTERIOR Dec 12 1902						
	8							
	9							
	10							
	11							
	12	On 1896 roll as Williamson Thomas						
	13							
	14							
	15							
	16							
	17							

TRIBAL ENROLLMENT OF PARENTS

	Name of Father	Year	County	Name of Mother	Year	County
1	Abel Thomas	Dead	Eagle	Sallie Bahotubbee	1896	Eagle
2						
3						
4						
5						
6						
7						
8						
9						
10						
11						
12						
13						
14				Date of Application for Enrollment.		
15						
16				April 25/99		
17						

Choctaw By Blood Enrollment Cards 1898-1914

RESIDENCE: Bok Tuklo COUNTY. **Choctaw Nation** **Choctaw Roll** CARD NO.
POST OFFICE: Lukfata, I.T. (Not Including Freedmen) FIELD NO. **831**

Dawes' Roll No.	NAME	Relationship to Person First Named	AGE	SEX	BLOOD	TRIBAL ENROLLMENT Year	County	No.
2124	DIED PRIOR TO SEPTEMBER 25, 1902 1 Watson, Louie	Named	22	M	Full	1896	Bok Tuklo	13425
	2							
	3							
	4							
	5							
	6							
	7							
	8							
	9							
	10							
	11							
	12							
	13	On 1896 roll as Lowa Watson						
	14	No1 died February 22, 1902; proof of death filed Dec 3, 1902.						
	15							
	16							
	17							

ENROLLMENT
OF NOS. 1 HEREON
APPROVED BY THE SECRETARY
OF INTERIOR DEC 12 1902

TRIBAL ENROLLMENT OF PARENTS

	Name of Father	Year	County	Name of Mother	Year	County
1	Thos. Watson	1896	Bok Tuklo	Salina Watson	Dead	Bok Tuklo
2						
3						
4						
5						
6						
7						
8						
9						
10						
11						
12						
13						
14					Date of Application for Enrollment.	
15						
16					April 25/99	
17						

231

Choctaw By Blood Enrollment Cards 1898-1914

RESIDENCE: Nashoba COUNTY. **Choctaw Nation** Choctaw Roll *(Not Including Freedmen)* CARD NO.
POST OFFICE: Alikchi, I.T. FIELD NO. **832**

Dawes' Roll No.	NAME		Relationship to Person First Named	AGE	SEX	BLOOD	TRIBAL ENROLLMENT		
							Year	County	No.
2125	1 Battiest, Wade	41	First Named	38	M	Full	1896	Nashoba	1187
2126	2 " , Sina	33	Wife	30	F	"	1896	"	1188
2127	3 " , Silean	15	Dau	12	"	"	1896	"	1189
2128	4 " , Nelly	11	"	8	"	"	1896	"	1190
2129	5 " , Viney	6	"	3	"	"	1896	"	1191
	6								
	7								
	8								
	9								
	10								
	11								
	12								
	13								
	14								
	15								
	16								
	17								

ENROLLMENT OF NOS. 1, 2, 3, 4 and 5 HEREON APPROVED BY THE SECRETARY OF INTERIOR Dec. 12, 1902

TRIBAL ENROLLMENT OF PARENTS

	Name of Father	Year	County	Name of Mother	Year	County
1	E-ma-ha-tubbee	Dead	Nashoba	Sibbie Battiest	1896	Nashoba
2	Colone Bond	"	"	Larkie Bond	Dead	"
3	No 1			No 2		
4	No 1			No 2		
5	No 1			No 2		
6						
7						
8	No2 on 1896 roll as Sarneh Battiest					
9	No3 " 1896 " " Sally A. "					
10	No5 " 1896 " " Samilli "					
	For child of No3 see N.B. (March 3, 1905) #953					
11	For child of Nos 1&2 see N.B. (March 3, 1905) #954					
12						
13						
14						
15					Date of Application for Enrollment.	
16					April 25/99	
17	P.O. Bethel, I.T. 12/11 '02					

232

Choctaw By Blood Enrollment Cards 1898-1914

RESIDENCE: Eagle COUNTY. POST OFFICE: Eagletown, I.T.	**Choctaw Nation**	**Choctaw Roll** (Not Including Freedmen)	CARD NO. FIELD NO. **833**

Dawes' Roll No.	NAME	Relationship to Person First Named	AGE	SEX	BLOOD	TRIBAL ENROLLMENT Year	County	No.
2130	1 Stephen, Lemus 43		40	M	Full	1896	Eagle	11428
DEAD	2 " , Emy DEAD	Wife	39	F	"	1896	"	1270
2131	3 " , Melissa 4	Dau	4mo	"	"			
	4							
	5							
	6	ENROLLMENT OF NOS. 1 and 3 HEREON APPROVED BY THE SECRETARY OF INTERIOR Dec. 12, 1902						
	7							
	8							
	9							
	10	No2 hereon dismissed under order of						
	11	the Commission to the Five Civilized						
	12	Tribes of March 31, 1905.						
	13							
	14							
	15							
	16							
	17							

TRIBAL ENROLLMENT OF PARENTS

Name of Father	Year	County	Name of Mother	Year	County
1 Stephen Untahealy	1896	Eagle	Netchie	1896	Eagle
2	Dead	"	Lo-lo-ha-ma	Dead	"
3 No 1			No 2		
4					
5					
6					
7 No2 on 1896 roll as Emy Billy					
8 No1 is now the husband of Linas Wade on Choctaw Card #1250 Aug. 10, 1901.					
9 No2 Died Nov. 10, 1899. Proof of death received and filed Dec. 24, 1902.					
10 For child of No1 see N.B. (March 3, 1905) #1181					
11					
12					
13					
14				Date of Application for Enrollment.	
15					
16				April 25/99	
17					

233

RESIDENCE: Eagle COUNTY.
POST OFFICE: Eagletown, I.T.

Choctaw Nation

Choctaw Roll *(Not Including Freedmen)*

CARD NO.
FIELD NO. 834

Dawes' Roll No.		NAME		Relationship to Person First Named	AGE	SEX	BLOOD	TRIBAL ENROLLMENT		
								Year	County	No.
2132	1	Harris, Adam	42		39	M	Full	1896	Eagle	5601
2133	2	" Bicksy		Wife	42	F	"	1896	"	5602
2134	3	" Allen		Son	15	M	"	1896	"	5603
2135	4	" Alfred	11	"	8	"	"	1896	"	5604
2136	5	" Isnie	8	Dau	5	F	"	1896	"	5623
	6									
	7									
	8									
	9									
	10									
	11									
	12									
	13									
	14									
	15									
	16									
	17									

(DIED PRIOR TO SEPTEMBER 25, 1902 — rows 2 and 3)

ENROLLMENT
OF NOS. 1 2 3 4 and 5 HEREON
APPROVED BY THE SECRETARY
OF INTERIOR DEC 12 1902

TRIBAL ENROLLMENT OF PARENTS

	Name of Father	Year	County	Name of Mother	Year	County
1	Harris	Dead	Eagle	Okla-hema	Dead	Eagle
2	Ho-ten-la-by	"	"	Che-mollie-hoke	"	"
3	No 1			No 2		
4	No 1			No 2		
5	No 1			No 2		
6						
7	No1 on 1896 roll as Adam Harrison					
8	No2 " 1896 " " Betsy "					
9	No3 " 1896 " " Allen "					
	No4 " 1896 " " Alfred "					
10	No5 " 1896 " " Iany "					
11	No2 died Jan 2 1903: Enrollment cancelled by Department July 8. 1904					
12	No3 died before Sept 25. 1902: Enrollment cancelled by Department May 2, 1906.					
13						
14					Date of Application for Enrollment.	
15						
16					April 25/99	
17	P.O. Hochetown, I.T. 6/20/05					

234

Choctaw By Blood Enrollment Cards 1898-1914

RESIDENCE: Eagle COUNTY.		
POST OFFICE: Eagletown, I.T.	**Choctaw Nation**	Choctaw Roll (Not Including Freedmen)

CARD NO.

FIELD NO. 835

Dawes' Roll No.	NAME	Relationship to Person	AGE	SEX	BLOOD	TRIBAL ENROLLMENT		
						Year	County	No.
2137	1 Jefferson, Watkin ³¹	First Named	28	M	Full	1893	Bok Tuklo	P.R. 158
	2							
	3							
	4							
	5	ENROLLMENT						
	6	OF NOS. 1 HEREON APPROVED BY THE SECRETARY						
	7	OF INTERIOR DEC 12 1902						
	8							
	9							
	10							
	11							
	12							
	13	Also on 1896 roll as Watson Jefferson,						
	14	Page 171, No 6969 – Eagle Co.						
	15							
	16							
	17							

TRIBAL ENROLLMENT OF PARENTS

Name of Father	Year	County	Name of Mother	Year	County
1 Edwin Jefferson	Dead	Eagle	Susan Jefferson	Dead	Bok Tuklo
2					
3					
4					
5					
6					
7					
8					
9					
10					
11					
12					
13					
14					
15					
16					
17					

DATE OF APPLICATION FOR ENROLLMENT April 25/99

235

Choctaw By Blood Enrollment Cards 1898-1914

RESIDENCE: Eagle COUNTY.
POST OFFICE: Eagletown, I.T.

Choctaw Nation

Choctaw Roll
(Not Including Freedmen)

CARD NO.
FIELD NO. 836

Dawes' Roll No.	NAME	Relationship to Person	AGE	SEX	BLOOD	TRIBAL ENROLLMENT		
						Year	County	No.
2138	DIED PRIOR TO SEPTEMBER 25, 1902 1 Onnahabbi, Garvin	First Named	38	M	Full	1896	Eagle	9932
2139	DIED PRIOR TO SEPTEMBER 25, 1902 2 Efin	Wife	49	F	"	1896	"	P.R. 556
	3							
	4							
	5							
	6 ENROLLMENT							
	7 OF NOS. 1 and 2 HEREON APPROVED BY THE SECRETARY							
	8 OF INTERIOR DEC 12 1902							
	9							
	10							
	11							
	12							
	13							
	14							
	15							
	16							
	17							

TRIBAL ENROLLMENT OF PARENTS

	Name of Father	Year	County	Name of Mother	Year	County
1	Onnahabbi	1896	Eagle	O-boch-tuna	Dead	Eagle
2	Pisa-chubbee	Dead	Bok Tuklo	Ish-tala-ho-tema	"	Bok Tuklo
3						
4						
5						
6						
7	No2 on 1893 roll as Efin Onahabe					
8						
9	No1 died April 20, 1902; proof of death filed Dec 3, 1902					
	No2 " June 1900; proof of death filed Dec 3, 1902					
10	No1 died April 20, 1902; No2 died June 1900; Enrollment cancelled by Department July 8 1904					
11						
12						
13						
14						
15						
16				Date of Application for Enrollment	April 25/99	
17						

236

Choctaw By Blood Enrollment Cards 1898-1914

RESIDENCE: Eagle COUNTY.
POST OFFICE: Eagletown, I.T.

Choctaw Nation

Choctaw Roll CARD NO.
(Not Including Freedmen) FIELD NO. **837**

Dawes' Roll No.		NAME		Relationship to Person First Named	AGE	SEX	BLOOD	TRIBAL ENROLLMENT Year	County	No.
DEAD	1	Wilson, Silas DEAD			35	M	Full	1896	Eagle	13544
2140	2	" , Jinnie	28	Wife	25	F	"	1896	"	13537
2141	3	" , Willie	10	Son	7	M	"	1896	"	13526
2142	4	" , Standley	8	"	5	"	"	1896	"	13505
2143	5	DIED PRIOR TO SEPTEMBER 25, 1902 , Josie		Dau	7mo	F	"			
2144	6	DIED PRIOR TO SEPTEMBER 25, 1902 " , Raiey		Son	7mo	M	"			
	7									
	8									
	9	ENROLLMENT								
	10	OF NOS. 2,3,4,5and6 HEREON APPROVED BY THE SECRETARY								
	11	OF INTERIOR Dec. 2, 1902								
	12									
	13	No 1 hereon dismissed under order of								
	14	the Commission to the five civilized tribes of March 31, 1905.								
	15									
	16									
	17									

TRIBAL ENROLLMENT OF PARENTS

	Name of Father	Year	County	Name of Mother	Year	County
1	Elija Wilson	Dead	Eagle	Ettie Wilson	Dead	Eagle
2	Bill Sam	"	"	Winnie Sam	"	"
3	No 1			No 2		
4	No 1			No 2		
5	No 1			No 2		
6	No 1			No 2		
7						
8	No.1 died September 2, 1900. Evidence of death filed March 22, 1901.					
9	No6 Enrolled March 25, 1901.					
10	No5 Died in 1899; No6 Died winter of 1901 or 1902; Enrollment cancelled by Department					
11	May 2, 1906.					
12	For child of No.2 see N.B. (March 3, 1905) #1006					
13						
14				Date of Application for Enrollment.		
15						
16				April 25/99		
17						

Choctaw By Blood Enrollment Cards 1898-1914

RESIDENCE: Nashoba COUNTY.
POST OFFICE: Alikchi, I.T.

Choctaw Nation

Choctaw Roll
(Not Including Freedmen)

CARD NO.
FIELD NO. 838

Dawes' Roll No.	NAME		Relationship to Person	AGE	SEX	BLOOD	TRIBAL ENROLLMENT		
							Year	County	No.
2145	1 Homer, Pierce	54	First Named	51	M	Full	1896	Nashoba	5546
2146	2 " , Limer	43	Wife	40	F	"	1896	"	5547
2147	3 " , Arbit	6	Son	3	M	"	1896	"	5548
2148	4 " , Emiline	13	Dau	10	F	"	1896	"	5523
	5								
	6								
	7	ENROLLMENT							
	8	OF NOS. 1 2 3 and 4 HEREON APPROVED BY THE SECRETARY							
	9	OF INTERIOR Dec 12, 1902							
	10								
	11								
	12								
	13								
	14								
	15								
	16								
	17								

TRIBAL ENROLLMENT OF PARENTS

	Name of Father	Year	County	Name of Mother	Year	County
1	John Homer	Dead	Eagle	Jincey Homer	Dead	Eagle
2	Took-lo-tubbee	"	Nashoba	E-la-pa-hona	"	Nashoba
3	No 1			No 2		
4	No 1			Milen Homer	Dead	Nashoba
5						
6						
7	No3 on 1896 roll as Sibet Homer					
8	No4 " 1896 " " Emeline "					
9	For child of No4 see NB (Apr 26-06) Card #637.					
	" " " " (Mar 3-05) " #940.					
10						
11						
12						
13						
14						Date of Application for Enrollment.
15						
16						April 25/99
17	No4 P.O. Bethel I.T. 4/6/05					

238

Choctaw By Blood Enrollment Cards 1898-1914

RESIDENCE: Towson COUNTY.
POST OFFICE: Fowlerville, I.T.

Choctaw Nation

Choctaw Roll *(Not Including Freedmen)*

CARD No.
FIELD No. **839**

Dawes' Roll No.	NAME	Relationship to Person First Named	AGE	SEX	BLOOD	TRIBAL ENROLLMENT Year	County	No.
2149	₁ James, Absalom B.		40	M	Full	1896	Towson	6756
2150	₂ " , Cornelia S. ³¹	Wife	28	F	"	1896	"	6757
2151	₃ " , William ²¹	Son	18	M	"	1896	"	6758
2152	₄ " , Josiah ¹⁹	"	16	"	"	1896	"	6759
2153	₅ " , Frances ¹⁴	Dau	11	F	"	1896	"	6760
2154	₆ " , Nancy ¹¹	"	8	"	"	1896	"	6761
2155	₇ " , Raphael ⁹	Son	6	M	"	1896	"	6762
2156	₈ " , Louella ⁶	Dau	2	F	"			
2157	₉ " , Betsey ⁴	"	7mo	"	"			
2158	₁₀ " , Dallas ¹	Son	1mo	M	"			
	₁₁							
	₁₂							
	₁₃							
	₁₄							
	₁₅							
	₁₆							
	₁₇							

(DIED PRIOR TO SEPTEMBER 25, 1902) — [annotation across row 1]

```
ENROLLMENT
OF NOS. 1,2,3,4,5,6,7,8,9 and 10 HEREON
APPROVED BY THE SECRETARY
OF INTERIOR Dec. 12, 1902
```

TRIBAL ENROLLMENT OF PARENTS

	Name of Father	Year	County	Name of Mother	Year	County
1	William James	Dead	Bok Tuklo	Betsey James	Dead	Bok Tuklo
2	Michael Christie	"	Towson	Agnes Christie	"	Towson
3	No.1			Narcissa James	"	"
4	No.1			"	"	"	"
5	No.1			"	"	"	"
6	No.1			No.2		
7	No.1			No.2		
8	No.1			No.2		
9	No.1			No.2		
10	No.1			No.2		
11						
12			No1 on 1896 roll as A.B. James			
13			No2 " 1896 " " Cornelia "			
14			No6 " 1896 " " Mary "			
			No10 born Oct 23d,1901: Enrolled Nov. 22d, 1901.			
15			No1 died May 16, 1902; Proof of death filed Dec 3, 1902			#1 to 9 inc
16		No1 died May 16,1902: Enrollment cancelled by Department July 8, 1904.				Date of Application for Enrollment.
17	P.O. Chula 11/26/02		For child of No.3 see NB (March 3, 1905) #1270			April 25/99

P.O. Valliant I.T. 3/14/07

239

Choctaw By Blood Enrollment Cards 1898-1914

RESIDENCE: Towson COUNTY.
POST OFFICE: Fowlerville, I.T.

Choctaw Nation

Choctaw Roll
(Not Including Freedmen)

CARD No.
FIELD No. 840

Dawes' Roll No.	NAME	Relationship to Person First Named	AGE	SEX	BLOOD	TRIBAL ENROLLMENT Year	County	No.
2159	1 Christie, Tennessee	First Named	30	F	Full	1896	Towson	2458
2160	2 Holman, Sallie	Dau	7mo	F	"			
	3							
	4							
	5							
	6	ENROLLMENT OF NOS. 1 and 2 HEREON						
	7	APPROVED BY THE SECRETARY OF INTERIOR DEC 12 1902						
	8							
	9							
	10							
	11							
	12							
	13	No 2 Enrolled Aug 20, 1901.						
	14							
	15							
	16							
	17							

TRIBAL ENROLLMENT OF PARENTS

Name of Father	Year	County	Name of Mother	Year	County
1 Michael Christie	Dead	Towson	Agnes Christie	Dead	Towson
2 Unknown			No.1		
3					
4					
5					
6					
7					
8					
9					
10					
11					
12					
13					
14					
15				#1	
16				Date of Application for Enrollment	April 25/99
17					

240

RESIDENCE: Red River   COUNTY.   **Choctaw Nation**   Choctaw Roll   CARD NO.
POST OFFICE: Janis, I.T.   *(Not Including Freedmen)*   FIELD NO. **841**

Dawes' Roll No.	NAME	Relationship to Person Named	AGE	SEX	BLOOD	TRIBAL ENROLLMENT		
						Year	County	No.
2161	1 Simmons, James ⁴⁴	First Named	41	M	Full	1896	Red River	11451
2162	2 " , Viney ⁴¹	Wife	38	F	"	1896	" "	5712
Dead	~~DEAD " , Towson~~	~~Son~~	~~19~~	~~M~~	~~"~~	~~1896~~	~~" "~~	~~11453~~
2163	4 " , Irvin ⁷	"	4	"	"	1896	" "	11454
2164	5 Holt, Siley ¹³	S Dau	10	F	"	1896	" "	5713
2165	6 " , Silin ¹¹	"	8	"	"	1896	" "	5714
2166	7 " , Houston ⁷	S.Son	4	M	"	1896	" "	5715
	8							
	9	ENROLLMENT OF NOS. 1,2,4,5,6 and 7HEREON APPROVED BY THE SECRETARY						
	10	OF INTERIOR Dec 12, 1902						
	11							
	12	No.3 hereon dismissed under order of						
	13	the Commission to the Five Civilized						
	14	Tribes of March 31, 1905.						
	15							
	16							
	17							

TRIBAL ENROLLMENT OF PARENTS

	Name of Father	Year	County	Name of Mother	Year	County
1	Ya-kom-bey	Dead	Red River	Ca-no-tame	Dead	Red River
2	Gibson Bilvin	"	" "	Ho-yo-ka	"	" "
3	~~No 1~~			~~Louisa Simmons~~	"	" "
4	No 1			" "	"	" "
5	Jim Holt	Dead	Red River	No 2		
6	" "	"	" "	No 2		
7	" "	"	" "	No 2		
8						
9	No.2 on 1896 roll as Viney Holt.					
10	No.6 " 1896 " " Selina "					
11	No.7 " 1896 " " Heuston "					
12	~~No3 Died about June 12, 1899. Evidence of death filed May 24, 1901~~					
13						
14						
15						
16				Date of Application for Enrollment April 25/99		
17						

Choctaw By Blood Enrollment Cards 1898-1914

RESIDENCE: Nashoba COUNTY. **Choctaw Nation** Choctaw Roll CARD No.
POST OFFICE: Smithville, I.T. (Not Including Freedmen) FIELD No. **842**

Dawes' Roll No.	NAME	Relationship to Person First Named	AGE	SEX	BLOOD	TRIBAL ENROLLMENT Year	County	No.
2167	1 Impalumbi, Adam ~~DIED PRIOR TO SEPTEMBER 25, 1902~~		55	M	Full	1896	Nashoba	6260
2168	2 " Lowinie 47	Wife	44	F	"	1896	"	6261
2169	3 " Josephine 16	Dau	13	"	"	1896	"	6264
2170	4 " Abbester 14	Son	11	M	"	1896	"	6265
2171	5 " Sylvester 11	"	8	"	"	1896	"	6266
2172	6 " Ennis 6	Dau	3	F	"	1896	"	6267
	7							
	8							
	9							
	10							
	11	ENROLLMENT						
	12	OF NOS. 1 2 3 4 5 and 6 HEREON APPROVED BY THE SECRETARY						
	13	OF INTERIOR Dec. 12, 1902						
	14							
	15							
	16							
	17							

TRIBAL ENROLLMENT OF PARENTS

	Name of Father	Year	County	Name of Mother	Year	County
1	~~Impalumbi~~	~~Dead~~	~~Nashoba~~		Dead	Eagle
2	Tith-la-yo-taby	"	"	Wol-lie	"	Nashoba
3	No.1			No.2		
4	No.1			No.2		
5	No.1			No.2		
6	No.1			No.2		
7						
8						
9		No6 on 1896 roll as Janis Impalumbi				
10		No.1 died July 15, 1900: Enrollment cancelled by Department July 8, 1904				
11		For child of No3 see NB (Apr 26-06) Card #608				
12						
13						
14						
15						
16						
17				Date of Application for Enrollment.	April 25/99	

242

Choctaw By Blood Enrollment Cards 1898-1914

RESIDENCE: Eagle   COUNTY.
POST OFFICE: Eagletown, I.T.   **Choctaw Nation**   Choctaw Roll _(Not Including Freedmen)_   CARD NO.
FIELD NO. **843**

Dawes' Roll No.	NAME	Relationship to Person First Named	AGE	SEX	BLOOD	TRIBAL ENROLLMENT Year	County	No.
2173	1 Jacob, Eli _38_		35	M	Full	1896	Eagle	13490
2174	2 " Milin _27_	Wife	24	F	"	1896	"	1303
2175	3 " Soffin _7_	Dau	4	"	"	1896	"	13491
2176	4 " Henry _1_	Son	1mo	M	"			
	5							
	6							
	7							
	8							
	9							
	10							
	11							
	12							
	13							
	14							
	15							
	16							
	17							

ENROLLMENT
OF NOS. 1 2 3 and 4 HEREON
APPROVED BY THE SECRETARY
OF INTERIOR Dec. 12, 1902

No4 died April 26, 1902; Enrollment cancelled by Department March 2, 1907

TRIBAL ENROLLMENT OF PARENTS

	Name of Father	Year	County	Name of Mother	Year	County
1	Jacob	Dead	Bok Tuklo	Jinnie Jacob	Dead	Bok Tuklo
2	Abel Thomas	"	Eagle	Sallie Thomas	1896	Eagle
3	No 1			Facie Battiest	Dead	"
4	No 1			No 2		
5						
6						
7	No.2 on 1896 roll as Milin Billy					
8	No.3 " 1896 " " Soffit William					
9	No.1 " 1896 " " Eli					
10	No.4 born Dec 30,1901; Enrolled Jany. 15, 1902					
11	No.1 identified from 1893 Pay Roll, Boktuklo Co., P.48, No. 315					
12	No.2 also on 1893 PayRoll, Eagle Co., P.11, No.123, as Melin Billy					
13	For child of Nos. 1&2 see N.B. (March 3,1905) #1020.					
14					#1 to 3 inc	
15					Date of Application for Enrollment.	
16					April 25/99	
17						

243

Choctaw By Blood Enrollment Cards 1898-1914

RESIDENCE: Nashoba COUNTY.　**Choctaw Nation**　Choctaw Roll (Not Including Freedmen)

POST OFFICE: Smithville, I.T.

CARD NO. FIELD NO. **844**

Dawes' Roll No.	NAME	Relationship to Person	AGE	SEX	BLOOD	TRIBAL ENROLLMENT		
						Year	County	No.
2177	1 McCoy, Wicklis 51	First Named	48	M	Full	1896	Nashoba	9277
2178	2 " Silian 53	Wife	50	F	"	1896	"	9278
2179	3 " Semensie 13	Dau	10	"	"	1896	"	9279
	4							
	5							
	6							
	7							
	8	ENROLLMENT						
	9	OF NOS. 1 2 and 3 HEREON						
	10	APPROVED BY THE SECRETARY OF INTERIOR Dec 12, 1902						
	11							
	12							
	13							
	14							
	15							
	16							
	17							

TRIBAL ENROLLMENT OF PARENTS

	Name of Father	Year	County	Name of Mother	Year	County
1	Ah-no-la	Dead	Eagle	Pisa-he-ma	Dead	Eagle
2	E-mey-a-tubbee	"	"		"	"
3	No. 1			No. 2		
4						
5						
6						
7						
8						
9						
10						
11						
12						
13						
14						
15						
16					Date of Application for Enrollment	April 25/99
17						

244

Choctaw By Blood Enrollment Cards 1898-1914

RESIDENCE: Nashoba   COUNTY.   **Choctaw Nation**   Choctaw Roll   CARD NO.
POST OFFICE: Smithville, I.T.   *(Not Including Freedmen)*   FIELD NO. **845**

Dawes' Roll No.	NAME	Relationship to Person First Named	AGE	SEX	BLOOD	TRIBAL ENROLLMENT Year	County	No.
2180	1 Jefferson, Edson ²⁹		26	M	Full	1896	Nashoba	6829
2181	2 " , Sealy ²⁴	Wife	21	F	"	1896	"	6830
2182	3 " , Madison ⁸	Son	5	M	"	1896	"	6831
2183	4 " , Nicholas ⁶	"	3	"	"	1896	"	6832
Dead	5 DEAD " , Hobson	"	1	"	"			
2184	6 " , Esean ²	Dau	1	F	"			
15826	7 " , Levicy	Dau	1	F	"			
	8							
	9	ENROLLMENT						
	10	OF NOS. 1 2 3 4 and 6 HEREON APPROVED BY THE SECRETARY						
	11	OF INTERIOR Dec. 12, 1902						
	12							
	13	No. 5 hereon dismissed under order of						
	14	the Commission to the Five Civilized						
	15	Tribes of March 31, 1905.			ENROLLMENT			
	16				OF NOS. 7 HEREON APPROVED BY THE SECRETARY			
	17				OF INTERIOR Jun 12, 1905			

TRIBAL ENROLLMENT OF PARENTS

	Name of Father	Year	County	Name of Mother	Year	County
1	King Jefferson	Dead	Eagle	Pollie Jefferson	1896	Eagle
2	Adam Impalumbi	1896	Nashoba	Luena Impalumbi	1896	Nashoba
3	No 1			No 2		
4	No 1			No 2		
5	No 1			No 2		
6	No 1			No 2		
7	No 1			No 2		
8						
9						
10	No2 on 1896 roll as Cillie Jefferson					
11	No6 Enrolled June 8th, 1902					
12	No.5 died June 25, 1901: Proof of death filed March 6, 1902.					
13	No7 was born March 22d, 1902: Application received and name placed on this card March 25, 1905, under provision of act of Congress, approved					
14	March 3d, 1905. For children of Nos 1 &2 see N.B. (March 3, 1905) #892					
15						
16					#1 to 5 inc	
17					Date of Application for Enrollment. April 25/99	

Choctaw By Blood Enrollment Cards 1898-1914

RESIDENCE: Nashoba COUNTY.
POST OFFICE: Alikchi, I.T.

Choctaw Nation

Choctaw Roll
(Not Including Freedmen)

CARD NO.
FIELD NO. **846**

Dawes' Roll No.	NAME	Relationship to Person First Named	AGE	SEX	BLOOD	TRIBAL ENROLLMENT Year	County	No.
2185	1 Gipson, James 69	First Named	66	M	Full	1896	Nashoba	4760
2186	2 " , Elizabeth 53	Wife	50	F	"	1896	"	4761
2187	3 " , Simon 12	Son	9	M	"	1896	"	4762
2188	4 " , Lula 7	Dau	4	F	"	1896	"	4763
	5							
	6							
	7							
	8							
	9							
	10							
	11	ENROLLMENT						
	12	OF NOS. 1 2 3 and 4 HEREON APPROVED BY THE SECRETARY						
	13	OF INTERIOR Dec 12, 1902						
	14							
	15							
	16							
	17							

TRIBAL ENROLLMENT OF PARENTS

	Name of Father	Year	County	Name of Mother	Year	County
1	Ho-yo-ho-ka	Dead	Nashoba	A-la-ma-ke-ka	Dead	Nashoba
2	Nok-ke-ne-homby	"	"		"	Sugar Load
3	No 1			No 2		
4	No 1			No 2		
5						
6						
7						
8						
9						
10						
11						
12						
13						
14						
15						
16				Date of Application for Enrollment		April 25/99
17						

RESIDENCE: Eagle	COUNTY.					

RESIDENCE: Eagle   COUNTY.   **Choctaw Nation**   Choctaw Roll   CARD NO.
POST OFFICE: Eagletown, I.T.   (Not Including Freedmen)   FIELD NO. **847**

Dawes' Roll No.	NAME	Relationship to Person First Named	AGE	SEX	BLOOD	TRIBAL ENROLLMENT		
						Year	County	No.
2189	₁ Johnson, Charles DIED PRIOR TO SEPTEMBER 25, 1902		20	M	Full	1896	Eagle	6973
2190	₂ " Nelis 20	Wife	17	F	"	1893	"	P.R. 308
2191	₃ " Lucy Ann DIED PRIOR TO SEPTEMBER 25, 1902	Dau	1	"	"			
15780	₄ Onahabbe, Silence 1	Dau of No.2	1	F	"	Died Dec 16,1902		
	₅							
	₆							
	₇	ENROLLMENT						
	₈	OF NOS. 1 2 and 3 HEREON APPROVED BY THE SECRETARY						
	₉	OF INTERIOR Dec 12 1902						
	₁₀							
	₁₁							
	₁₂							
	₁₃							
	₁₄	ENROLLMENT						
	₁₅	OF NOS. 4 HEREON APPROVED BY THE SECRETARY						
	₁₆	OF INTERIOR Mar 15 1905						
	₁₇							

TRIBAL ENROLLMENT OF PARENTS

	Name of Father	Year	County	Name of Mother	Year	County
₁	Peter Johnson	Dead	Eagle	Siekie Johnson	Dead	Eagle
₂	Thompson Hotambe	"	"	Jincey Hotambe	"	"
₃	No. 1			No. 2		
₄	Calvin Onahabbe	"	Eagle	No.2		
₅						
₆						
₇						
₈	No.2 on 1893 Pay Roll as Nelis Hotambe also on 1896					
₉	roll as Nilis Hotambi, Page 137, No. 5631					
₁₀	Eagle Co					
	No.1 died in 1901: proof of death filed Dec. 3, 1902					
₁₁	No.3 " May1901: " " " " " 3, 1902.					
₁₂	No.1 died - - 1901: No3 died May-1901: Enrollment cancelled by Department July 8, 1904.					
₁₃	No.4 was born Nov.25,1901: application for her enrollment was made at					
	Garvin, I.T. in Nov. 1902: proof of birth filed and placed on this card				#1 to 3	
₁₄	Dec 23d, 1904				Date of Application	
₁₅					for Enrollment.	
₁₆					April 25/99	
₁₇						

Choctaw By Blood Enrollment Cards 1898-1914

RESIDENCE: Red River   COUNTY.   **Choctaw Nation**   Choctaw Roll   CARD NO.
POST OFFICE: Kullituklo, I.T.   *(Not Including Freedmen)*   FIELD NO. **848**

Dawes' Roll No.	NAME	Relationship to Person First Named	AGE	SEX	BLOOD	TRIBAL ENROLLMENT		
						Year	County	No.
2192	1 Frazier, Wilson E ³²	First Named	29	M	Full	1896	Red River	4203
2193	2 " Mollie ³¹	Wife	28	F	"	1896	" "	4204
2194	3 " Cornelius ⁷	Son	4	M	"	1896	" "	4206
2195	4 " Cornelia ³	Dau	1mo	F	"			
	5							
	6							
	7							
	8							
	9							
	10							
	11							
	12							
	13							
	14							
	15							
	16	No 1 on 1896 roll as W E Frazier						
	17	For child of nos[sic] 1&2 see NB (March 3, 1905) #1466						

ENROLLMENT
OF NOS. 1 2 3 and 4 HEREON
APPROVED BY THE SECRETARY
OF INTERIOR Dec 12 1902

TRIBAL ENROLLMENT OF PARENTS

	Name of Father	Year	County	Name of Mother	Year	County
1	Elum Frazier	Dead	Red River	Jincey Frazier	Dead	Red River
2	Robison Choate	"	" " "	Lottie Choate	"	" " "
3	No.1			No.2		
4	No.1			No.2		
5						
6						
7						
8						
9						
10						
11						
12						
13					Date of Application for Enrollment.	
14						
15				No 4 enrolled Nov 24/99		
16				April 25/99		
17						

248

Choctaw By Blood Enrollment Cards 1898-1914

RESIDENCE: Eagle COUNTY.
POST OFFICE: Eagletown, I.T.

Choctaw Nation

Choctaw Roll
(Not Including Freedmen)

CARD NO.
FIELD NO. **849**

Dawes' Roll No.	NAME	Relationship to Person First Named	AGE	SEX	BLOOD	TRIBAL ENROLLMENT Year	County	No.
2196	1 Ebahotubbi, Davis 28	First Named	25	M	Full	1896	Eagle	3756
2197	2 " Sallie 48	Wife	45	F	"	1893	"	P.R. 119
2198	3 Billy, Nelly 14	S.Dau	11	"	"	1896	"	1308
2199	4 Thomas, Melena 18	"	15	"	"	1893	"	P.R. 123
2200	5 Amos, Hickman 9	Ward	6	M	"	1893	"	53
14602	6 Ebahotubbi, Aaron 1	Son	6mo	M				
	7							
	8							
	9	ENROLLMENT OF NOS. 1 2 3 4 and 5 HEREON APPROVED BY THE SECRETARY OF INTERIOR Dec 12 1902						
	10							
	11							
	12							
	13	ENROLLMENT OF NOS. 6 HEREON APPROVED BY THE SECRETARY						
	14							
	15	OF INTERIOR May 20 1903						
	16							
	17							

TRIBAL ENROLLMENT OF PARENTS

	Name of Father	Year	County	Name of Mother	Year	County
1	Johon[sic] Ebahotubbi	Dead	Eagle	Susan Ebahotubbi	Dead	Eagle
2	Lasso Billy	"	"	Ellen Billy	"	"
3	Hampton Billy	"	"	No. 2		
4	Abel Thomas	"	"	No.2		
5	Onsen Amos	"	"	Sarah Amos	Dead	Eagle
6	No. 1			Nancy Ebahotubbi	1893	Wade

7 No.1 now the husband of Nancy Billy on Choctaw card #D140: Evidence of marriage filed Oct 11, 1902
8 No.2 on 1893 Pay roll as wife of Hampton Billy
9 No.2 " 1893 " " " Sallie Billy
No.4 " 1893 " " " Lena "
10 No.2 also on 1896 Choctaw Census roll: page 33: #132 as Sallie Billy
11 Evidence of divorce between Nos. 1 and 2 filed Oct 11, 1902
12 No6 Born April 10, 1902, enrolled Oct 11, 1902
No.4 is now wife of Ziad Harrison, Choc #739: certificate of marriage filed
13 Dec. 11, 1902
14 No.5 on 1896 Roll as Hickman Billy, P. 232, #1280
15 Wife of no.1 is Nancy Ebahotubbi Choctaw card #5638 Jany 31, 1903

#1 to 5 inc

Date of Application for Enrollment April 25/99

249

Choctaw By Blood Enrollment Cards 1898-1914

RESIDENCE: Towson COUNTY.
POST OFFICE: Doaksville, I.T.

Choctaw Nation

Choctaw Roll
(Not Including Freedmen)

CARD NO.
FIELD NO. **850**

Dawes' Roll No.	NAME		Relationship to Person First Named	AGE	SEX	BLOOD	TRIBAL ENROLLMENT		
							Year	County	No.
2201	1 Tims, Mitchell	33	First Named	30	M	1/2	1896	Towson	12117
2202	2 " Mildred	22	Wife	19	F	Full	1896	"	1098
2203	3 " Egnes E	1	Dau	2wks	F	3/4			
2204	4 DIED PRIOR TO SEPTEMBER 25, 1902 Else		Dau	2wks	F	3/4			
	5								
	6								
	7								
	8								
	9								
	10								
	11								
	12								
	13								
	14								
	15								
	16								
	17								

ENROLLMENT
OF NOS. 1 2 3 and 4 HEREON
APPROVED BY THE SECRETARY
OF INTERIOR Dec 12 1902

TRIBAL ENROLLMENT OF PARENTS

	Name of Father	Year	County	Name of Mother	Year	County
1	Benson Tims	Dead	Towson	Emiline Tims	1896	Towson
2	Nuck-a-mash	"	Jacks Fork	Me-ley	Dead	Jacks Fork
3	N⁰ 1			N⁰ 2		
4	N⁰ 1			N⁰ 2		
5						
6						
7						
8						
9	No.2 on 1896 roll as Mildred Billy					
10	For child of nos.1&2 see NB (March 3, 1905) #1170					
11	New born child. Else on Card D529					
12	No.3 Born Dec. 21, 1901: enrolled Jan. 3, 1902.					
13	No.4 born November 9, 1899: transferred to this card					
14	July 11, 1902.					#1&2
15	No.4 died Nov. 25, 1900: proof of death filed Dec. 5. 1902					Date of Application for Enrollment.
16	No.4 died Nov. 25, 1900: Enrollment cancelled by Department July 8. 1904					April 25/99
17	P.O. Fort Towson I.T. 3/25/05					

250

Choctaw By Blood Enrollment Cards 1898-1914

RESIDENCE: Red River   COUNTY. **Choctaw Nation**   **Choctaw Roll** CARD NO.
POST OFFICE: Goodwater, I.T.   *(Not Including Freedmen)*   FIELD No. **851**

Dawes' Roll No.	NAME	Relationship to Person First Named	AGE	SEX	BLOOD	TRIBAL ENROLLMENT Year	County	No.
2205	1 Brown, Michael J. ⁴¹	First Named	38	M	Full	1896	Red River	1360
2206	2 " Susan ³⁸	Wife	35	F	"	1896	" "	1361
2207	3 " Rachael ¹³	Dau	10	"	"	1896	" "	1362
2208	4 " Hinmon ¹¹	Son	8	M	"	1896	" "	1363
2209	5 " Leila ³	Dau	3mo	F	"			
	6							
	7							
	8							
	9							
	10							
	11							
	12							
	13							
	14							
	15							
	16							
	17							

ENROLLMENT OF NOS. 1 2 3 4 and 5 HEREON APPROVED BY THE SECRETARY OF INTERIOR Dec 12 1902

TRIBAL ENROLLMENT OF PARENTS

	Name of Father	Year	County	Name of Mother	Year	County
1	James Brown	Dead	Red River	Sina Brown	1896	Red River
2	Isaac Hopakonaby	"	" " "	Eliz Hopakonaby	1896	" "
3	No.1			No.2		
4	No.1			No.2		
5	No.1			No.2		
6						
7	No.3 on 1896 Roll as Rachel Brown					
8	No.4 on 1896 roll as Hammon Brown					
9	No.5 Enrolled June 28, 1901					

#1 to 4

Date of Application for Enrollment.
April 25/99

251

Choctaw By Blood Enrollment Cards 1898-1914

RESIDENCE: Red River COUNTY. **Choctaw Nation** Choctaw Roll CARD No.

POST OFFICE: Goodwater, I.T. *(Not Including Freedmen)* FIELD No. **852**

Dawes' Roll No.	NAME	Relationship to Person First Named	AGE	SEX	BLOOD	TRIBAL ENROLLMENT Year	County	No.
~~2210~~	~~1 Brown, Sina~~ DIED PRIOR TO SEPTEMBER 25, 1902	~~First Named~~	~~75~~	~~F~~	~~Full~~	~~1896~~	~~Red River~~	~~1364~~
2211	2 " Harriet 39	Dau	36	"	"	1896	" "	1365
2212	3 Byington, Thomas A 24	G. Son	21	M	"	1896	" "	1366
	4							
	5							
	6							
	7							
	8							
	9							
	10							
	11							
	12							
	13							
	14							
	15							
	16							
	17							

ENROLLMENT OF NOS 1 2 and 3 HEREON APPROVED BY THE SECRETARY OF INTERIOR Dec 12 1902

TRIBAL ENROLLMENT OF PARENTS

	Name of Father	Year	County	Name of Mother	Year	County
1	~~Capt. Shoney~~	~~Dead~~	~~Eagle~~		~~Dead~~	~~Eagle~~
2	James Brown	"	Red River	No. 1		
3	Thos. A. Byington	"	" "	Adeline Byington	Dead	Red River
4						
5						
6						

7 No.1 died August 31, 1902 Enrollment cancelled by Department May 2, 1906

8 No.1 on 1896 roll as Sannie Brown

9 No.3 " 1896 " " Ainsworth Byington

~~No.3 " 1893 payroll Redriver Co., P.11, N° 96 as F.A. Byington~~

10 No.3 is now husband of Miney James on Choc. #1160

11 No.1 died Aug 31, 1902: proof of death filed Dec 3, 1902.

12

13

14 Date of Application for Enrollment.

15

16 April 25/99

17

252

Choctaw By Blood Enrollment Cards 1898-1914

RESIDENCE: Red River COUNTY.
POST OFFICE: Kullituklo, I.T.

Choctaw Nation

Choctaw Roll
(Not Including Freedmen)

CARD NO.
FIELD NO. **853**

Dawes' Roll No.	NAME	Relationship to Person First Named	AGE	SEX	BLOOD	TRIBAL ENROLLMENT		
						Year	County	No.
I.W. 507	1 Herndon, Sidney J ²⁹	First Named	26	M	I.W.	1896	Red River	14632
2213	2 " Emma J ²⁴	Wife	21	F	1/8	1896	" "	5672
2214	3 " Arthur S ⁷	Son	4	M	1/16	1896	" "	5673
2215	4 " Bertha M ⁵	Dau	2	F	1/16			
2216	5 " Elmer ³	Son	1mo	M	1/16			
2217	6 " Claude D. ¹	Son	2wk	M	1/16			
2218	7 " Clide H. ¹	Son	2wk	M	1/16			
	8							
	9 ENROLLMENT							
	OF NOS. 2 3 4 5 6 and 7 HEREON							
	10 APPROVED BY THE SECRETARY							
	OF INTERIOR Dec 12 1902							
	11							
	12							
	13 ENROLLMENT							
	OF NOS. ~~ 1 ~~ HEREON							
	14 APPROVED BY THE SECRETARY							
	OF INTERIOR Dec 24 1903							
	15							
	16							
	17							

TRIBAL ENROLLMENT OF PARENTS

Name of Father	Year	County	Name of Mother	Year	County
1 Harrison Herndon	1896	Non Citz.	Alice R. Herndon	1896	Non Citz
2 John Pebsworth	Dead	Towson	Mary C. Pebsworth	Dead	Intermarried
3	No.1			No.2	
4	No.1			No.2	
5	No.1			No.2	
6	No.1			No.2	
7	No.1			No.2	
8					
9	Affidavits as to birth of Nos 4 and 5 to be supplied: Recd May 4/99				
10					
11	No.6 Enrolled Aug 9, 1901				
	No.7 " Aug 9, 1901				
12	Nos 6 and 7 are twins.				
13	For child of nos 1&2 see NB (March 3, 1905) #884				
14					
15				#1 to 5	
16				Date of Application for Enrollment April 25/99	
17	P.O. Idabel I.T. 4/12/05				

RESIDENCE: Towson COUNTY.
POST OFFICE: Fowlerville, I.T.

Choctaw Nation

Choctaw Roll
(Not Including Freedmen)

CARD NO.
FIELD NO. **854**

Dawes' Roll No.		NAME	Relationship to Person	AGE	SEX	BLOOD	TRIBAL ENROLLMENT		
							Year	County	No.
I.W.508	1	Herndon, Edgar B ³⁰	First Named	27	M	I.W.	1896	Towson	14622
2219	2	" Lucy ³⁵	Wife	32	F	Full	1896	"	5511
2220	3	" Alice ⁶	Dau	2	"	1/2			
2221	4	" Harrison ³	Son	1mo	M	1/2			
2222	5	Townsend, Charles J ¹⁷	S.Son	14	"	1/2	1896	Towson	12106
2223	6	" Sarah ¹⁴	S.Dau	11	F	1/2	1896	"	12107
2224	7	" Susan ¹²	"	9	"	1/2	1896	"	12108
2225	8	" Clark ¹⁰	S.Son	7	M	1/2	1896	"	12109
2226	9	" Benjamin ⁸	"	5	"	1/2	1896	"	12110
2227	10	Herndon, James ²	Son	1mo	M	1/2			
	11	ENROLLMENT							
	12	OF NOS. 23456789and10 HEREON							
	13	APPROVED BY THE SECRETARY OF INTERIOR Dec 12 1902							
	14								
	15						ENROLLMENT OF NOS. 1 HEREON		
	16						APPROVED BY THE SECRETARY OF INTERIOR Dec 24 1903		
	17	For child of nos1&2 see NB(Apr26-06) card#632							

TRIBAL ENROLLMENT OF PARENTS

	Name of Father	Year	County	Name of Mother	Year	County
1	Harrison Herndon	1896	Non Citz	Alice R. Herndon	1896	Non Citz
2	McCann	Dead	Bok Tuklo	Mary McCann	Dead	Bok Tuklo
3	No.1			No.2		
4	No.1			No.2		
5	W.J. Townsend	Dead	Non Citz	No.2		
6	" " "	"	" " "	No.2		
7	" " "	"	" " "	No.2		
8	" " "	"	" " "	No.2		
9	" " "	"	" " "	No.2		
10	No.1			No.2		
11	Affidavits as to birth of Nos 3 and 4 to be supplied. Recd May 9/99					
12	No.5 on 1896 roll as Charles Townsend			For child of nos.1&2 see NB(Mar 3'05) #526		
13	No.8 " 1896 " " Clarke "					
14	No.10 Enrolled March 15th, 1901			#1 to 9 Date of Application for Enrollment.		
15						
16	P.O. Parsons I.T. 3/27/05			April 25/99		
17	P.O. Chula, I.T. 11/26/02					

Choctaw By Blood Enrollment Cards 1898-1914

RESIDENCE: Red River   COUNTY.   **Choctaw Nation**   **Choctaw Roll**   CARD NO.
POST OFFICE: Kullituklo, I.T.   *(Not Including Freedmen)*   FIELD NO.   **855**

Dawes' Roll No.	NAME		Relationship to Person First Named	AGE	SEX	BLOOD	Year	County	No.
I.W. 785	1 Herndon, Quintus	41		38	M	I.W.	1896	Red River	14634
14603	2 " Rosa	31	Wife	28	F	1/8	1896	" "	5685
14604	3 " May	11	Dau	8	"	1/16	1896	" "	5686
14605	4 " Edna	9	"	6	"	1/16	1896	" "	5687
14606	5 " Wilma	7	"	4	"	1/16	1896	" "	5688
14607	6 " Henry E.	4	Son	6mo	M	1/16			
14608	7 " Mayo	2	Son	1mo	M	1/16			
14609	8 " Raphiel	1	Son	5wks	M	1/16			
	9								
	10								
	11								

ENROLLMENT
OF NOS. 2,3,4,5,6,7 and 8 HEREON
APPROVED BY THE SECRETARY
OF INTERIOR May 20 1903

Judgement[sic] of U.S.Court admitting No1 vacated and set
aside by decree of Choctaw-Chickasaw Citizen Court Dec 17 '02.
13

1No.1 now in C.C.C.C. Case #21

15For child of Nos.1&2 see NB(Apr 26-06)Card-#413

Further action in connection with allotment to Nos. 2 to 8 inclusive suspended under protest of
attorney for Choctaw and Chickasaw Nations Jan23-1904 Protest withdrawn by Attys Mch24,1904
17

TRIBAL ENROLLMENT OF PARENTS

	Name of Father	Year	County	Name of Mother	Year	County
1	Harrison Herndon	1896	Non Citz	Alice R. Herndon	1896	Non Citz.
2	John Pebsworth	Dead	Towson	Mary Pebsworth	Dead	Blue
3	No.1			No.2		
4	No.1			No.2		
5	No.1			No.2		
6	No.1			No.2		
7	No.1			No.2		
8	No.1			No.2		
9						

* No.1 admitted by C.C.C.C. Case #21 March 21 '04.
11 No.5 on 1896 roll as Wilma Herndon
12 No.1 Denied by Dawes Com in 96 Case #430
No.6 Affidavit of birth to be supplied. Recd May 4/99
13 No.7 Enrolled December 15, 1900.
14 No.1 admitted as an intermarried citizen by U.S Court for Central
15 District, I.T. South McAlester I.T. July 13, 1897 Court Case #164.
16 No.8 Born Aug. 26, 1902, enrolled Oct. 12, 1902.
17

ENROLLMENT
OF NOS. 1 HEREON
APPROVED BY THE SECRETARY
OF INTERIOR May 9 1904

Date of Application for Enrollment. For Nos. 1to6incl

April 25/99

255

Choctaw By Blood Enrollment Cards 1898-1914

RESIDENCE: Eagle   COUNTY.   **Choctaw Nation**   Choctaw Roll *(Not Including Freedmen)*   CARD NO.

POST OFFICE: Eagletown, I.T.   FIELD NO. **856**

Dawes' Roll No.	NAME	Relationship to Person First Named	AGE	SEX	BLOOD	TRIBAL ENROLLMENT Year	County	No.
2228	1 Billy, Green ~~DIED PRIOR TO SEPTEMBER 25, 1902~~		49	M	Full	1896	Eagle	1338
2229	2 " Sias ¹⁷	Son	14	"	"	1896	"	1324
2230	3 " Ben ¹⁴	"	11	"	"	1896	"	1266
2231	4 " Loli ¹¹	Dau	8	F	"	1896	"	1294
	5							
	6							
	7							
	8							
	9							
	10							
	11							
	12							
	13							
	14							
	15							
	16							
	17							

ENROLLMENT OF NOS. 1 2 3 and 4 HEREON APPROVED BY THE SECRETARY OF INTERIOR Dec 12 1902

TRIBAL ENROLLMENT OF PARENTS

	Name of Father	Year	County	Name of Mother	Year	County
1	Billy	Dead	Eagle	Phene Billy	Dead	Eagle
2	No 1			Millie Billy	"	"
3	No 1			" "	"	"
4	No 1			" "	"	"
5						
6						
7			No.2 on 1896 roll as Silas Billy			
8						
9			No.1 died in May or June 1901; Enrollment cancelled by Department May 2, 1906.			
10						
11						
12						
13						
14						
15					Date of Application for Enrollment.	
16					April 25/99	
17						

Choctaw By Blood Enrollment Cards 1898-1914

RESIDENCE: Red River   COUNTY. **Choctaw Nation**   **Choctaw Roll**   CARD No.
POST OFFICE: Garvin, I.T.   (Not Including Freedmen)   FIELD No. **857**

Dawes' Roll No.	NAME		Relationship to Person First Named	AGE	SEX	BLOOD	TRIBAL ENROLLMENT		
							Year	County	No.
2232	₁ James, Watson	40	First Named	37	M	Full	1896	Red River	7039
2233	₂ " Winey	38	Wife	35	F	"	1896	" "	7040
2234	₃ " Moses	21	S.Son	18	M	"	1896	" "	7041
2235	₄ " Dixon	13	Son	10	"	"	1896	" "	7042
2236	₅ Willis, Emma	17	S.Dau	14	F	"	1896	" "	7043
	6								
	7								
	8								
	9								
	10								
	11								
	12								
	13								
	14								
	15								
	16								
	17								

ENROLLMENT
OF NOS. 1 2 3 4 and 5 HEREON
APPROVED BY THE SECRETARY
OF INTERIOR Dec 12 1902

TRIBAL ENROLLMENT OF PARENTS

	Name of Father	Year	County	Name of Mother	Year	County
1	Joe James	Dead	Red River	Sandie James	Dead	Red River
2	Foster	"	Bok Tuklo	Beckie Foster	"	" "
3	Gibson	"	Towson	No.2		
4	No.1			No.2		
5	Cisson Willis	Dead	Red River	No.2		
6						
7						
8			No.5 on 1896 roll as Emma James			
9			For child of No.3 see N.B. (Act. Mar 3-05) Card #288			
10			" " " " " " " " " " " " #963			
11						
12						
13						
14					Date of Application	
15					for Enrollment.	
16					April 25/99	
17						

257

Choctaw By Blood Enrollment Cards 1898-1914

Choctaw Nation

Choctaw Roll
(Not Including Freedmen)

CARD NO.
FIELD NO. **858**

Dawes' Roll No.	NAME		Relationship to Person First Named	AGE	SEX	BLOOD	TRIBAL ENROLLMENT		
							Year	County	No.
DEAD	1	Williams, Solomon	Named	57	M	Full	1896	Nashoba	13362
2237	2	" Wycie 58	Wife	55	F	"	1896	"	13363
2238	3	Jacob, Isaac 19	Ward	16	M	"	1896	"	6835
2239	4	Hicks, Holton 18	"	16	"	"	1896	"	5554
	5								
	6								
	7								
	8								
	9	ENROLLMENT							
	10	OF NOS. 2 3 and 4 HEREON							
		APPROVED BY THE SECRETARY							
	11	OF INTERIOR Dec 12, 1902				No			
	12								
	13	No. 1 hereon dismissed under order of							
	14	the Commission to the Five Civilized							
	15	Tribes of March 31, 1905.							
	16								
	17								

TRIBAL ENROLLMENT OF PARENTS

	Name of Father	Year	County	Name of Mother	Year	County
1	Williams	Dead	Nashoba	Pollie Williams	Dead	Nashoba
2	Charles Noah	"	"		"	
3	Jacob	"	Skullyville	Rhoda Jacob	"	Skullyville
4	Jacks Hicks	"	Nashoba	Jennie Hicks	"	Nashoba
5						
6						
7			Name of mother of No 2 could not be ascertained			
8						
9		No.1 died April, 1902: Evidence of death filed Dec. 9, 1902.				
10						
11						
12						
13						
14						
15						
16					Date of Application for Enrollment	April 25/99
17	No.2 P.O. Bethel I.T.	12/15/02				

Choctaw By Blood Enrollment Cards 1898-1914

RESIDENCE: Nashoba   COUNTY.   **Choctaw Nation**   **Choctaw Roll**   CARD No.
POST OFFICE: Alikchi, I.T   (Not Including Freedmen)   FIELD No.   **859**

Dawes' Roll No.	NAME	Relationship to Person First Named	AGE	SEX	BLOOD	TRIBAL ENROLLMENT		
						Year	County	No.
2240	1 Momintubbi, Jackson 63		60	M	Full	1896	Nashoba	8619
2241	2 Jackson, Silas 21		18	M	"	"	1896	"	10361
	3							
	4							
	5							
	6							
	7							
	8							
	9							
	10							
	11							
	12							
	13							
	14							
	15							
	16							
	17							

ENROLLMENT
OF NOS. 1 and 2 HEREON
APPROVED BY THE SECRETARY
OF INTERIOR Dec 12 1902

TRIBAL ENROLLMENT OF PARENTS

	Name of Father	Year	County	Name of Mother	Year	County
1	Achunatubbee	Dead	Nashoba	Unknown		
2	No.1	1896	Nashoba	Apa ba hona	Dead	
3						
4						
5						
6	No.1 died Nov. 30, 1899. Enrollment cancelled under Departmental authority					
7	of March 2, 1907 (I.T.D. 6614-1907) D.C. 12687-1907.					
8						
9	No.2 Silas Jackson enrolled as "Pisaletubbe".					
10						
11	No.1 died Nov. 30, 1899. Cancellation recommended 11/2/06.					
12						
13						
14				Date of Application for Enrollment.		
15						
16				April 25/99		
17						

259

Choctaw By Blood Enrollment Cards 1898-1914

RESIDENCE: Nashoba   COUNTY.   **Choctaw Nation**   Choctaw Roll   CARD NO.
POST OFFICE: Alikchi, I.T.   (Not Including Freedmen)   FIELD NO. **860**

Dawes' Roll No.	NAME	Relationship to Person First Named	AGE	SEX	BLOOD	TRIBAL ENROLLMENT		
						Year	County	No.
2242	1 Williams, Adeline 43		40	F	Full	1896	Nashoba	2513
2243	2 Baken, Morris 2	Son	1	M	"			
	3							
	4							
	5							
	6							
	7							
	8							
	9							
	10							
	11							
	12							
	13							
	14							
	15							
	16							
	17							

ENROLLMENT
OF NOS. 1 and 2 HEREON
APPROVED BY THE SECRETARY
OF INTERIOR Dec 12, 1902

TRIBAL ENROLLMENT OF PARENTS

	Name of Father	Year	County	Name of Mother	Year	County
1	Leonard Wright	Dead	Kiamitia	Sallie Wright	Dead	Kiamitia
2	Brazil Bacon[sic]	1896	Nashoba	No 1		
3						
4						
5						
6	No1 was formerly the wife of Brazil Bacon on Choctaw Card #745, from whom					
7	she was divorced Dec 6, 1901. Evidence of divorce filed June 2, 1902.					
8	No1 is now the wife of Morris Williams on Choctaw card #630 Evidence of marriage filed June 3, 1902.					
9	No2 Born March 2, 1901; enrolled June 3, 1902.					
10						
11						
12						
13						
14						
15					#1	
16					Date of Application for Enrollment	
17					April 25/99	

RESIDENCE: Nashoba COUNTY. **Choctaw Nation** Choctaw Roll CARD NO.
POST OFFICE: Alickchi[sic], I.T. *(Not Including Freedmen)* FIELD NO. **861**

Dawes' Roll No.	NAME		Relationship to Person First Named	AGE	SEX	BLOOD	TRIBAL ENROLLMENT		
							Year	County	No.
2244	1 Willis, Rayson	43	First Named	40	M	Full	1896	Nashoba	13342
2245	2 " Betsy	73	Wife	70	F	"	1896	"	13343
2246	3 " Vicey	21	Dau	18	F	"	1896	"	13344
2247	4 " Silen	17	Dau	14	F	"	1896	"	13345
2248	5 " Synwell	19	Son	16	M	"	1896	"	13346
	6								
	7	ENROLLMENT							
	8	OF NOS. 1,2,3,4 and 5 HEREON APPROVED BY THE SECRETARY							
	9	OF INTERIOR Dec. 12, 1902							
	10								
	11								
	12								
	13								
	14	March 14, 1909, Department requests report as to No.2							
	15	April 2, 1909 Report to Department							
	16	June 14, 1909 Department holds case of Betsy Willis is no analogous to Goldsby case and declines to							
	17	to[sic] take any action looking to her enrollment.							

TRIBAL ENROLLMENT OF PARENTS

	Name of Father	Year	County	Name of Mother	Year	County
1	Willis Willis	Dead		Abaiya Soply	Dead	
2	Going Robinson	"		Chi ho yo	"	
3	No.1	1896	Nashoba	No 2	1896	
4	No.1	1896	"	No 2	1896	
5	No.1	1896	"	No 2	1896	
6						
7	No.2 died in November, 1900: enrollment cancelled by Secretary of Interior					
8	Oct. 4th, 1905 (I.T.D. 12682-1905).					
9						
10			No.3 on 1896 Roll as Visie Willis			
11			No.4 Enrolled as Sillen Willis			
12			No.4 is female Change made under Departmental directions of			
13			July 3, 1905 (I.TD. 7950-1905) D.C. #33220-1905.			
14			For child of No.4 see NB (March 3, 1905) #1309.			
15					Date of Application for Enrollment.	
16					April 25/99	
17						

Choctaw By Blood Enrollment Cards 1898-1914

RESIDENCE: Red River COUNTY.		**Choctaw Nation**			**Choctaw Roll** (Not Including Freedmen)	CARD NO.
POST OFFICE: Garvin, I.T.						FIELD NO. **862**

Dawes' Roll No.	NAME	Relationship to Person First Named	AGE	SEX	BLOOD	TRIBAL ENROLLMENT		
						Year	County	No.
2249	1 LeFlore, Lonie M. ³⁸	First Named	35	M	Full	1896	Red River	8051
2250	2 " Salena ³⁷	Wife	34	F	"	1896	"	8052
2251	3 Jones, Hannah ²¹	Guardian	18	F	"	1896	"	7038
~~2252~~	~~4 Leflore, George ⁵~~	~~Ward~~	~~2~~	~~M~~	~~"~~			
	5							
	6							
	7							
	8	ENROLLMENT						
	9	OF NOS. 1 2 3 and 4 HEREON APPROVED BY THE SECRETARY						
	10	OF INTERIOR Dec 12 1902						
	11							
	12							
	13							
	14							
	15							
	16							
	17							

TRIBAL ENROLLMENT OF PARENTS

	Name of Father	Year	County	Name of Mother	Year	County
1	LeFlore Mitchell	Dead	Towson	LeFlore Mahaley	1896	Towson
2	Battiest McKinsey	"	Red River	Suckey Betsy	Dead	Red River
3	Jones Cornelius	"	" "	Cobb Julia	"	" "
4	~~Pistokcha Gibson~~	~~"~~	~~Kimitia[sic]~~	~~Carrie Pistokcha~~	~~1896~~	~~Kiamitia~~
5						
6	No.2 Enrolled as Cerena LeFlore					
7	No.3 Orphan living with No.1					
8	No.4 Adopted child of No.1					
	~~For child of No.3 see NB (March 3, 1905) #887~~					
9	~~No.4 Affidavit of birth to be supplied. Rec'd May 8/99~~					
10	No.1 on 1896 roll as L.M. LeFlore.					
11	No.4 Died June 12, 1902; proof of death filed Dec 3, 1902					
	~~No.4 died June 12, 1902: Enrollment cancelled by Department July 8, 1904~~					
12						
13						
14						
15				Date of Application for Enrollment		
16				April 25/99		
17						

Choctaw By Blood Enrollment Cards 1898-1914

RESIDENCE: Eagle   COUNTY.
POST OFFICE: Eagletown, I.T.

Choctaw Nation

Choctaw Roll
(Not Including Freedmen)

CARD No.
FIELD No.   **863**

Dawes' Roll No.	NAME	Relationship to Person First Named	AGE	SEX	BLOOD	TRIBAL ENROLLMENT		
						Year	County	No.
2253	1 Bunnup, William 34		31	M	Full	1896	Eagle	1331
2254	2 Sillen DIED PRIOR TO SEPTEMBER 25, 1902	Wife	28	F	"	1896	"	1321
2255	3 " Nollis 8	Son	5	M	"	1896	"	1301
2256	4 " Wisey 7	Dau	4	F	"	1896	"	1332
2257	5 Farics DIED PRIOR TO SEPTEMBER 25, 1902	Son	1	M	"			
	6							
	7							
	8							
	9							
	10							
	11	ENROLLMENT OF NOS. 1 2 3 4 and 5 HEREON						
	12	APPROVED BY THE SECRETARY						
	13	OF INTERIOR Dec 12 1902						
	14							
	15							
	16							
	17							

TRIBAL ENROLLMENT OF PARENTS

	Name of Father	Year	County	Name of Mother	Year	County
1	Joe Bunnup	Dead	Eagle	Wisey Bunnup	Dead	Eagle
2	John Stephens	"	"	Melvina Stephens	"	"
3	No.1			No.2		
4	No.1			No.2		
5	No.1			No.2		
6						
7						
8						
9						

No.1 on 1896 roll as Wᵐ Bump.
No.3 " 1896 " " Morris "
No.4 " 1896 " " Wisey "
No.2 died Jan'y 2, 1900: proof of death filed Dec 15, 1902
No.3 " Feby 19, 1900: " " " " Dec 15, 1902
No.2 died Jan 21[sic] 1901 No.3 died Feb 19, 1900: Enrollment cancelled by Department July 8, 1904
No.3 living on Sept 25, 1902. Restored to roll under Departmental authority of November 6, 1906
(I.T.D. 21716-1906) D.C. 48941-1906.

No.5 died February 19, 1900: Enrollment cancelled by Department Nov. 6, 1906.

Date of Application for Enrollment.

April 25/99

263

Choctaw By Blood Enrollment Cards 1898-1914

RESIDENCE: Nashoba   COUNTY.   **Choctaw Nation**   Choctaw Roll   CARD NO.
POST OFFICE: Alikchi, I.T.   (Not Including Freedmen)   FIELD NO. **864**

Dawes' Roll No.		NAME		Relationship to Person First Named	AGE	SEX	BLOOD	TRIBAL ENROLLMENT		
								Year	County	No.
DEAD	1	Battiest, Byington			40	M	Full	1896	Nashoba	1143
2258	2	" Mary	44	Wife	41	F	"	1896	"	1144
2259	3	" Agnes	18	Dau	15	"	"	1896	"	1145
2260	4	" Johnnie	15	Son	12	M	"	1896	"	1146
	5									
	6									
	7	ENROLLMENT								
	8	OF NOS. 2 – 3 and 4 HEREON APPROVED BY THE SECRETARY								
	9	OF INTERIOR Dec 2 1902								
	10									
	11	No. 1 hereon dismissed under order of								
	12	the Commission to the Five Civilized Tribes of March 31, 1905.								
	13									
	14									
	15									
	16									
	17									

TRIBAL ENROLLMENT OF PARENTS

	Name of Father	Year	County	Name of Mother	Year	County
1	Gaines Battiest	Dead	Nashoba	Pollie Battiest	Dead	Nashoba
2	Plannie Fisk	"	"	Annie Fisk		
3	No.1			No.2		
4	No.1			No.2		
5						
6						
7	For child of No.3 see NB (Apr 26-06) No. 568					
8	No.1 died Jan'y 14,1902: proof of death filed Dec. 16, 1902.					
9						
10						
11						
12						
13						
14						
15						
16				Date of Application for Enrollment	April 25/99	
17	P.O. Chula, I.T. 12/18/02					

RESIDENCE: Towson COUNTY.
POST OFFICE: Fowlerville, I.T.

Choctaw Nation

Choctaw Roll (Not Including Freedmen)

CARD NO. FIELD NO. **865**

Dawes' Roll No.		NAME		Relationship to Person First Named	AGE	SEX	BLOOD	TRIBAL ENROLLMENT		
								Year	County	No.
2261	1	Fowler, Jane	28	First Named	25	F	Full	1896	Towson	4128
2262	2	" Willie	9	Son	6	M	1/2	1896	"	4129
2263	3	" Louella	7	Dau	4	F	1/2	1896	"	4130
2264	4	" Mary E.	4	"	1	"	1/2			
W509	5	" David A.	35	Hus.	31	M	I.W.	1896	Towson	14528
2265	6	" Lena J.	2	Dau.	1mo	F	1/2			
	7									
	8	ENROLLMENT								
	9	OF NOS. 1 2 3 4 and 6 HEREON APPROVED BY THE SECRETARY								
	10	OF INTERIOR Dec 12 1902								
	11									
	12									
	13									
	14									
	15			ENROLLMENT							
	16			OF NOS. ~~~ 5 ~~~ HEREON APPROVED BY THE SECRETARY							
	17			OF INTERIOR Dec 24, 1903							

TRIBAL ENROLLMENT OF PARENTS

	Name of Father	Year	County	Name of Mother	Year	County
1	John Johnson	1896	Kiamitia	Fillis Johnson	Dead	Red River
2	David Fowler	1896	Non Citz	No.1		
3	" "	1896	" "	No.1		
4	" "	1896	" "	No.1		
5	Mears N. Fowler		" "	Martha Fowler		Non Citizen
6	No.5			No.1		
7						
8	No.3 on 1896 roll as Fonella Fowler					
9						
10	No.5 Enrolled Feby 16, 1900; Affidavits					
11	and correspondence attached. Feby 16, 1900.					
12	No.6 Enrolled December 21, 1900.					
13	No.5 also on 1896 Choctaw census roll page 387 #14528 as David Fowler				#1 to 4 inc	
14					Date of Application for Enrollment.	
15					April 25/99	
16	P.O. 11/26/02 Chula, I.T.					
17	P.O. Valliant, I.T. -/29/05[sic]	For child of Nos. 1&5 see NB (March 3-1905) Card No. 35 (32)				

"   "   "   "   "   "   " (April 26-1906) "   " 214
M-

Choctaw By Blood Enrollment Cards 1898-1914

RESIDENCE: Eagle COUNTY.				
POST OFFICE: Eagletown, I.T.				

Choctaw Nation

Choctaw Roll *(Not Including Freedmen)*

CARD NO.

FIELD NO. **866**

Dawes' Roll No.	NAME	Relationship to Person	AGE	SEX	BLOOD	TRIBAL ENROLLMENT		
						Year	County	No.
2266	1 Colbert, Simpson ⁴³	First Named	40	M	Full	1896	Eagle	2636
2267	² DIED PRIOR TO SEPTEMBER 25, 1902 Winny	Wife	35	F	"	1896	"	2642
2268	³ DIED PRIOR TO SEPTEMBER 25, 1902 Silva Ann	S.Dau	14	"	"	1896	"	4194
2269	4 " Milly ¹³	Dau	10	"	"	1896	"	2625
2270	5 " Osborne ¹¹	Son	8	M	"	1896	"	2631
2271	6 " Jesse ⁹	"	6	"	"	1896	"	2614
2272	7 " ✓Golton ⁵	"	2	"	"			
	8							
	9							
	10							
	11	ENROLLMENT						
	12	OF NOS. 1 2 3 4 5 6 and 7 HEREON APPROVED BY THE SECRETARY						
	13	OF INTERIOR Dec 12 1902						
	14							
	15							
	16							
	17							

TRIBAL ENROLLMENT OF PARENTS

	Name of Father	Year	County	Name of Mother	Year	County
1	Davis Colbert	Dead	Eagle		Dead	Eagle
2	Billie Barlow	"	"	Siney Barlow	"	"
3	Parro Farver	"	"	No 2		
4	No 1			No 2		
5	No 1			No 2		
6	No 1			No 2		
7	No 1			No 2		
8						
9						
10			No3 on 1896 roll as Silveann Farner			
11						
12		No2 died June 25, 1900: proof of death filed Dec 5, 1902				
13		No3 " June 24, 1900: " " " " " "				
		N°7 Born Jany. 28, 1896: proof of birth filed April 28, 1903				
14	No.2 died June25,1900:No.3 died June24,1900: Enrollment cancelled by Department July8,1904					
15		For child of No.1 see NB (March 3, 1905) #931				
16				Date of Application for Enrollment April 25/99		
17						

266

Choctaw By Blood Enrollment Cards 1898-1914

RESIDENCE: Red River COUNTY.
POST OFFICE: Kully Tuklo I.T

Choctaw Nation

Choctaw Roll
(Not Including Freedmen)

CARD No.

FIELD No. 867

Dawes' Roll No.	NAME	Relationship to Person First Named	AGE	SEX	BLOOD	TRIBAL ENROLLMENT Year	County	No.
2273	1 Watkins Wesley 56	First Named	53	M	Full	1896	Red River	13569
	2							
	3							
	4							
	5							
	6	ENROLLMENT						
	7	OF NOS. 1 HEREON APPROVED BY THE SECRETARY						
	8	OF INTERIOR DEC 12 1902						
	9							
	10							
	11							
	12							
	13							
	14							
	15							
	16							
	17							

TRIBAL ENROLLMENT OF PARENTS

Name of Father	Year	County	Name of Mother	Year	County
1 Watkins Isaac	Dead	Red River	Winnie Watkins	Dead	Red River
2					
3					
4					
5					
6					
7					
8					
9					
10					
11					
12					
13					
14			Date of Application for Enrollment.		
15					
16			April 25, 1899		
17					

267

Choctaw By Blood Enrollment Cards 1898-1914

RESIDENCE: Red River COUNTY. **Choctaw Nation** **Choctaw Roll** CARD NO.
POST OFFICE: Kully Tuklo I.T. (Not Including Freedmen) FIELD NO. 868

Dawes' Roll No.	NAME	Relationship to Person First Named	AGE	SEX	BLOOD	TRIBAL ENROLLMENT		
						Year	County	No.
2274	1 Edward Moses 27	First Named	24	M	Full	1896	Bok Tuklo	3742
2275	2 " Susan 56	Wife	53	F	"	1896	" "	251
	3							
	4							
	5							
	6							
	7							
	8							
	9							
	10							
	11	ENROLLMENT OF NOS. 1 and 2 HEREON						
	12	APPROVED BY THE SECRETARY						
	13	OF INTERIOR DEC 12 1902						
	14							
	15							
	16	No. 2 Enrolled as Susan Anderson						
	17							

TRIBAL ENROLLMENT OF PARENTS

	Name of Father	Year	County	Name of Mother	Year	County
1	Thomas Edwards[sic]	Dead	Bok Tuklo	Ilantima	Dead	Bok Tuklo
2	Kanotubbe	"	" "	Unknown		
3						
4						
5						
6						
7						
8						
9						
10						
11						
12						
13						
14						
15				Date of Application for Enrollment.		
16				April 25, 1899		
17						

268

RESIDENCE: Red River COUNTY. **Choctaw Nation** **Choctaw Roll** CARD No.
POST OFFICE: Kullituklo, I.T. *(Not Including Freedmen)* FIELD No. 869

Dawes' Roll No.	NAME	Relationship to Person First Named	AGE	SEX	BLOOD	TRIBAL ENROLLMENT Year	County	No.
2276	₁ Jones, Solomon ⁶¹		58	M	Full	1896	Red River	7023
DEAD	₂ " Liksey DEAD	Wife	70	F	"	1896	" "	7024
	₃							
	₄							
	₅							
	₆							
	₇							
	₈	ENROLLMENT						
	₉	OF NOS. 1 HEREON APPROVED BY THE SECRETARY						
	₁₀	OF INTERIOR DEC 12 1902						
	₁₁							
	₁₂							
	₁₃							
	₁₄	No. 2 HEREON DISMISSED UNDER ORDER OF THE COMMISSION TO THE FIVE CIVILIZED TRIBES OF MARCH 31, 1905.						
	₁₅							
	₁₆							
	₁₇							

TRIBAL ENROLLMENT OF PARENTS

	Name of Father	Year	County	Name of Mother	Year	County
₁	Joshn[sic] Jones	Dead	Red River	Pollie Jones	Dead	Red River
₂		"			"	
₃						
₄						
₅						
₆	No2 on 1896 roll as Letsy Jones					
₇						
₈	Parents of No2 never came to the Choctaw Nation. Their names could not be ascertained.					
₉	No.2 died May 16, 1901: Proof of death filed Nov. 30, 1901					
₁₀						
₁₁						
₁₂						
₁₃						
₁₄						
₁₅						
₁₆			Date of Application for Enrollment April 25/99			
₁₇						

Choctaw By Blood Enrollment Cards 1898-1914

RESIDENCE: Red River COUNTY. **Choctaw Nation** Choctaw Roll CARD NO.
POST OFFICE: Kully Tuklo I.T (Not Including Freedmen) FIELD NO. 870

Dawes' Roll No.	NAME		Relationship to Person	AGE	SEX	BLOOD	TRIBAL ENROLLMENT		
							Year	County	No.
2277	1 Willis Bicy	48	First Named	45	F	Full	1896	Red River	3590
2278	2 Stewart Siney	47	Sister	44	F	"	1896	" "	11434
	3								
	4								
	5								
	6								
	7	ENROLLMENT							
	8	OF NOS. 1 and 2 HEREON APPROVED BY THE SECRETARY							
	9	OF INTERIOR DEC 12 1902							
	10								
	11								
	12								
	13								
	14								
	15	No.1 on 1896 roll as Bycy Willis							
	16	No.2 " 1896 " " Siney Steward							
	17								

TRIBAL ENROLLMENT OF PARENTS

	Name of Father	Year	County	Name of Mother	Year	County
1	Solomon Stewart	Dead	Eagle	Hotaiona	Dead	Eagle
2	Solomon Stewart	"	"	"	"	"
3						
4						
5						
6						
7						
8						
9						
10						
11						
12						
13						
14						
15			Date of Application for Enrollment.	April 25th 1899		
16						
17						

Choctaw By Blood Enrollment Cards 1898-1914

RESIDENCE: Eagle   COUNTY.   **Choctaw Nation**   **Choctaw Roll**   CARD NO.
POST OFFICE: Lukfata, I.T.   *(Not Including Freedmen)*   FIELD NO. **871**

Dawes' Roll No.	NAME	Relationship to Person First Named	AGE	SEX	BLOOD	TRIBAL ENROLLMENT		
						Year	County	No.
2279	1 Apototubi, Jefferson 43	First Named	40	M	Full	1896	Eagle	284
2280	2 " Soki 53	Wife	50	F	"	1896	"	308
2281	3 " Greek 17	Son	14	M	"	1896	"	277
2282	4 " Judy 15	Dau	12	F	"	1896	"	285
2283	5 Wilson, Littie 18	Ward	15	"	"	1896	"	3753
2284	6 Wilson, Lena 4	Dau of No 5	5mo	F	"			
	7							
	8							
	9							
	10							
	11	ENROLLMENT OF NOS. 1 2 3 4 5 and 6 HEREON						
	12	APPROVED BY THE SECRETARY						
	13	OF INTERIOR Dec. 12, 1902						
	14							
	15							
	16							
	17							

TRIBAL ENROLLMENT OF PARENTS

	Name of Father	Year	County	Name of Mother	Year	County
1	A-po-to-tubi	Dead	Eagle	Jennie	Dead	Eagle
2	Wilson	"	"	Hah-lo-te-ma	"	"
3	No 1			Por-ne-fka	"	"
4	No 1			Lis-nie	"	"
5	E-ba-fo-ka	Dead	Eagle	Jennie	"	"
6	William P. Wilson	1896	Eagle	No 5		
7						
8						
9						
10						
11	No5 on 1896 roll as Littie Ebafokka					
12	Surnames on 1896 roll as "Apototubbi"					
13	No5 is now the wife of William P. Wilson on Choctaw Card #1264. See letter of					
14	William P. Wilson filed July 20,1901 Evidence of marriage requested Filed Oct 2, 1902					
15	No.6 Enrolled July 20, 1901					
	For child of No.5 see N.B. (Apr 26-06) No. 543					#1 to 5
16	" " " " " " (Mar 3-05) " 1143					Date of Application for Enrollment.
	" " " No3 " " " " " " 1147					April 25/99
17						

271

Choctaw By Blood Enrollment Cards 1898-1914

RESIDENCE:	Eagle	COUNTY.					CARD No.		
POST OFFICE:	Eagletown, I.T.	**Choctaw Nation**				Choctaw Roll *(Not Including Freedmen)*	FIELD No.	**872**	

Dawes' Roll No.	NAME		Relationship to Person	AGE	SEX	BLOOD	TRIBAL ENROLLMENT		
							Year	County	No.
2285	1 Fobb, Simeon	23	First Named	20	M	Full	1896	Eagle	4180
15750	2 " Eliza	29	Wife	26	F	"	1896	"	275
2286	3 " Linnie	19	Sister	16	F	"	1896	"	4171
	4								
	5								
	6								
	7	ENROLLMENT OF NOS. 1 and 3 HEREON							
	8	APPROVED BY THE SECRETARY OF INTERIOR Dec. 12, 1902							
	9								
	10	ENROLLMENT							
	11	OF NOS. ~~ 2 ~~ HEREON APPROVED BY THE SECRETARY							
	12	OF INTERIOR Dec. 15, 1904							
	13								
	14								
	15								
	16								
	17								

TRIBAL ENROLLMENT OF PARENTS

	Name of Father	Year	County	Name of Mother	Year	County
1	John Fobb	Dead	Eagle	Sallie Fobb	Dead	Eagle
2	John Chalubbi	"	"	Louisa Chalubbi	1896	"
3	John Fobb	Dead	Eagle	Sallie Fobb	Dead	Eagle
4						
5	No3 died about Dec. 1, 1901: Enrollment cancelled by Department					
6	Nov. 5, 1906					
7	For child of Nos 1&2 see N.B. (March 3, 1905) #910					
8						
9	No.2 enrolled as Eliza Achayatubbi					
10						
11	No.3 on 1896 Census roll as "Linnie"					
12						
13						
14						
15			Date of Application for Enrollment.	April 25th 1899		
16						
17						

Choctaw By Blood Enrollment Cards 1898-1914

RESIDENCE: Red River
POST OFFICE: Kullituklo, I.T.

COUNTY. **Choctaw Nation**

Choctaw Roll (*Not Including Freedmen*)

CARD NO.
FIELD NO. **873**

Dawes' Roll No.	NAME		Relationship to Person First Named	AGE	SEX	BLOOD	TRIBAL ENROLLMENT		
							Year	County	No.
2287	1 James, Allen	53	First Named	50	M	Full	1896	Red River	6980
2288	2 " Fillis	37	Wife	34	F	"	1896	" "	6981
2289	3 " Willis	24	Son	21	M	"	1896	" "	6982
2290	4 " Kitsie	17	Dau	14	F	"	1896	" "	6984
2291	5 " Sarah	15	"	12	"	"	1896	" "	7015
2292	6 " Lucy	14	S.Dau	11	"	"	1896	" "	6985
	7								
	8								
	9								
	10								
	11	ENROLLMENT OF NOS. 1 2 3 4 5 and 6 HEREON							
	12	APPROVED BY THE SECRETARY OF INTERIOR Dec. 12, 1902							
	13								
	14								
	15								
	16								
	17								

TRIBAL ENROLLMENT OF PARENTS

	Name of Father	Year	County	Name of Mother	Year	County
1	Fille-a-te-by	Dead	Red River	Ela-pin-tuna	Dead	Red River
2	Smith	"	Eagle	Beckie Smith	"	Eagle
3	No 1			Lizzie James	"	Red River
4	No 1			" "	"	" " "
5	No 1			" "	"	" " "
6	Wattie Ellis	Dead	Red River	No 2		
7						
8						
9	No3 on 1896 roll as Willie James					
10	No2 " 1896 " " Filis "					
11	Husband of #6 on Choctaw card #996 Roll #2622 as Johnson Wesley.					
12	now the No.3 is Husband of Isim Ontontabi on Choctaw card #909					
13						
14	For child of No6 see N.B. (Apr 26-06) #863					
15	" " " " 5 " (Mar 3 '05) #881				Date of Application for Enrollment.	
16					April 26/99	
17	P.O. Goodsprings IT. 7-11-1902					

Choctaw By Blood Enrollment Cards 1898-1914

RESIDENCE: Nashoba COUNTY.			**Choctaw Nation**			Choctaw Roll *(Not Including Freedmen)*	CARD NO.
POST OFFICE: Alikchi, I.T.							FIELD NO. **874**

Dawes' Roll No.	NAME	Relationship to Person First Named	AGE	SEX	BLOOD	TRIBAL ENROLLMENT		
						Year	County	No.
2293	1 Carterby, Almon ²⁶	First Named	23	M	Full	1896	Nashoba	2523
	2							
	3							
	4	ENROLLMENT						
	5	OF NOS. 1 HEREON APPROVED BY THE SECRETARY						
	6	OF INTERIOR Dec 12 1902						
	7							
	8							
	9							
	10							
	11							
	12							
	13							
	14							
	15	No. 1 is Husband of Sophie Noahobi, Choctaw Card #1055						
	16							
	17							

TRIBAL ENROLLMENT OF PARENTS

	Name of Father	Year	County	Name of Mother	Year	County
1	Phillie Carterby	Dead	Nashoba	Emiline Carterby	1896	Nashoba
2						
3						
4						
5						
6						
7						
8						
9						
10						
11						
12						
13						
14						
15				Date of Application for Enrollment.		
16				April 26/99		
17						

Choctaw By Blood Enrollment Cards 1898-1914

RESIDENCE: Red River   COUNTY.   **Choctaw Nation**   **Choctaw Roll** *(Not Including Freedmen)*   CARD No.

POST OFFICE: Garvin, I.T.   FIELD No. **875**

Dawes' Roll No.	NAME		Relationship to Person First Named	AGE	SEX	BLOOD	TRIBAL ENROLLMENT		
							Year	County	No.
DEAD	Austin, John	DEAD		41	M	Full	1893	Red River	P.R. 17
2594	" Alice	53	Wife	50	F	"	1893	" "	18
	3								
	4								
	5								
	6								
	7	ENROLLMENT OF NOS. 2 HEREON							
	8	APPROVED BY THE SECRETARY OF INTERIOR Dec. 12, 1902							
	9								
	10								
	11	No 1 Hereon dismissed under order							
	12	of the Commission to the Five Civilized							
	13	Tribes of March 31, 1905.							
	14								
	15								
	16								
	17								

TRIBAL ENROLLMENT OF PARENTS

	Name of Father	Year	County	Name of Mother	Year	County
1	William Austin	Dead	Red River	E-law-ta-huna	Dead	Bok Tuklo
2	Tow-a-by	"	Towson	Te-ho-ya	"	Towson
3						
4						
5	No2 on 1893 Pay roll as Ilias Auston					
6						
7	No1 on 1896 roll, Page 8, No.310, Red River Co, as Jordan Austin					
8	No2 " 1896 " " 8 No 311 " " " " Ilis "					
9	No1 Died Oct. 28, 1901: proof of death filed May 7, 1902					
10						
11						
12						
13						
14						
15						
16			Date of Application for Enrollment.	April 26/99		
17						

275

Choctaw By Blood Enrollment Cards 1898-1914

RESIDENCE: Nashoba COUNTY. **Choctaw Nation** Choctaw Roll CARD NO.
POST OFFICE: Alikchi, I.T. *(Not Including Freedmen)* FIELD NO. **876**

Dawes' Roll No.	NAME	Relationship to Person First Named	AGE	SEX	BLOOD	TRIBAL ENROLLMENT		
						Year	County	No.
2295	1 Ishcomer, Adam ³⁴	First Named	31	M	Full	1896	Nashoba	6274
2296	2 " , Betsy ²⁴	Wife	21	F	"	1896	"	6275
2297	3 " , Hudson ¹³	Son	10	M	"	1896	"	6273
2298	4 " , Wilton ⁷	"	4	"	"	1896	"	6277
2299	5 " , Joshua ³	"	6mo	M	"			
2300	6 " , Colberson ¹	Son	10mo	M	"			
	7							
	8							
	9							
	10							
	11	ENROLLMENT						
	12	OF NOS. 1 2 3 4 5 and 6 HEREON APPROVED BY THE SECRETARY						
	13	OF INTERIOR Dec 12, 1902						
	14							
	15							
	16							
	17							

TRIBAL ENROLLMENT OF PARENTS

	Name of Father	Year	County	Name of Mother	Year	County
1	Nelson Ischomer[sic]	Dead	Bok Tuklo	Staohke Ishomer[sic]	Dead	Bok Tuklo
2	John Baker	"	Nashoba	Elsie Baker	1896	Nashoba
3	No 1			Isabelle Ishcomer	Dead	"
4	No 1			No 2		
5	No 1			No 2		
6	No 1			No 2		
7						
8						
9	No 2 on Choctaw roll as Betsie Ishcomer					
10	No 6 Born Nov. 7, 1901, enrolled Sept. 17, 1902.					
11						
12						
13						
14						
15						
16					Date of Application for Enrollment April 26/99	
17	P.O. Glover I.T. 9/17/02				No.5 enrolled Nov 1/99	

Choctaw By Blood Enrollment Cards 1898-1914

RESIDENCE: Nashoba   COUNTY. **Choctaw Nation**   **Choctaw Roll**   CARD NO.
POST OFFICE: Alikchi, I.T.   *(Not Including Freedmen)*   FIELD NO.   **877**

Dawes' Roll No.	NAME	Relationship to Person	AGE	SEX	BLOOD	TRIBAL ENROLLMENT Year	County	No.
2301	1 Ishcomer, Sinsie ²¹	First Named	18	F	Full	1896	Nashoba	6276
2302	2 John, Smallwood ~~DIED PRIOR TO SEPTEMBER 25, 1962~~	Son	1	M	"			
15391	3 Hicks, Hobe ²	Son	3	M	"			
	4							
	5							
	6	ENROLLMENT OF NOS. 1 and 2 HEREON APPROVED BY THE SECRETARY OF INTERIOR Dec. 12, 1902						
	7							
	8							
	9	ENROLLMENT OF NOS. ~~~ 3 ~~~ HEREON APPROVED BY THE SECRETARY OF INTERIOR May 9, 1904						
	10							
	11							
	12							
	13							
	14							
	15							
	16							
	17							

TRIBAL ENROLLMENT OF PARENTS

	Name of Father	Year	County	Name of Mother	Year	County
1	Nelson Ishcomer	Dead	Bok Tuklo	Staohke Ishcomer	Dead	Bok Tuklo
2	~~Keon John~~	~~1896~~	~~Nashoba~~	~~No 1~~		
3	Cephus Hicks	1896	"	No 1		
4						
5						
6			No2 died May 1898; proof of death filed Dec. 3, 1902			
7			No3 born Dec. 13, 1900, application first received May 11, 1901, Returned for			
8			correction, corrected affidavits received and No3 enrolled Jany. 28, 1904.			
			~~No2 died May ~ 1898: Enrollment cancelled by Department July 8, 1904.~~			
9						
10						
11						
12						
13						
14				#1 & 2		
15				Date of Application for Enrollment.		
16				April 26/99		
17						

Choctaw By Blood Enrollment Cards 1898-1914

RESIDENCE: Nashoba   COUNTY.   **Choctaw Nation**   Choctaw Roll   CARD No.

POST OFFICE: Alikchi, I.T.   *(Not Including Freedmen)*   FIELD No. **878**

Dawes' Roll No.	NAME	Relationship to Person First Named	AGE	SEX	BLOOD	TRIBAL ENROLLMENT		
						Year	County	No.
2303	1 Edwards, Morton 28		25	M	Full	1896	Nashoba	3731
2304	2 Noelsie DIED PRIOR TO SEPTEMBER 25, 1902	Wife	42	F	"	1896	Jacks Fork	1926
	3							
	4							
	5							
	6							
	7							
	8							
	9							
	10							
	11	ENROLLMENT						
	12	OF NOS. 1 and 2 HEREON APPROVED BY THE SECRETARY						
	13	OF INTERIOR Dec 12 1902						
	14							
	15							
	16							
	17							

TRIBAL ENROLLMENT OF PARENTS

	Name of Father	Year	County	Name of Mother	Year	County
1	Bunbus Edwards	1896	Nashoba	Sallie Edwards	1896	Nashoba
2	Hullie	Dead	"	Okla-homa	Dead	"
3						
4						
5						
6						
7	No.2 on 1896 roll as Noelsie Baker					
8	No.1 " 1896 " " Mooten Edwards					
9	N².2 Died Nov. 15, 1900. Proof of death filed Dec. 24, 1902.					
10	No.2 died Nov. 15, 1900: Enrollment cancelled by Department July 8, 1904.					
11						
12						
13						
14						
15						
16				Date of Application for Enrollment		April 26/99
17	P.O. Bethel I.T. 12/26/02					

278

Choctaw By Blood Enrollment Cards 1898-1914

RESIDENCE: Nashoba   COUNTY.   **Choctaw Nation**   **Choctaw Roll** *(Not Including Freedmen)*   CARD NO.

POST OFFICE: Alikchi, I.T.   FIELD NO. **879**

Dawes' Roll No.	NAME	Relationship to Person First Named	AGE	SEX	BLOOD	Year	County	No.
2305	1 ~~Edwards, Barnabas~~ ~~DIED PRIOR TO SEPTEMBER 25, 1902~~	~~First Named~~	~~56~~	~~M~~	~~Full~~	~~1896~~	~~Nashoba~~	~~3739~~
2306	2 " Sallie ³⁹	Wife	36	F	"	1896	"	3723
2307	3 " Maneffie ²⁷	Dau	24	"	"	1896	"	3724
2308	4 " Silway ²⁰	"	17	"	"	1896	"	3727
2309	5 " Louisa ¹⁷	"	14	"	"	1896	"	3725
*2310	6 " Ebenezer ¹⁵	Dau ~~Son~~	12	F ~~M~~	"	1896	"	3726
~~2311~~	~~7 Kinsie~~ ~~DIED PRIOR TO SEPTEMBER 25, 1903~~	~~Dau~~	~~10~~	~~F~~	~~"~~	~~1896~~	~~"~~	~~3728~~
~~2312~~	~~8 Jinsie~~ ~~DIED PRIOR TO SEPTEMBER 25, 1903~~	~~"~~	~~6~~	~~"~~	~~"~~	~~1896~~	~~"~~	~~3729~~
2313	9 " Betsy ⁷	"	4	"	"	1896	"	3730

* 6-3-31 – Sex of No6 changed from "M to F". Approved May 28.1931 (See letter #2534-31)
No.7 died Aug.20,1900:No.8 died Sept-1901:No.1 died Aug.16,1900: Enrollment cancelled by
Department July 8,1904

ENROLLMENT
OF NOS. 12345678and9 HEREON
APPROVED BY THE SECRETARY
OF INTERIOR Dec 12 1902

For child of No3 see NB (Apr 26-06) Card No 838
   " " " No4 " " (Mar 3-05) " " 876
   " " " No3 " " " " " 1452

TRIBAL ENROLLMENT OF PARENTS

	Name of Father	Year	County	Name of Mother	Year	County
1	~~Nate Edwards~~	~~Dead~~	~~Nashoba~~	~~Meley Edwards~~	~~Dead~~	~~Nashoba~~
2	Reuben Calvin	"	"	Knih-me	"	Cedar
3	No 1			No 2		
4	No 1			No 2		
5	No 1			No 2		
6	No 1			No 2		
7	~~No 1~~			~~No 2~~		
8	~~No 1~~			~~No 2~~		
9	No 1			No 2		

No2 on 1896 roll as Sallie Edward
No6 " 1896 " " Ebenizie Edwards
No1 " 1896 " " Barnebas "
No1 died Aug 19: proof of death filed Dec 16, 1902.
No8 " Sept 1901: " " " " 16, 1902.
N⁰8 Died Aug 15, 1901: " " " " Dec. 24, 1902
N⁰7 Died Aug 20.1900: " " " " Dec. 24, 1902
No1 Died Aug16,1900 " " " " Dec. 24, 1902

Date of Application for Enrollment.
April 26/99

279

Choctaw By Blood Enrollment Cards 1898-1914

RESIDENCE: Eagle COUNTY. **Choctaw Nation** Choctaw Roll CARD NO.
POST OFFICE: Lukfata, I.T. *(Not Including Freedmen)* FIELD NO. **880**

Dawes' Roll No.	NAME	Relationship to Person First Named	AGE	SEX	BLOOD	TRIBAL ENROLLMENT		
						Year	County	No.
2314	1 Tashka, Wallace 39		36	M	Full	1896	Eagle	12234
2315	2 ~~Eatona~~ DIED PRIOR TO SEPTEMBER 25, 1902	Wife	38	F	"	1896	"	12237
2316	3 Pisahakubbi, Malwit 21	S.Son	18	M	"	1896	"	10407
2317	4 " Sallie 19	S.Dau	16	F	"	1896	"	10408
	5							
	6							
	7							
	8							
	9							
	10							
	11	ENROLLMENT						
	12	OF NOS. 1, 2, 3 and 4 HEREON APPROVED BY THE SECRETARY						
	13	OF INTERIOR Dec. 2, 1902						
	14							
	15							
	16							
	17							

TRIBAL ENROLLMENT OF PARENTS

	Name of Father	Year	County	Name of Mother	Year	County
1	Tashka	Dead	Eagle	I-o-wa-ta-ua	Dead	Eagle
2	~~Ele um ly~~	"	"	~~Ona tama~~	"	"
3	Pisahakubbi	"	"	No 2		
4	"	"	"	No 2		
5						
6			No2 on 1896 roll as Iatona Tashka			
7						
8						
9			No's 2 and 3 supposed to be dead			
10			No.2 Died Feb. 5, 1901: Enrollment cancelled by Department July 8, 1904. For child of No1 see N.B. (Apr. 26-06) Card No. 691			
11						
12						
13						
14					Date of Application for Enrollment.	
15						
16					April 26/99	
17						

Choctaw By Blood Enrollment Cards 1898-1914

RESIDENCE: Nashoba COUNTY. **Choctaw Nation** Choctaw Roll CARD No.
POST OFFICE: Alikchi, I.T. (Not Including Freedmen) FIELD No. **881**

Dawes' Roll No.	NAME	Relationship to Person First Named	AGE	SEX	BLOOD	TRIBAL ENROLLMENT Year	TRIBAL ENROLLMENT County	TRIBAL ENROLLMENT No.
2318	1 Noahobi, Williamson 32		29	M	Full	1896	Nashoba	9684
2319	2 " Semy 23	Wife	20	F	"	1896	"	9685
2320	3 " Easter 8	Dau	5	"	"	1896	"	9701
2321	4 " Laynus 3	Son	1	M	"			
2322	5 " Jamyson 1	Son	3mo	M	"			
	6	Is reference given above to No.2 a mistake?						
	7							
	8							
	9							
	10							
	11	ENROLLMENT						
	12	OF NOS. 1,2,3,4 and 5 HEREON APPROVED BY THE SECRETARY						
	13	OF INTERIOR Dec. 12, 1902						
	14							
	15							
	16							
	17							

TRIBAL ENROLLMENT OF PARENTS

	Name of Father	Year	County	Name of Mother	Year	County
1	Noahobi	Dead	Nashoba	Yo-tu-na	1896	Nashoba
2	William	"	Eagle	Elsie Johnson	1896	"
3	No 1			Jennie Noahobi	Dead	"
4	No 1			No 2		
5	No 1			No 2		
6						
7	No 2 on 1896 Amy Noahobi					
8	No 3 " 1896 roll as Esther "					
9	No4 Enrolled January 3 1901.					
10	No5 Born March 9, 1901. Enrolled June 11, 1902					
11	No.2 identified from 1896 Roll No. 6855, as Simmie Johnson					
12						
13						
14						
15					#1 to 3	
16					Date of Application for Enrollment April 26/99	
17	Preset P.O. Address Bethel I.T. Jany 3, 1901					

281

Choctaw By Blood Enrollment Cards 1898-1914

RESIDENCE: Eagle COUNTY, **Choctaw Nation** Choctaw Roll CARD No.
POST OFFICE: Eagletown, I.T. *(Not Including Freedmen)* FIELD No. **882**

Dawes' Roll No.	NAME		Relationship to Person	AGE	SEX	BLOOD	TRIBAL ENROLLMENT		
							Year	County	No.
2323	1 Wilson, Esey	33	First Named	30	F	Full	1896	Eagle	13545
2324	2 " Jimison	15	Son	12	M	"	1896	"	13510
2325	3 " Allington	5	"	2	"	"			
	4								
	5								
	6								
	7								
	8								
	9								
	10								
	11								
	12								
	13								
	14								
	15								
	16								
	17								

ENROLLMENT
OF NOS. 1 2 and 3 HEREON
APPROVED BY THE SECRETARY
OF INTERIOR Dec. 12, 1902

TRIBAL ENROLLMENT OF PARENTS

	Name of Father	Year	County	Name of Mother	Year	County
1	Sam Pisahokeby	Dead	Eagle	Yah-tee-na	1896	Eagle
2	Joe Wilson	"	"	No 1		
3	" "	"	"	No 1		
4						
5						
6						
7						
8						
9						
10						
11						
12						
13						
14				Date of Application for Enrollment.		
15						
16				April 26/99		
17						

Choctaw By Blood Enrollment Cards 1898-1914

RESIDENCE: Eagle	COUNTY.		
POST OFFICE: Lukfata, I.T.			

Choctaw Nation

Choctaw Roll *(Not Including Freedmen)*

CARD NO.

FIELD NO. **883**

Dawes' Roll No.	NAME	Relationship to Person First Named	AGE	SEX	BLOOD	TRIBAL ENROLLMENT		
						Year	County	No.
2326	1 Loman, Sarah ⁵¹	First Named	48	F	Full	1893	Eagle	P.R. 499
	2							
	3							
	4							
	5							
	6							
	7							
	8	ENROLLMENT OF NOS. 1 HEREON APPROVED BY THE SECRETARY OF INTERIOR Dec 12 1902						
	9							
	10							
	11							
	12							
	13	Also on 1896 roll as Sarah Onatambi						
	14	Page 252, No 9930, Eagle Co.						
	15							
	16							
	17							

TRIBAL ENROLLMENT OF PARENTS

Name of Father	Year	County	Name of Mother	Year	County
1 Ona-tambe	Dead	Eagle	Ta-lo-wa-to-na	Dead	Eagle
2					
3					
4					
5					
6					
7					
8					
9					
10					
11					
12					
13					
14					
15					
16			Date of Application for Enrollment.	April 26/99	
17					

Choctaw By Blood Enrollment Cards 1898-1914

RESIDENCE: Eagle   COUNTY.   **Choctaw Nation**   Choctaw Roll   CARD NO.
POST OFFICE: Lukfata, I.T.   *(Not Including Freedmen)*   FIELD NO. **884**

Dawes' Roll No.	NAME	Relationship to Person First Named	AGE	SEX	BLOOD	TRIBAL ENROLLMENT Year	County	No.
2327	1 Bunce, Susan ³³		30	F	Full	✳1896	Eagle	12226
2328	2 Tonihka, Charles ⁸	Son	5	M	"	1896	"	10409
2329	3 Bunce, Dyer ¹	Son	1mo	M	"			
4								
5								
6								
7								
8								
9								
10								
11	ENROLLMENT							
12	OF NOS. 1 2 and 3 HEREON APPROVED BY THE SECRETARY							
13	OF INTERIOR Dec 12 1902							
14								
15								
16								
17								

TRIBAL ENROLLMENT OF PARENTS

	Name of Father	Year	County	Name of Mother	Year	County
1	Sam Pisahakobey	Dead	Eagle	E-o-to-na	Dead	Eagle
2	Albert Tonihka	"	"	No 1		
3	Jerry Bunce	1896	"	№ 1		
4						
5	For child of No1 see NB (Apr 26-06) Card #581					
6	#This seems to be an error					
7						
8	No2 On 1896 roll as Charles Pisahakubbi					
9						
10	No 2: Also on 1896 roll No 12227: page 318 as					
11	Intsey Tonihka. This seems to be error.					
12	No1 also on 1896 Choctaw census roll page 318 #12235 as Susie Tashka					
13	No1 is now wife of Jerry Bunce on Choctaw card #753. See her statement					
14	and that of Jerry Bunce filed July 29, 1902.					
15	№ 3 Born July 11, 1902: enrolled Aug. 22, 1902					
16					Date of Application for Enrollment.	April 26/99
17						

284

Choctaw By Blood Enrollment Cards 1898-1914

RESIDENCE: Red River   COUNTY.   **Choctaw Nation**   Choctaw Roll   CARD NO.

POST OFFICE: Kullituklo, I.T.   (Not Including Freedmen)   FIELD NO. **885**

Dawes' Roll No.	NAME		Relationship to Person	AGE	SEX	BLOOD	TRIBAL ENROLLMENT		
							Year	County	No.
2330	1 Wright, Thomas	48	First Named	45	M	Full	1896	Red River	13570
2331	2 " Elsie	35	Wife	32	F	"	1896	" "	13571
~~2332~~	~~3 " Alfred~~ DIED PRIOR TO SEPTEMBER 25, 1902		~~Son~~	~~2~~	~~M~~	"			
2333	4 " Andy	3	Son	4mo	M	"			
14610	5 " Leslie	1	Son	4mo	M	"			
	6								
	7								
	8								
	9								
	10								
	11	ENROLLMENT OF NOS. 1 2 3 and 4 HEREON APPROVED BY THE SECRETARY OF INTERIOR Dec. 12, 1902							
	12								
	13								
	14	ENROLLMENT OF NOS. 5 HEREON APPROVED BY THE SECRETARY OF INTERIOR May 20 1903							
	15								
	16								
	17								

TRIBAL ENROLLMENT OF PARENTS

	Name of Father	Year	County	Name of Mother	Year	County
1	A-ha-yok-tubbee	Dead	Bok Tuklo	Annie	Dead	Red River
2	Roberson Battiest	"	Jackson	Liney LeFlore	"	Jackson
3	~~No 1~~			~~No 2~~		
4	No. 1			No.2		
5	Nº1			Nº2		
6						
7			No.4 Enrolled June 23d, 1900			
8			Nº5 Born June 4, 1902: enrolled Oct. 6, 1902.			
9			No3 died May 15, 1900: proof of death filed Dec 3, 1902.			
10			~~No 3 died May 15, 1900: Enrollment cancelled by Department July 8, 1904~~			
11						
12						
13			#1 to 3			
14			Date of Application for Enrollment.			
15						
16			April 26/99			
17						

Choctaw By Blood Enrollment Cards 1898-1914

RESIDENCE: Nashoba COUNTY.			**Choctaw Nation**			**Choctaw Roll** *(Not Including Freedmen)*	CARD No.	
POST OFFICE: Alikchi, I.T.							FIELD No. **886**	

Dawes' Roll No.	NAME		Relationship to Person First Named	AGE	SEX	BLOOD	TRIBAL ENROLLMENT		
							Year	County	No.
2334	1 Battiest, Joel	34	First Named	31	M	Full	1896	Nashoba	1219
2335	2 " Melvina	30	Wife	27	F	"	1896	"	13315
2336	3 " Sina	5	Dau	1	"	"			
2337	4 Wood, Leanie	10	S.Dau	7	"	"	1896	Nashoba	13316
	5								
	6								
	7								
	8								
	9								
	10								
	11	ENROLLMENT OF NOS. 1 2 3 and 4 HEREON							
	12	APPROVED BY THE SECRETARY							
	13	OF INTERIOR Dec 12 1902							
	14								
	15								
	16								
	17								

TRIBAL ENROLLMENT OF PARENTS

	Name of Father	Year	County	Name of Mother	Year	County
1	Carson Battiest	Dead	Nashoba	Sais Battiest	Dead	Nashoba
2	James Wood	1896	"	Ka-no-te-ma		
3	No 1			No 2		
4	Nias Watson	1896	Nashoba	No 2		
5						
6	No 2 on 1896 roll as Melvina Wood					
7						
8	Nᵒˢ 1 and 2 were divorced in July 1903. Copy of Bill of Divorce filed Aug. 5, 1903					
9						
10						
11						
12						
13						
14				Date of Application for Enrollment.		
15						
16				April 26/99		
17						

Choctaw By Blood Enrollment Cards 1898-1914

RESIDENCE: Bok Tuklo   COUNTY.   **Choctaw Nation**   Choctaw Roll   CARD NO.
POST OFFICE: Lukfata, I.T.   *(Not Including Freedmen)*   FIELD NO. **887**

Dawes' Roll No.	NAME	Relationship to Person	AGE	SEX	BLOOD	TRIBAL ENROLLMENT		
						Year	County	No.
2338	1 Watson, Allen T. ³¹	First Named	28	M	Full	1896	Bok Tuklo	13400
2339	2 " Minerva ²⁸	Wife	25	F	"	1896	" "	4198
2340	3 Forbis, Nancy ¹⁰	S.Dau	7	"	"	1896	" "	4199
	4							
	5							
	6							
	7							
	8							
	9							
	10							
	11	ENROLLMENT OF NOS. 1 2 and 3 HEREON APPROVED BY THE SECRETARY OF INTERIOR Dec 12 1902				No1 on 1896 roll as A.T. Watson		
	12					No2 " 1896 " " Minnie Forbis		
	13							
	14							
	15							
	16							
	17							

TRIBAL ENROLLMENT OF PARENTS

	Name of Father	Year	County	Name of Mother	Year	County
1	Thos Watson	1896	Bok Tuklo	Salina Watson	Dead	Bok Tuklo
2	Wilmon Mehatubbee	Dead	Towson	Sallie Mehatubbee	"	Towson
3	Eddie Forbis	1896	Red River	No 2		
4						
5						
6						
7						
8						
9						
10						
11						
12						
13						
14						
15						
16					Date of Application for Enrollment.	April 26/99
17						

Choctaw By Blood Enrollment Cards 1898-1914

RESIDENCE: Bok Tuklo   COUNTY.   **Choctaw Nation**   **Choctaw Roll**   CARD NO.
POST OFFICE: Lukfata, I.T.   (Not Including Freedmen)   FIELD NO. **888**

Dawes' Roll No.	NAME		Relationship to Person First Named	AGE	SEX	BLOOD	TRIBAL ENROLLMENT		
							Year	County	No.
2341	1 Crosby, Wallace	54	First Named	51	M	Full	1896	Bok Tuklo	2566
2342	2 " Licksie	38	Wife	35	F	"	1896	" "	12186
2343	3 Tisho, Fliston	16	S.Son	13	M	"	1896	" "	12187
2344	4 " George	14	"	11	"	"	1896	" "	12188
2345	5 " Lincie	10	S.Dau	7	F	"	1896	" "	12189
2346	6 " Wesley	8	S.Son	5	M	"	1896	" "	12190
2347	7 " Rogers	6	"	3	"	"	1896	" "	12191
2348	8 Crosby, Ida	2	Dau	3mo	F	"			
	9								
	10								
	11								
	12								
	13								
	14								
	15								
	16								
	17								

ENROLLMENT
OF NOS. 1234567and8 HEREON
APPROVED BY THE SECRETARY
OF INTERIOR Dec 12 1902

TRIBAL ENROLLMENT OF PARENTS

	Name of Father	Year	County	Name of Mother	Year	County
1	Ca-na-le-tubbee	Dead	Bok Tuklo	Ka-ne-a-huna	Dead	Bok Tuklo
2	Ka-nich-tubbee	"	" " "	Sillen	"	" " "
3	Thomas Tisho	"	" " "	No.2		
4	" "	"	" " "	No.2		
5	" "	"	" " "	No.2		
6	" "	"	" " "	No.2		
7	" "	"	" " "	No.2		
8	No.1			No.2		
9						
10	No.2 on 1896 roll as Licksie Tisho					
11	No.7 " 1896 " " Rojis "					
12	No.8 Enrolled June 25, 1901					
13						
14						
15				Date of Application for Enrollment.	#1 to 7 inc	
16				April 26/99		
17						

RESIDENCE: Bok Tuklo	COUNTY.	**Choctaw Nation**	**Choctaw Roll**	CARD No.
POST OFFICE: Lukfata, I.T.			*(Not Including Freedmen)*	FIELD No. **889**

Dawes' Roll No.	NAME		Relationship to Person Named	AGE	SEX	BLOOD	TRIBAL ENROLLMENT		
							Year	County	No.
2349	1 Crosby, Josiah	48	First	45	M	Full	1896	Bok Tuklo	2581
2350	2 " Sissy	33	Wife	30	F	"	1896	" "	2582
2351	3 " Susan	29	Dau	26	"	"	1896	" "	2583
DEAD	4 " Stephen DEAD		Son	22	M	"	1896	" "	2584
2352	5 " Seanis	23	Dau	20	F	"	1896	" "	2585
2353	6 " Davis	19	Son	16	M	"	1896	" "	2586
2354	7 " Bettie	13	Dau	10	F	"	1896	" "	2587
2355	8 " Paul	11	Son	8	M	"	1896	" "	2588
2356	9 " Lesian	6	Dau	3	F	"	1896	" "	2589
2357	10 " Lucie	2	"	1½	F	"			
14611	11 Louis, Gilbert	1	Son of No3	4mo	M	"			
	12	ENROLLMENT							
	13	OF NOS. 1,2,3,6,7,8,9 and 10 HEREON APPROVED BY THE SECRETARY							
	14	OF INTERIOR Dec 12 1902							
	15	No11 Born Aug 21, 1901: Enrolled Dec 18/02							
	16	No3 is now the wife of Johnson Louis on Choctaw Card #1321- Nov. 28, 1902.							
	17								

TRIBAL ENROLLMENT OF PARENTS

	Name of Father	Year	County	Name of Mother	Year	County	
1	Aka-na-la-tuby	Dead	Bok Tuklo	Ca-ne-a-hu-na	Dead	Bok Tuklo	
2	Minte-hi-ah	"	" "	Ah-hu-na	1896	" "	
3	No 1			Sillen Crosby	Dead	" "	
4	No 1			" "	"	" "	
5	No 1	ENROLLMENT		" "	"	" "	
6	No 1	OF NOS. 11 HEREON APPROVED BY THE SECRETARY		" "	"	" "	
7	No 1	OF INTERIOR May 20 1903		No 2			
8	No 1			No 2	No 4 hereon dismissed		
9	No 1			No 2	under order of the Commission to the Five		
10	No 1			No 2	Civilized Tribes of March		
11	Johnson Louis			No 3	31, 1905.		
12	No5 on 1896 roll as Simus Crosby, a male						
13	No9 " 1896 " " Lucy "						
14	No1 said to be father of No5 on Choctaw card #916 May 11,1901 relative to which see letter of Notary Public H.L. Fowler filed in Choctaw Case #916 May 13,1901						#1 to 9
15	No4 Died June 13, 1901. Evidence of death filed Oct. 10, 1901						Date of Application for Enrollment.
16	No10 Enrolled Oct. 10, 1901.						
17	For child of No.5 see NB (March 3, 1905) #1446						April 26/99

289

Choctaw By Blood Enrollment Cards 1898-1914

RESIDENCE: Cedar COUNTY.
POST OFFICE: Doaksville I.T.

Choctaw Nation

Choctaw Roll (Not Including Freedmen)

CARD NO.
FIELD NO. **890**

Dawes' Roll No.	NAME		Relationship to Person	AGE	SEX	BLOOD	TRIBAL ENROLLMENT		
							Year	County	No.
2358	1 Luce, Lefen	31	First Named	28	M	Full	1893	Cedar	P.R. 324
15751	2 " Lita	40	Wife	37	F	"	1893	Kimitia[sic]	897
2359	3 Anderson, Tobias	17	Step son	14	M	"	1896	"	346
2360	4 Outahyabbi, Louie	13	Step son	10	M	"	1896	Cedar	9927
	5								
	6								
	7								
	8								
	9								
	10								
	11								
	12								
	13								
	14								
	15								
	16								
	17								

ENROLLMENT
OF NOS. ~~2~~~~ HEREON
APPROVED BY THE SECRETARY
OF INTERIOR Dec 15 1904

ENROLLMENT
OF NOS. 1 3 and 4 HEREON
APPROVED BY THE SECRETARY
OF INTERIOR Dec 12 1902

No.2 on 1885 Choctaw Census Roll
Towson County No.14 as Liddy
William No.3 on said roll, No.15,
as Tobias William

TRIBAL ENROLLMENT OF PARENTS

Name of Father	Year	County	Name of Mother	Year	County
1 Wallen Lewis	Dead	Cedar	Silmy Lewis	Dead	Cedar
2 Adam William	"	Towson	Celia William	"	Kimitia[sic]
3 Sampson Anderson	"	"	No 2	1896	Cedar
4 Outahyabbi	1896	Bok Tuklo	No.2	1896	"
5					
6	No.1 on Pay roll 1893 Cedar Co. No.324, Page 30				
7	No2 enrolled as Lottie Williams				
8	No3 child of No2				
9	No4 " " No2				
10					
11	It is found that the number on the 1896 roll given to No2 is incorrect, No 13779 belongs to Lottie Christie Card				
12	No 1587 May 10/99.				
13	No.2 on 1893 Pay Roll Kiamitia County page 108 No. 897 (as Lilla Williams)				
14	No.2 Enrollment number a mistake – See card #1587				
15				Date of Application for Enrollment.	
16				April 26/99	
17					

290

Choctaw By Blood Enrollment Cards 1898-1914

RESIDENCE: Nashoba COUNTY. **Choctaw Nation** **Choctaw Roll** CARD NO.
POST OFFICE: Alikchi I.T. *(Not Including Freedmen)* FIELD NO. **891**

Dawes' Roll No.	NAME	Relationship to Person	AGE	SEX	BLOOD	TRIBAL ENROLLMENT		
						Year	County	No.
2361	1 Battiest, Loren ²¹	First Named	18	M	Full	1896	Nashoba	1221
	2							
	3							
	4							
	5							
	6	ENROLLMENT						
	7	OF NOS. ~ 1 ~ HEREON APPROVED BY THE SECRETARY						
	8	OF INTERIOR Dec 12 1902						
	9							
	10							
	11							
	12							
	13	No. 1 on 1896 Roll as Lorin Battiest						
	14							
	15							
	16							
	17							

TRIBAL ENROLLMENT OF PARENTS

Name of Father	Year	County	Name of Mother	Year	County
1 Casson Battiest	Dead	Nashoba	Sis Battiest	Dead	Nashoba
2					
3					
4					
5					
6					
7					
8					
9					
10					
11					
12					
13					
14					
15					
16			Date of Application for Enrollment		April 26/99
17					

Choctaw By Blood Enrollment Cards 1898-1914

RESIDENCE: Eagle COUNTY.
POST OFFICE: Eagletown I.T.

Choctaw Nation

Choctaw Roll *(Not Including Freedmen)*

CARD NO.
FIELD NO. 892

Dawes' Roll No.	NAME		Relationship to Person First Named	AGE	SEX	BLOOD	TRIBAL ENROLLMENT		
							Year	County	No.
2362	1 E-ba-ho-tubbi	49	First Named	46	M	Full	1896	Eagle	3763
2363	2 E-ba-ho-tubbi, Kizzie A	41	Wife	38	F	"	1896	"	3749
*2364	3 " Moffin	10	~~Dau~~ Son	7	~~F~~ M	"	1896	"	3750
2365	4 " Elliston	7	Son	4	M	"	1896	"	3748
2366	5 " Graven	9	Son	6	M	"	1896	"	3746
2367	6 " Minnie	4	Dau	1mo	F	"			
2368	7 " Nicey	4	Dau	1mo	F	"			
2369	8 " Fannie	1	Dau	1mo	F	"			
2370	9 " Abner	1	Son	1mo	M	"			
	10								
	11	ENROLLMENT OF NOS. 12345678and9 HEREON APPROVED BY THE SECRETARY OF INTERIOR Dec 12 1902							
	12								
	13								
	14								
	15								
	16								
	17								

TRIBAL ENROLLMENT OF PARENTS

	Name of Father	Year	County	Name of Mother	Year	County
1	No-yo-pa-tubbi	Dead	Mississippi	A-pis-an-tona	1896	Eagle
2	Stewart Mitchell	1896	Blue	Annie Mitchell	Dead	Red River
3	No.1	1896	Eagle	Lucy Noley	1896	Bok Tuklo
4	No.1	1896	"	No.2	1896	Eagle
5	No.1	1896	"	No.2	1896	Eagle
6	No.1	1896	"	No.2	1896	Eagle
7	No.1	1896	"	No.2	1896	Eagle
8	No.1		"	No.2		"
9	No.1		"	No.2		"
10						
11			No.3 enrolled as Moffin Ebahotubbi			
12			No.8 Born Sept. 8, 1901: Enrolled Nov. 5, 1901			
13			No.9 " " 8, 1901: " " 5, 1901			
14			Nos 8 and 9 twins			
			as to name of No.1 see letter of J.W. Costilow filed Nov. 5, 1901			
15		*7-28-31 Sex of No.3 changed from "F to M" by authority of letter July 16, 1931				
16					Date of Application for Enrollment.	#1 to 7
17						April 26/99

RESIDENCE: Cedar COUNTY. **Choctaw Nation** Choctaw Roll CARD No.
POST OFFICE: Doaksville, I.T. (Not Including Freedmen) FIELD No. 893

Dawes' Roll No.	NAME	Relationship to Person First Named	AGE	SEX	BLOOD	TRIBAL ENROLLMENT		
						Year	County	No.
2371	1 Nehka, Solomon 36	First Named	33	M	Full	1896	Cedar	9650
2372	2 " Mintihona 55	Wife	52	F	"	1896	"	9651
	3							
	4							
	5							
	6							
	7							
	8							
	9							
	10							
	11	ENROLLMENT						
	12	OF NOS. 1 and 2 HEREON APPROVED BY THE SECRETARY						
	13	OF INTERIOR Dec. 12, 1902						
	14							
	15							
	16							
	17							

TRIBAL ENROLLMENT OF PARENTS

	Name of Father	Year	County	Name of Mother	Year	County
1	Farlis Nehka	1896	Cedar	Jinnie Nehka	Dead	Cedar
2	Nak-a-cha	Dead	Towson	Ta-lin-na	"	Nashoba
3						
4						
5						
6						
7						
8						
9						
10						
11						
12						
13						
14				Date of Application for Enrollment.		
15						
16				April 26/99		
17						

293

Choctaw By Blood Enrollment Cards 1898-1914

RESIDENCE: Cedar   COUNTY.   **Choctaw Nation**   **Choctaw Roll**   CARD NO.
POST OFFICE: Antlers, I.T.   (Not Including Freedmen)   FIELD NO. **894**

Dawes' Roll No.	NAME	Relationship to Person First Named	AGE	SEX	BLOOD	TRIBAL ENROLLMENT		
						Year	County	No.
2373	1 Bacon, Silas 37	First Named	34	M	Full	1896	Cedar	1075
2374	2 " Sallie 24	Wife	21	F	"	1896	"	1076
2375	3 " Joseph 16	Son	13	M	"	1896	"	1077
2376 ~~DEAD~~	4 " Johnson 12	"	9	"	"	1896	"	1078
~~Dau~~	5 " ~~Lita~~ DEAD	~~Dau~~	~~11~~	~~F~~	"	~~1896~~	"	~~1049~~
2377	6 " Susan 10	S.Dau	7	"	"	1896	"	1079
	7							
	8 ENROLLMENT							
	9 OF NOS. 1 2 3 4 and 6 HEREON	APPROVED BY THE SECRETARY						
	10 OF INTERIOR Dec 12. 1902							
	11							
	12 No. 5 Hereon Dismissed under order							
	13 of the Commission to the Five Civilized	Tribes of March 31, 1905.						
	14							
	15							
	16							
	17							

TRIBAL ENROLLMENT OF PARENTS

	Name of Father	Year	County	Name of Mother	Year	County
1	Dennis Bacon	Dead	Cedar	Litey Bacon	Dead	Cedar
2	Allen Bacon	"	Kiamitia	Finey Bacon	"	Kiamitia
3	No 1			Elizabeth Anderson	"	Cedar
4	No 1			" "	"	"
5	~~No 1~~			" "	"	"
6	James Durant	1896	Jackson	No 2		
7						
8						
9	No5 on 1896 roll as Lidy Bacon					
10	No5 died in May 1899: Evidence of death filed Feby. 11, 1902					
11						
12						
13						
14				Date of Application for Enrollment.		
15						
16				April 26/99		
17						

294

Choctaw By Blood Enrollment Cards 1898-1914

RESIDENCE: Nashoba   COUNTY. **Choctaw Nation**   Choctaw Roll   CARD No.
POST OFFICE: Smithville, I.T.   *(Not Including Freedmen)*   FIELD No. **895**

Dawes' Roll No.	NAME	Relationship to Person First Named	AGE	SEX	BLOOD	TRIBAL ENROLLMENT		
						Year	County	No.
2378	1 Wilson, Norwood 33	First Named	30	M	Full	1896	Nashoba	13277
2379	2 " Toby 34	Wife	31	F	1/2	1896	"	13278
2380	3 " Sina 14	Dau	11	F	3/4	1896	"	13279
2381	4 " Johnnie 12	Son	9	M	3/4	1896	"	13280
2382	5 " Willie 6	"	3	"	3/4	1896	"	13281
2383	6 " Minnie 4	Dau	3mo	F	3/4			
2384	7 " Anney 1	Dau	1yr	F	3/4			
	8							
	9							
	10							
	11	ENROLLMENT						
	12	OF NOS. 123456and7 HEREON APPROVED BY THE SECRETARY						
	13	OF INTERIOR Dec 12, 1902						
	14							
	15							
	16							
	17							

TRIBAL ENROLLMENT OF PARENTS

	Name of Father	Year	County	Name of Mother	Year	County
1	O-ko-chan-toby	Dead	Eagle	Sissie Nollitt	1896	Nashoba
2	Robison Cohn	"	"		Dead	Eagle
3	No.1			No.2		
4	No.1			No.2		
5	No.1			No.2		
6	No.1			No.2		
7	No.1			No.2		
8						
9	No.2 on 1896 roll as Atterbie Wilson					
10	No.3 " 1896 " " Sairey "					
11						
12	No.6 Affidavit of birth to be subblied[sic]: Recd May 9/99					
13	No.7 Born March 26, 1901: Enrolled May 17, 1907					
14	For child of nos 1&2 see NB (March 3 1905) #888				Date of Application for Enrollment.	
15						
16					April 26/99	
17						

Choctaw By Blood Enrollment Cards 1898-1914

RESIDENCE: Nashoba COUNTY. **Choctaw Nation** Choctaw Roll CARD No.
POST OFFICE: Smithville, I.T. (Not Including Freedmen) FIELD No. **896**

Dawes' Roll No.	NAME		Relationship to Person First Named	AGE	SEX	BLOOD	TRIBAL ENROLLMENT		
							Year	County	No.
2385	1 Narlett, Sissie	62	First Named	59	F	Full	1896	Nashoba	9676
~~DEAD~~ ~~Dead~~	~~2 Mambi, Willis~~	~~DEAD~~	~~Ward~~	~~14~~	~~M~~	~~"~~	~~1896~~	~~Eagle~~	~~8647~~
2386	3 " Ramus	15	"	12	"	"	1896	"	8649
2387	4 Robinson Emma	24	"	21	F	"	1896	"	8613
2388	5 Robinson James	2	Son of No.4	21mo	M	3/4			
2389	6 " Phebe	1	Dau of No.4	3mo	F	3/4			
	7								
	8								
	9								
	10								
	11								
	12								
	13								
	14								
	15								
	16								
	17								

ENROLLMENT
OF NOS. 1 3 4 5 and 6 HEREON
APPROVED BY THE SECRETARY
OF INTERIOR Dec 12 1902

No. 2 hereon dismissed under order of the Commission to the Five Civilized Tribes of March 31, 1905

TRIBAL ENROLLMENT OF PARENTS

	Name of Father	Year	County	Name of Mother	Year	County
1	Narlett	Dead	Eagle	Pa-hem-ma	Dead	Eagle
2	~~Dennis Mambi~~	"	"	~~Sillen Mambi~~	"	~~Nashoba~~
3	" "	"	"	" "	"	"
4	" "	"	"	" "	"	"
5	Amsiah Robinson	1896	Nashoba	No.4		
6	" "	1896	"	No.4		
7						
8						
9						
10						
11						
12	No3 on 1896 roll as Olemus Mambi No. 8649 also the same as Lamus Marbie No. 8614					
13	No.2 died Oct 15" 1899: Evidence of death filed July 14th 1902					
14	No.4 on 1896 roll as Emma Marbie					
15	No.4 is now the wife of Amsiah Robinson on Choctaw card #2073: Evidence of marriage requested. Received and filed June 14, 1902				#1 to 4	
16	No.5 Born July 12, 1900: Enrolled April 15, 1902				Date of Application for Enrollment April 26/99	
17	No.6 Born Jany 5, 1902: Enrolled April 15, 1902				No.4 enrolled May 30/99	

Choctaw By Blood Enrollment Cards 1898-1914

RESIDENCE: Eagle   COUNTY.   **Choctaw Nation**   **Choctaw Roll** *(Not Including Freedmen)*   CARD No.
POST OFFICE: Eagletown, I.T.   FIELD No. **897**

Dawes' Roll No.		NAME		Relationship to Person First Named	AGE	SEX	BLOOD	TRIBAL ENROLLMENT Year	County	No.
~~2390~~	1	~~Louis, Kellis~~ DIED PRIOR TO SEPTEMBER 25, 1902			~~25~~	~~M~~	~~Full~~	~~1896~~	~~Eagle~~	~~8011~~
2391	2	" Ennis	42	Wife	39	F	"	1896	"	12222
2392	3	Tonihka, Otson	23	S.Son	20	M	"	1896	"	12211
2393	4	" Salean	19	S.Dau	16	F	"	1896	"	12212
2394	5	" Richmond	1	Son of No3	1mo	M	"			
	6									
	7									
	8									
	9									
	10									
	11									
	12									
	13									
	14									
	15									
	16									
	17									

ENROLLMENT
OF NOS. 1 2 3 4 and 5 HEREON
APPROVED BY THE SECRETARY
OF INTERIOR Dec 12 1902

No.4 is now the wife of Lewis Wesley Lenas
Choctaw Card #1251
~~No.1 died June – 1902: Enrollm3n5~~
~~cancelled by Department July 8, 1904~~

TRIBAL ENROLLMENT OF PARENTS

	Name of Father	Year	County	Name of Mother	Year	County
1	~~Cholman Louie~~	~~Dead~~	~~Red River~~	~~Lincy Tonihka~~	~~1896~~	~~Eagle~~
2	Washington Hudson	"	Eagle	Elizabeth Hudson	Dead	"
3	Silas Tonihka	"	"	No 2		
4	" "	"	"	No 2		
5	No 3			Lucy Tonehka[sic]		Choctaw
6						
7						
8	No2 on 1896 roll as Ennis Tonihka					
9	No3 " 1896 " " Atson "					
10	No4 " 1896 " " Seleam "					
11	No5 Born Aug. 7, 1902. Enrolled Sept. 18, 1902					
12	No3 is now the husband of Lucy Leandis on 1893 Leased District					
13	payment roll Towson Co, page 56 #51. See affidavit of Batties Tolubbee					
14	and Anderson Harris as to marriage and copy of letter of Jeff Gardner as					
15	~~to enrollment of Lucy Leandis filed Sept 18, 1902. See also letter of Jeff Gardner~~					
16	~~filed with papers in Choctaw #1249 idetifying[sic] mother of No5 as Lucy Wesley on~~					
	Choctaw Card #1249.					
17	No1 died June – 1902: proof of death filed Dec. 20. 1902					
	No2 P.O. Lukfata I.T. 4/17/05					

Date of Application for Enrollment. #1 to 4

April 26/99

Choctaw By Blood Enrollment Cards 1898-1914

RESIDENCE: Eagle COUNTY.
POST OFFICE: Eagletown I.T.

Choctaw Nation

Choctaw Roll (Not Including Freedmen)

CARD NO.
FIELD NO. 898

Dawes' Roll No.	NAME	Relationship to Person First Named	AGE	SEX	BLOOD	TRIBAL ENROLLMENT Year	County	No.
2395	1 Ho-tambi ~~DIED PRIOR TO SEPTEMBER 25, 1902~~		79	M	Full	1896	Eagle	5625
2396	2 A-pis-an-tona 79	Wife	76	F	"	1896	"	266
2397	3 Ho-tambi, Louisin 11	Grand Son	8	F	"	1896	"	5630
	4							
	5							
	6							
	7							
	8							
	9							
	10							
	11	ENROLLMENT OF NOS. 1 2 and 3 HEREON APPROVED BY THE SECRETARY OF INTERIOR Dec 12 1902						
	12							
	13							
	14							
	15							
	16							
	17							

TRIBAL ENROLLMENT OF PARENTS

	Name of Father	Year	County	Name of Mother	Year	County
1	~~Ones-hubbi~~	~~Dead~~	~~Eagle~~	~~E-ma-ho-ke~~	~~Dead~~	~~Eagle~~
2	Ila-pe-subbi	"	Mississippi	Mi-ha-hoke	"	"
3	Thompson Hotambi	"	Eagle	Nus Hotambi	"	"
4						
5						
6	No.2 enrolled as Apisatona					
7	No.3 " " Lowesin Hotambi					
8	No1 died Oct. 15, 1899: proof of death filed Dec 6, 1902 ~~No.1 died Oct 15, 1899: Enrollment cancelled by Department Sept 16, 1904~~					
9						
10						
11						
12						
13						
14						
15						
16				Date of Application for Enrollment	April 26/99	
17	P.O. Lukfata, I.T. 12/12 '02					

RESIDENCE: Nashoba   COUNTY.   **Choctaw Nation**   Choctaw Roll   CARD No.
POST OFFICE: Doaksville, I.T.   (Not Including Freedmen)   FIELD No.   **899**

Dawes' Roll No.	NAME	Relationship to Person First Named	AGE	SEX	BLOOD	TRIBAL ENROLLMENT Year	County	No.
2398	1 LeFlore Henry 35	First Named	32	M	Full	1896	Cedar	7903
2399	2 " Minnie 38	Wife	36	F	"	1896	"	7904
2400	3 " Levina 11	Dau	8	"	"	1896	"	7907
2401	4 " Mitchell 5	Son	2	M	"			
2402	5 Holman, Ellen 16	S.Dau	13	F	Full	1896	Towson	5508
2403	6 LeFlore, Nancy 12	"	9	"	Full	1896	Cedar	7905
2404	7 " Johnny 10	S.Son	7	M	"	1896	"	7906
	8							
	9							
	10							
	11							
	12							
	13							
	14							
	15							
	16							
	17							

ENROLLMENT
OF NOS. 123456and7 HEREON
APPROVED BY THE SECRETARY
OF INTERIOR Dec 12, 1902

For child of No5 see N.B (Mar. 3, 1905) #627

TRIBAL ENROLLMENT OF PARENTS

	Name of Father	Year	County	Name of Mother	Year	County
1	Edmund LeFlore	1896	Cedar	Winnie LeFlore	Dead	Cedar
2	E-la-ish-ubbee	Dead	Towson	E-cha-pe-hona	"	Towson
3	No 1			Frances Noah	1896	Nashoba
4	No 1			No 2		
5	Martin Holman	Dead	Towson	No 2		
6	Michael LeFlore	"	Cedar	No 2		
7	" "	"	"	No 2		
8						
9						
10						
11						
12						
13						
14						
15						
16						
17						

Date of Application for Enrollment   April 26/99

299

Choctaw By Blood Enrollment Cards 1898-1914

RESIDENCE: Cedar   COUNTY.   **Choctaw Nation**   Choctaw Roll   CARD No.
POST OFFICE: Doaksville, I.T.   *(Not Including Freedmen)*   FIELD No. **900**

Dawes' Roll No.	NAME		Relationship to Person First Named	AGE	SEX	BLOOD	TRIBAL ENROLLMENT		
							Year	County	No.
2405	1 Nehka Farris	65	First Named	62	M	Full	1896	Cedar	9^$7
2406	2 " Amy	55	Wife	52	F	"	1896	"	9648
2407	3 " Noel	19	Son	16	M	"	1896	"	9649
	4								
	5								
	6								
	7								
	8								
	9								
	10								
	11	ENROLLMENT OF NOS. 1 2 and 3 HEREON							
	12	APPROVED BY THE SECRETARY							
	13	OF INTERIOR Dec 12, 1902							
	14								
	15								
	16								
	17								

TRIBAL ENROLLMENT OF PARENTS

	Name of Father	Year	County	Name of Mother	Year	County
1	Nehka	Dead	Cedar	Pis-a-hona	Dead	Cedar
2	Hina-homa	"	Red River	Unknown	"	Red River
3	No 1	1896	Cedar	Jennie Nehka	Dead	Cedar
4						
5						
6	No 2 enrolled as Amma Nehka					
7						
8	No 3 is now the husband of Ellen Billy, Choctaw Card #1243 12/2 02					
9						
10						
11						
12						
13						
14				Date of Application for Enrollment.		
15						
16				April 26/99		
17						

306

309

Index